Business model shifts

Six ways to create new value for customers

written by Patrick van der Pijl, Roland Wijnen, Justin Lokitz
designed by Maarten van Lieshout

Published by John Wiley & Sons, Inc., Hoboken, New Jersey.

Published simultaneously in Canada.

For general information on our other products and services or for technical support, please contact our Customer Care Department within the United States at (800) 762-2974, outside the United States at (317) 572-3993 or fax (317) 572-4002.

Wiley publishes in a variety of print and electronic formats and by print-on-demand. Some material included with standard print versions of this book may not be included in e-books or in print-on-demand. If this book refers to media such as a CD or DVD that is not included in the version you purchased, you may download this material at http://booksupport.wiley.com. For more information about Wiley products, visit www.wiley.com.

Library of Congress Cataloging-in-Publication Data:
ISBN 9781119525349 (Paperback)
ISBN 9781119525332 (ePDF)
ISBN 9781119525356 (ePub)

Cover Design: Wiley

Printed in the United States of America

SKY10021915 102820

Dedicated to your
(future) customers.

Table of contents

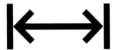

132 | From pipeline to platform

Throughout history, the biggest companies used pipeline business models to become what they are today. It took only a decade for new entrants, using platform business models, to eat their lunch.

172 | From incremental to exponential

Most business models begin with a short burst of exponential growth followed by a long period of linear growth. What if you could inject your business model with some secret sauce that would take it from 10% improvement to 10X growth?

214 | From linear to circular

Our traditional economy has limited growth potential because linear business models exhaust resources to make products that eventually go to waste. Circular business models overcome these limits.

Intro

Conclusion

The customer wins!

As Jean-Baptiste Alphonse Karr, a French critic, journalist, and novelist, once said, "The more things change, the more they remain the same." This statement has never been truer or more evident than it is at this very moment.

As this book is being finalized, the world is in the throes of a global pandemic, known as COVID-19. Not only has this pandemic strained the very fabric of society, it has cast a spotlight on the economy, pointing out businesses (and business models) that must change or die trying.

To say this time is an exciting time to live is an understatement to say the least. Change—very visibly—is accelerating, compounding on itself, creating even more change, faster. We can see that change is not linear. We see this in technology, where only a few years ago technologies like Artificial Intelligence (AI) were the province of a handful of people, who created algorithms used to "suggest" the word in a search term. Today, deep learning, a subset of machine learning, which is itself a subset of AI, is being used to create its own algorithms. In other words, in only a few years' time, we've come from a time when humans owned and published the math used to create efficiencies in various computer systems, to a time when humans actually know very little about why the system chooses (itself) to make certain decisions. AI, in a sense, is sowing the seeds for better AI, which is in turn creating better AI, and so on.

The same goes for people's attitudes and behaviors. Although at a high level our wants and needs remain somewhat constant in that we desire and need things like security, connectedness, and freedom, as technology changes—thereby changing the world around us—the way people go about achieving their wants and needs is also changing. For example, just as many companies finalized their shiny new open office plans, we found ourselves in the middle of a global paradigm shift. Due to the pandemic, we could no longer meet in "meatspace" (the physical world). This quickly changed peoples' perceptions of what it meant to meet face-to-face, creating a new world of face-to-face online meetings that had previously been mostly niche or relegated to a few scattered people or groups within any company. In fact, at the time of this writing, people are meeting virtually even for weekly happy hours with their family and friends.

The same goes for transportation in and around most cities around the world. Before 2009, hailing, calling, or waiting in line for taxis was commonplace. Today we grab our smartphones and use ride-hailing apps to magically summon vehicles to take us from point A to point B. When these services don't work or aren't available we're at a loss, having little idea about what to do next.

These changes have in many respects made the world more connected and easier to navigate, even if some of the underlying information is obfuscated from our view. With these changes, people expect the companies they do business with to adapt to the new paradigm. Just as traditional taxi companies around the world have had to adapt or face extinction, so will your businesses if you're not willing to change to meet your future customers' wants and needs.

How to respond?

As an organization, you can certainly choose to resist change, thinking your customers will eventually become tired of the latest trend. This, of course, is how most paradigm shifts start. When in the late 1970s Sony introduced Betamax (and VCRs), Universal Studios sued Sony for copyright infringement, stating that consumers would use Sony's technology to steal content. Sony not only won the case, but once the paradigm shifted, Universal Studios and every other movie studio found themselves in a place where they had to release movies to videotape for home rental or they would become less relevant to customers and risk extinction.

This is not an isolated case. Wherein 50 years ago the average lifespan of a company was about 61 years, today that lifespan has decreased to less than 20 years. In most cases, companies die because they're no longer relevant, having become fixated on fighting for the current business model rather than shifting to a newer, more relevant one. This is the fate of the survival mindset.
The good news is that you have agency here! You and the leaders in your organization can also commit to change, focusing on what's truly relevant for your customers and stakeholders, now and in the future. This is

what innovation is all about. To succeed, you must adopt a mindset that is open to exploration and continually searches for (unmet) customer needs and contextual changes in the business, technology, regulatory, and competitive landscape.

If you commit to change in this way, you can shift your business and business model as needed to outlast the competition, perhaps even cannibalizing the value you created in the past and creating more value for the future.

Companies die because they've become fixated on fighting for their current business model rather than shifting to a more relevant one.

Where is value now and next?

A single business model

Many traditional businesses that deal in buying, manufacturing, brokering, and selling goods are fairly static where their business models are concerned. This makes sense for businesses that historically have dealt with a stable or slowly changing context. How about this: "To fulfill customer demand, traditional businesses manufacture more goods while raising capital to continually increase production and scale distribution." Expansion in this case often comes down to investing in product development and/or acquisitions and expanding to new geographies and markets, selling the same goods. Because those goods and the underlying (single) business model are the lifeblood of the organization, protecting intellectual property (IP) is a constant endeavor. Consider the aforementioned example of Universal Studios. With a single business model in play for content production and distribution—even if that business model had multiple customer segments and revenue streams—if the content can no longer be protected, in Universal's eyes, the business model will die.

Keeping this in mind, it's no wonder that many organizations, including Universal Studios, did quite well through most of the twentieth century, spending little effort on new business models or innovation within their existing business models. Traditional companies of this period that worked with a single business model often attempted to innovate by engaging in disparate activities that were not tied tightly to their business goals. In these cases, the return on innovation was often pretty low because innovation that is not tied tightly to a company's business goals seldom leads to new value being created for new and existing customers.

Grow a portfolio of business models

By now, we've established that the business world continuously shifts as technology changes at an accelerating rate, and customer behavior and expectations change. Just as Universal Studios and its competitors were forced to create new business models to remain relevant, organizations today must develop, build, grow, and manage not just one business model but a portfolio of business models to serve an entire spectrum of evolving customer needs.

Such a business model portfolio consists of mature business models that generate current cash flow; adjacent business models that are on a growth trajectory (potentially) leading to future cash flow; emerging business models that are being incubated with the idea that they may help gain traction in another market; and declining business models that are losing relevance and subsequently declining in revenue. Organizations that employ a business model portfolio approach are always in search of future value, particularly in customer segments and markets where they may not yet play. What's more, a portfolio approach helps to reinforce strategic decision-making around how technologies and customers' needs are evolving and what business models must come to the fore, evolve, or be sunsetted in order to create, deliver, and capture future value. Portfolios are about continuous innovation and not stasis as a strategy.

Recombine to innovate . . . and shift

New business models and the portfolios they're managed within need not be created from scratch. In fact, given that you may already know your customer and market well, some of the best business model innovations and shifts are brought about by combining various elements in existing business models in order to create new value.

Perdiodic table

Likewise, every organization has a collection of business model elements that together make up the current business model(s), resulting in value being created, delivered, and captured. To demonstrate how business model shifts work, this book uses real-world case studies. For the large case studies in this book, you'll find what we call a Periodic Table of Business Model Elements or simply, the *Periodic Table* for a particular organization,

meant to help surface important elements in the company's business models—and overarching strategy, and culture—that the company uses (or has used) to create new business models via recombining elements. The Periodic Table is separated into four sections: the aspirational elements related to the vision and ambition of an organization; energy elements related to how an organization fuels the interaction and engagement among its people, customers, and partners; informational elements related to how information flows throughout the organization as part of the value creation process; and operational elements that show the nuts and bolts of the business model that are crucial for enabling value creation.

While in no way are the Periodic Tables of any organization described in this book inclusive of everything that goes on in that organization, what we've attempted to do here is make clear how the various elements are brought together and connected for strategic endeavors, such as shifting business models. What we hope you'll see in the case studies in this book is that forward-looking, continuously innovating organizations always combine various elements in such a way that new and unique value is created.

After all, business model innovation is about finding new combinations from existing business model elements, enhanced elements, and completely new elements. Just as important, it's crucial to get rid of those elements that no longer work and hamper growth.

Example Periodic Table from BMW case study in Services Shift page 26.

Business model shift

A deliberate and systematic move toward more relevance and value for your customers.

No overnight success

Just as with the case studies in this book, the success stories online and in other media often paint a picture that shows innovative companies in the best light, as if they made no mistakes and placed only winning bets, as if it is easy to turn ideas into viable new businesses that disrupt entire markets. Overnight success does not exist. In reality, innovating is hard work and the journey to success is a long and rocky road. Even in the case studies presented in this book you'll find that the backstories, which in many cases are simply left out due to space constraints and other editorial criteria, are littered with failures and near constant pivots. That is to say, in order to consistently create, deliver, and capture future value, you must constantly invest time and resources in business model innovation.

Evolve, one shift at a time

Just as it's important to understand that there's no such thing as an overnight success where business model shifts are concerned, It's just as Important to focus on one business model shift at a time rather than some multifaceted "big bang" form of disruption. In fact, for most companies wanting (or needing) to shift their business models, it's more informative to start small, with a single business model shift initiative that everyone can learn from, identifying what works, what doesn't work, and ultimately what customers need and want.

Successfully shifting business models is tough and requires guts and perseverance. Innovation and shifts are all about seeing and discovering new customer needs and experimenting to find out what works and more often what doesn't work. Most of all, making shifts is about customers. If you don't have customers or cannot keep them, what good is your business model?

Business model shift

A business model shift is a deliberate and systematic move toward more relevance and value for customers, and as a result growth of your organization. Business model shift can reflect bold moves into wholly new business models. But more often, shifts start as small moves inside an existing business model that evolve into entirely new ways of creating value and relevance.

Six ways to create new value for customers

In this book we have identified six kinds of business model shifts, each addressing a structural flaw in the current economic system. While these are discrete shifts that follow some specific business model patterns, it's important to note that like individual business model elements, these shifts can also be combined and recombined to create new business models and customer value specific to the organization, its mission, vision, culture, and resources. The six business model shifts are as follows:

1. The Services Shift

The move from a product-oriented business model to a service-oriented business model focused on getting some job done for the customer.

2. The Stakeholder Shift

The move from a shareholder orientation to creating value for all stakeholders in the greater ecosystem and business model context.

3. The Digital Shift

The move from fragmented online and offline business operations to an always-on business model that is connected to customers and their needs.

4. The Platform Shift

The move from a disintegrated ecosystem of businesses and uneven value exchange to directly connecting people and businesses facilitating value exchange in an orderly way.

5. The Exponential Shift

The move from improving businesses and revenue streams in terms of single- or double-digit percentage growth to exponential thinking and 10x growth and impact.

6. The Circular Shift

The move from take-make-dispose to restorative, regenerative, and circular value creation.

How to use this book

Business model canvas 101

How value is created, delivered, and captured

When it comes to business models and their underlying shifts, there is no framework better for demonstrating the mechanisms by which business models work and shift than the business model canvas. This tool, developed by Alexander Osterwalder and published in the best-selling book, *Business Model Generation: A Handbook for Visionaries, Game Changers, and Challengers,* by Alexander Osterwalder and Yves Pigneur (published by John Wiley and Sons), is composed of nine interconnecting boxes that together describe and illustrate how organizations create, deliver, and capture value. What's more, it shows the big picture of a business such that anybody can understand how the business works. And, just as business models shift over time, by layering business model canvases on top of one another as if there's a Z-axis running through them, they can be used to represent both points in time as well as shifts.

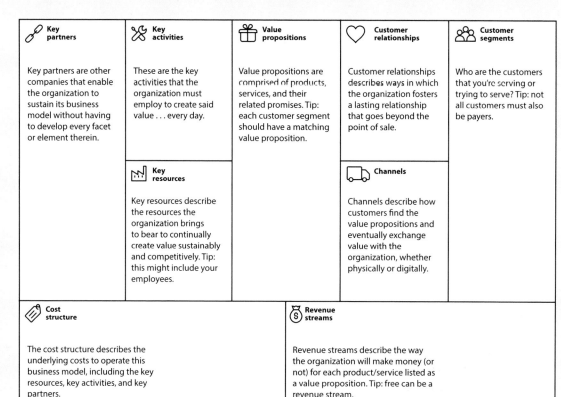

Key partners

Key partners are other companies that enable the organization to sustain its business model without having to develop every facet or element therein.

Key activities

These are the key activities that the organization must employ to create said value . . . every day.

Key resources

Key resources describe the resources the organization brings to bear to continually create value sustainably and competitively. Tip: this might include your employees.

Value propositions

Value propositions are comprised of products, services, and their related promises. Tip: each customer segment should have a matching value proposition.

Customer relationships

Customer relationships describes ways in which the organization fosters a lasting relationship that goes beyond the point of sale.

Channels

Channels describe how customers find the value propositions and eventually exchange value with the organization, whether physically or digitally.

Customer segments

Who are the customers that you're serving or trying to serve? Tip: not all customers must also be payers.

Cost structure

The cost structure describes the underlying costs to operate this business model, including the key resources, key activities, and key partners.

Revenue streams

Revenue streams describe the way the organization will make money (or not) for each product/service listed as a value proposition. Tip: free can be a revenue stream.

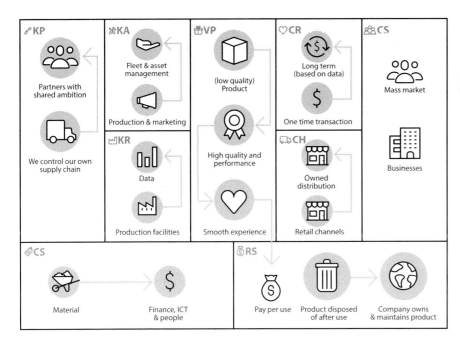

The business model canvas diagram includes:

KP (Key Partners)
- Partners with shared ambition
- We control our own supply chain

KA (Key Activities)
- Fleet & asset management
- Production & marketing

KR (Key Resources)
- Data
- Production facilities

VP (Value Proposition)
- (low quality) Product
- High quality and performance
- Smooth experience

CR (Customer Relationships)
- Long term (based on data)
- One time transaction

CH (Channels)
- Owned distribution
- Retail channels

CS (Customer Segments)
- Mass market
- Businesses

CS (Cost Structure)
- Material
- Finance, ICT & people

RS (Revenue Streams)
- Pay per use
- Product disposed of after use
- Company owns & maintains product

The shift from products to services

An example of shifts you might expect in a business model when moving from products towards services.

the customer get their job done and so on. In each chapter, the specific business model shift is illustrated as one large case study, a couple of medium case studies, and several short case studies, all of which tell a story about how a value creation was brought to life.

Learn to apply

Our goal is to encourage you to think and act strategically by illustrating how business model shifts have been made in various industries and by a huge number of companies of all sizes. Of course, while we've attempted to cover as many industries and examples as we could, this book is in no way an encyclopedia of every business model shift in every industry.

We urge you to apply what you learn from this book to become skilled in making your own business model shift(s). Have fun! We're here when you need us . . .

Structure of the book

This book has been structured to show how each business model shift moves away from a traditional, outdated, and inefficient business model to one that highlights the unique elements that exist in a particular shift, such as the services shift. This is visualized by showing the high-level "from" and "to" business model patterns. We have also identified so-called successor patterns, which are distinct lower level patterns that show different business model dynamics within each shift.

For instance, where the services shift is concerned, there are a number of patterns at play that together tell the bigger story about how a product-to-service shift is made. The dynamic interplay of the shifting elements happening in a single business model canvas would look something like this.

Here you can see that for this business model, the value proposition shifts from some (close to) commodity product to a higher quality one with a promise of helping

From normal to new normal

The COVID-19 pandemic is presently an ongoing tragedy and an existential threat to businesses around the world, but it can have the positive effect of helping leaders think in new ways about their business models. Businesses we have relied on for decades are finding new ways to make ends meet, or thrive, or going bankrupt. Every organization, including yours, is being forced to question and rethink its business model. We are excited about the timing of this book because we are confident it will help your organization adapt in the wake of the COVID-19 pandemic and energetically adapt when facing any other great threats and opportunities in years to come.

For business owners and managers whose businesses were—and still are—affected by COVID-19, the crucial question is, "What can I do now?" Faced with this question, you have several options: 1) You could close your business and walk away; 2) You could work on cutting costs to a bare minimum in order to stay alive another day; 3) You could wait for things to work out, ignoring the fact that they may not, and even if they do, we may find ourselves in a similar position in the future; or 4) You can immediately shift your business model for the short and long term. As you might guess, this book focuses on shifting your business model.

It is our point of view that we are collectively at the point of no return: The paradigm shift is happening, and we can no longer afford to wait for some new tech to save us. At this point, we must focus on business model innovation with both a short- and long-term view. Yes, this takes resources that might be scarce today. Yet the urgency to invest in business model innovation has never been clearer or more needed than right now. So, what can you do right now?

1

The first thing you need to do to get started innovating your business model is to **dive deep into what your current/old business model looks like and how it used to work.** The best way to do this is to break out a Business Model Canvas—described in this book's introduction—and use this, with your team, business partners, or confidants, to detail exactly how your business created, delivered, and captured value up until now. Don't worry about every iteration your business has taken. Rather, focus on the most recent and relevant past. What makes (or made) your business tick? What do you produce and how? Whom do you serve? The best way to answer these questions is by scribbling down (or drawing) each detail or element as its own sticky note and applying that to the corresponding section of the Business Model Canvas. Don't leave out important details. And don't be wishful. Your job is to capture what is or once was such that you can zoom out and interrogate

The big challenge: what can I do right now?

the complete collection of elements that was your business model. If you don't know how your business created, delivered, and captured value, simply because you just did that on autopilot, this is the time to take a step back and get introspective.

2 Once you've captured what you believe is a complete picture of your business model, on a separate piece of paper, a flip chart, or a whiteboard, **identify the weak points and strong points of your current (or old) business model.** What used to work that now doesn't? What value propositions simply aren't being delivered or purchased by your customers? What key resources are underutilized and costing you money to keep around? What are you doing well? What are customers continuing to come back for? What key resources are you proud of? At this point, you might even zoom out further and consider cultural elements related to your business model that made your business what it is. Now is the time to truly understand your Periodic Table—the

core of your overall value creation—and use it to create a shift. Don't hold back. One of the best ways to pivot in the short and long term is to use what you already have.

3 Once you've gone through this introspective exercise, and your business model is broken (or at least fractured), you can **create new ways to reach your customers.** For many companies, this might be **the perfect moment to go through a digital shift** (see Chapter 3 of this book), which is a business model strategy that focuses on using digital technology to create and deliver great customer experiences unencumbered by physical-only value propositions, resources, and activities. If your business deals with physical goods and/or services, technology is the enabler and not the value proposition. This strategy may use existing and/or new technologies to enable organizations to create relevancy with and for customers. At its core, the digital shift is about figuring out how to use digital technologies to drive

You don't have the luxury to wait, ponder, and research your future to death. You never did. It is just more obvious now.

Barebottle's response to COVID-19

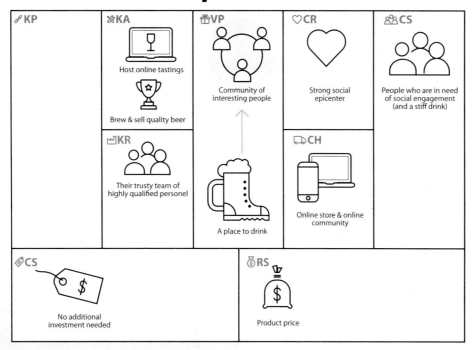

🔧 KP	⚒ KA	🎁 VP	♡ CR	👥 CS
	Host online tastings	Community of interesting people	Strong social epicenter	People who are in need of social engagement (and a stiff drink)
	Brew & sell quality beer			
	⚒ KR		🚚 CH	
	Their trusty team of highly qualified personel	A place to drink	Online store & online community	
🏷 CS			💰 RS	
No additional investment needed			Product price	

From brewery to online community
While diving in their strategic intro-spection—forced by COVID-19—Barebottle realized that at its core, it was not just a bar; its core value was delivering community to people who love good beer. Here's what Barebottle's shift looks like.

value creation as well as deliver that value to current and new customer segments.

At BMI, a business model innovation and strategy firm run by the authors of this book that used to do most of its business face-to-face in facilitated workshops, we have had to undergo an entire digital shift in order to

help our company deliver on its core value propositions. This has meant that, like most companies, we have had to move fully to online collaboration tools, like Microsoft Teams, Zoom, and Mural, while also chang-ing the very nature of how we run what used to be several day workshops. Though you might think that this is a stopgap for us, that couldn't be further from the truth. Through doing—and continuing to do—the work to shift our business model and ways of work-ing to be completely digital, we have found that we're able to respond to our clients' needs in new ways that we could have never done before.

Likewise, as with many people, you may be thinking **now would be a good time to use your business to give back to the world or your community**. We call this a stakeholder shift (see page 49), which is a business model strategy that seeks to ensure that value is created for all stakeholders—customers, employees, partners, society, and investors—simultaneously. Organizations that undergo this shift find ways to actively engage each and every stakeholder to make sure they achieve their goals as well.

Examples of businesses that have undergone a stakeholder shift—often simultaneously with a digital shift—abound. One such company is Barebottle, which markets itself as "a San Francisco crowd-inspired craft brewery." When the COVID-19 calamity forced everyone to shelter in place, Barebottle, which has a brewery and large taproom that serves in many ways as a de facto community center in the Bernal Heights neighborhood of San Francisco, found itself in a place where it needed to go through its own shift to meet the needs of the community. Although drinking beer is certainly one of those needs, what Barebottle's team discovered early on was that just like most any other restaurant or bar, people went to Barebottle not just for a drink; they went there for the community. Rather than wait for that community to come back to its physical space, Barebottle created an online community, complete with virtual craft beer tastings led by its employees. What's more, these are all free for anyone to join. This has been a way for Barebottle to give back to the community while also establishing new relationships with its customers, employees, partners, and investors.

4 So, how might you **make these shifts for your business?** By far, the most straightforward, actionable way to generate new options for your business is a technique called *epicenter-based ideation*. With epicenter-based ideation, you'll effectively use your current business model to generate ideas for the future by focusing on the core of what you do and who you deliver value to. One way to start ideating in this way is to clear your business model of eight boxes, leaving the focus on one single box. What would you build if you kept all the existing elements (or sticky notes) for only that one box? For instance, what if you were able to bring to bear your company's resources to create an entirely new business model? During COVID-19, many restaurants realized that one of their key resources was fresh ingredients, which they bought in bulk. Out of this key resource came new business models wherein restaurants are selling things you can't find at the grocery store or creating cook-at-home meal boxes.

Using epicenter-based ideation, it's best to start by zeroing in on the elements in your

Start by zeroing in on the core of your business: the elements in your business model where you shine!

business model where you shine. For many businesses, this might be your core value proposition (the product plus its promises). Focusing on that, if you had to remove most of the elements except your core value proposition and your customers, in what new ways might customers experience your value proposition that they cannot do today?

What's unique about epicenter-based ideation is that once you have a good handle on the big picture of how your business used to work, you can mine it for constituent pieces that would work really well in future business models.

5 Once you and your team have created a number of ideas, you'll want to assess them all, and using your own point of view (and company culture) as a guide, identify the ones that stand out as something you believe you'd want to do . . . or at least try. In fact, you'll likely find that some of the ideas you've written down will fit nicely together as larger or branching parts of your future business. With these in hand, expand upon what's written on the sticky notes or on your whiteboard, by **applying the ideas to new Business Model Canvases**. In this way, you'll essentially take what may be a simple term or sentence and blow it out into a full business model. By doing this, you'll quickly figure out what you'll need to create, deliver, and capture value in new ways.

As with the idea stage, the goal of this prototyping stage—even if it's simply business model prototyping—is to build out more than one option. Having multiple options will enable you to pivot very quickly when your customers or key partners react or invalidate some of what you've designed.

6 With a few business model options in hand, you'll want to **find ways to quickly test the ones you're most excited about directly with your customers**. You might think customers will be appalled at being test subjects for your new ideas, but this couldn't be further from the truth. If you're up-front with your customers about what you're doing and why you're doing

it, they will provide valuable feedback. Moreover, they'll feel like they're part of the "club," empowered to help a business they value. Your job in this case is to ask lots of open-ended questions and capture their honest feedback. Don't try to sell them on something they don't want. Just put it out there and listen.

7 As you digest the feedback, **continue to iterate the business model(s) and prototype(s) until you believe you're ready to scale (or pivot)**. There's a lot here. Just know that you're not the only business going through this strange time. If you're systematic in your efforts to create and test new options, you will afford yourself the possibility to create something new. At the very least, you will gain insights that just might help you create stronger connections with your existing customers.

The keys to any shift you make are the following. People's basic needs, such as connecting with friends/family, health, and fitness, have not changed, even if they've

been reprioritized. Whatever you deliver, it must be highly relevant for customers and society and should address their immediate needs. Your customers may also have new needs that have arisen out of COVID-19, such as social distancing and hand hygiene. You'll likely need to address these in some way. Where your value proposition and revenue streams are concerned, you'll need to think through what "free" means to your business model. In crises such as these, many businesses make some services free as a way to help society and communities. This isn't pure altruism at work. Free offers provide a way to create deeper connections with customers, which play out in the long term. No shift is mutually exclusive. Whatever shift you make, it's clear that you must add digital value propositions—and in an accelerated fashion. With those digital value propositions, you might consider offering specific COVID-19-related products and services. Finally, don't do this all in a vacuum. Reach out to your customers and listen/observe for new needs and reinforce working together in the long term.

If you need more resources about building new business models for the future, check out our books *Design a Better Business* and *Business Model Generation*!

iFixit: another COVID-19-inspired shift

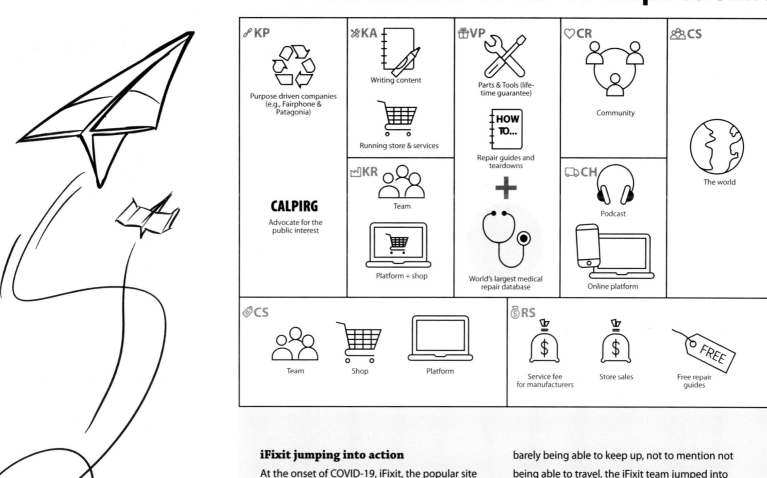

KP

Purpose driven companies (e.g., Fairphone & Patagonia)

CALPIRG
Advocate for the public interest

KA

Writing content

Running store & services

KR

Team

Platform + shop

VP

Parts & Tools (life-time guarantee)

HOW TO...

Repair guides and teardowns

+

World's largest medical repair database

CR

Community

CH

Podcast

Online platform

CS

The world

CS

Team

Shop

Platform

RS

Service fee for manufacturers

Store sales

Free repair guides

iFixit jumping into action

At the onset of COVID-19, iFixit, the popular site for fixing personal electronics, released the world's largest medical device repair database. With medical device companies and service representatives barely being able to keep up, not to mention not being able to travel, the iFixit team jumped into action and created an entirely new offering for medical professionals and others by focusing 50% of their staff (key resources) on the problem.

From products to services

Most of us may be drawn to certain products due to their newness, features, and perceived quality. We tend to praise these products, perhaps even knowing deep down that our praise is not about the products but the benefits that they provide. The advantage services have over products is that services deliver those benefits to customers directly, getting the job done without the hassle of owning and maintaining one or several products.

products →

As Theodore Levitt, American economist and a professor at the Harvard Business School, told his students, **"People don't want a quarter-inch drill. They want a quarter-inch hole."** The gist here is this: whatever products companies sell, ultimately, the customers who buy these products do so to address a goal or achieve an ambition that may have nothing to do with owning the product. Service shifts then are about moving from a product exchange to an approach in which the product or service can be "rented" out to **help customers get their jobs done**, which is often more convenient for customers than owning the product outright. And, as change continues to accelerate, service business models can deliver the latest and greatest services to customers without requiring them to rebuy something they already have, thereby **increasing customer relationships and the lifetime value they provide**.

services

Shift stories
Large
↗ BMW

Medium
↗ Medtronic
↗ Rolls-Royce

Short
↗ Dollar Shave Club
↗ Swapfiets
↗ Rent the Runway

"We have new expectations as consumers. We prefer outcomes over ownership. We prefer customization, not standardization. And we want constant improvement, not planned obsolescence. We want services, not products. The one-size-fits-all approach isn't going to cut it anymore. And to succeed in this new digital world, companies have to transform."

Source: Tien Tzuo, Subscribed: Why the Subscription Model Will Be Your Company's Future—and What to Do About It

Access, not ownership

Whatever you're producing, at the end of the day, your customers only care about getting a job done. While your product may satisfy some of that need, you're just as likely to be in a constant arms race to sell more and more product. Not every shift starts with an outdated business model, however. Many start by satisfying a need.

How might you instead offer a better service, enabling customers to use something that you maintain for them . . . forever?

In doing so, you might provide new opportunities to stay connected with your customers, enabling you to create better and more unique value propositions that help them to achieve their ambitions, making for happier customers, and . . . more value for everyone!

Strategic questions
What are your customers' jobs-to-be-done? What service can you provide that will help your customers get their jobs done while also addressing their pains and helping them achieve their ambitions? How can you use your product portfolio as a resource for creating new value with services? Do you still need a product, or should you offer your customers a pure service?

What can you learn and apply from companies that are making this shift or have already made this shift and will never go back?

From products

The product business model is specifically designed to develop and manufacture products in an efficient way. It's the job of the marketing and sales team to put those products out into the market and ensure there's demand from customers.

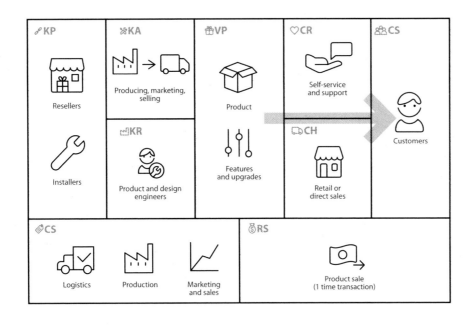

Into the hands of customers
Customers have a need that is satisfied by the product they buy. The relationship with customers is fairly transactional. You may not know who exactly your customer is or how they use your product, especially if you sell through indirect channels. Customers are urged to upgrade or buy the next version of a product by seducing them with new features. If customers are still satisfied with the previous version and are happily using it, revenue streams may shrink significantly.

Market and sell
A push strategy and big launches are used to convince new customers to buy now. Existing customers are targeted to buy the latest version. A brand can be important to distinguish a product from the competition. Product designers and engineers need to come up with a new and better version of the product. In some sectors, services around the product are introduced for free to make sure customers keep buying. Resellers are brought in as partners to sell even more of the product ("move boxes") or to add additional value around using the product.

The figure is a Business Model Canvas with the following labeled sections and items:

- **KP** — Resellers; Installers
- **KA** — Producing, marketing, selling; **KR** — Product and design engineers
- **VP** — Product; Features and upgrades
- **CR** — Self-service and support; **CH** — Retail or direct sales
- **CS** — Customers
- **CS** — Logistics; Production; Marketing and sales
- **RS** — Product sale (1 time transaction)

to services

Getting the job done

The overall value proposition is to keep customers "moving" so they can focus on what's important to them. A service business model takes over an important job and ensures that it is well-done. The outcome is delivered consistently every time. Customers pay for the delivery of the service on a subscription, consumption, or performance basis, with an agreed upon contract that is renewed or renegotiated at an end date. The relationship is all about making it work for customers and being "at their service."

Manage to engage

Addressing and fully understanding the job-to-be-done requires constant engagement with customers. Assets need to be managed really well so that each customer has access to the service they need, when they need it. A high-quality product and infrastructure is required as a key resource for providing the service. Usage data is important for asset management as well as input for innovating the service fed by new customer needs. Partners are included for providing technology and IT systems and for financing assets.

The services business model is specifically designed to get a job done for customers. A service business model is about understanding the lives of your customers and meeting their ongoing needs throughout time.

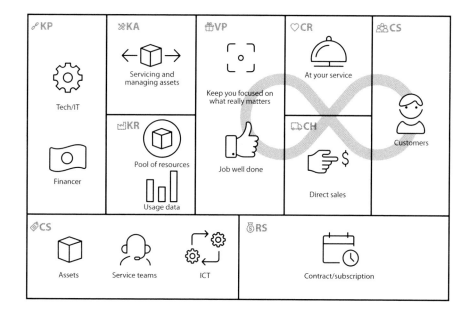

Product plus services

❶

Services, such as installation, maintenance, advice, etc., are core parts of the value proposition, which improve the overall experience, performance, and other benefits of using the product. These business models focus on benefits rather than features and functions. Although services may have their own revenue stream, they're often added to an already commoditized product, ensuring customers keep purchasing your product.

Examples: BMW

Consumables

❷

This pattern focuses on regular delivery of a consumable product that is used on a frequent basis. Subscription agreements may also enable flexibility in the quantity of a product and which products are delivered, based on customers' preferences. Consistent delivery is crucial as customers require these consumables in their daily routine.

Examples: Dollar Shave Club, HelloFresh

Services subscription

❸

These are often categorized as utilities or facilities wherein customers pay a subscription that may be fixed or usage based. Key to this pattern is constant supply and reliability of the core service. If customers use a facility as part of this service, the facility must maintain hours that are reasonable for customers and not just for the service owner.

Examples: Metromile, ClassPass

Patterns

Information goods & services

Rental or lease

Managed services

This is about providing access to media or information customers rely on. Information-based business models often utilize paid subscription packages that provide a premium experience and/or access to more information or content. Paramount in this pattern is the design, development, and maintenance of robust infrastructure to ensure uninterrupted service.

Examples: The New York Times, Apple

This is about providing access to a product that can be (flexibly) used. Leases may provide exclusive access to products or shared access, wherein customers access a shared pool of products. The company employing this business model owns the products and must efficiently manage a pool of products. The service provider is responsible for maintenance, repair, and control of products.

Examples: BMW DriveNow, Swapfiets, Zilok, Rent the Runway, Le Tote, LoveHomeSwap

This focuses on performing some important job to be done, often guaranteeing a specific level of performance, even when there is no predetermined product involved. Contracts may be performance based, which may include specific operational activities (e.g., cleaning), the output of a product (e.g., prints instead of a copying machine), or a functional result (e.g., a pleasant climate). Revenue streams may be fixed or based on shared risk.

Examples: Medtronic, Rolls-Royce, BMW YourNow

L

BMW

BMW started as a manufacturer of engines for various applications. It has evolved into a company that innovates to deliver sheer driving pleasure— whether you drive a car or motorcycle. Its next evolution is offering people the freedom to move around in a pleasant and sustainable way.

Founders
Camillo Castiglioni, Franz Josef Popp, and Karl Rapp

Founded in 1916

Total revenue
€104 billion (2019)

Industry
Automotive
Mobility

Scale
Offices in 14 countries
Sales network
over 140 countries
133,778 employees (2019)

Timeline

1916-1952
Founded

Founded in 1916 as Bayerische Flugzeugwerke AG and renamed to Bayerische Motoren Werke (BMW) in 1922. In 1933 the BMW 303 was launched, a new and self-developed car. In 1952, it launched the BMW 501.

1953-1959
Almost bankrupt

Luxury cars were too expensive for most people. The Isetta was introduced, a microcar produced in license. This car is still the world's best-selling single cylinder car, with over 160,000 cars sold from 1954-1962.

1960-1971
Focus on niche

BMW established a new segment in the car market: the quality production salon, positioned between the mass production and handcrafted cars. This led to a reputation as a leading manufacturer of sports cars.

It is both exciting and challenging to imagine the future: how will society, the economy, living conditions, and therefore mobility—change?"

BMW website: The next 100 years.

Innovate for driving pleasure

BMW originated from Bayerische Flugzeugwerke (BFW), a company that sold aircraft engines, which is still reflected in the logo representing a propeller slashing through a bright blue sky. In 1928, the company began to produce and sell cars. After World War II, many people could not afford luxury cars, which forced BMW to look for different ways to generate revenue. The company discovered the Isetta, an Italian-designed microcar, which it licensed and began to build in its German plant. Also called Motocoupé or Knutschkugel, it was affordable, perfect for city travel, and fit for the lifestyle of those times. Profit margins from the Isetta were however small and the slow sales of luxury cars brought BMW to the verge of bankruptcy in 1959. Management suggested selling the whole company to Daimler-Benz, but because of opposition from the workforce and trade unions, this was ultimately blocked. Herbert Quandt, one of BMW's early investors, even increased his share in BMW to 50% against the advice of his bankers. This investment was used to finance the BMW 700, a traditional car that became very successful.

The BMW New Class compact sedans, introduced in 1962, was the beginning of its reputation as a leading manufacturer of sports cars. Just as it does today, BMW used its sophisticated technical skills and brand to fill this niche.

BMW

1972-1989
The ultimate driving machine

Expansion of its range by adding coupe and luxury sedan models, such as the 5 Series (1972), the 3 Series (1975), the 6 Series (1976) and the 7 Series (1978). The slogan "The Ultimate Driving Machine" launched in the US in 1974.

1990
Forschungs- und Innovationszentrum

Research and Innovation Centre opened. Acquired Rover in 1994. This acquisition was not a success, leading to big financial losses. Most of it sold in 2000, except for MINI. The roadster Z3 was introduced in 1995. SUV market entered in 1999.

Most sustainable brand

In 1999 acknowledged as the most sustainable brand by the Dow Jones Sustainability Index. Since then featured every year in the index.

Product plus services
Since 1962, BMW has gained the reputation as the leading manufacturer of sports cars, offering quality-minded people the "ultimate driving experience".

Ultimate driving experience

BMW offers what it calls the ultimate driving machine. There are over 700 BMW Motor Clubs with over 200,000 members, all of whom love to share their experiences. A drive in a BMW is facilitated by exceptional design and technology, all to enhance the pleasure of driving and arriving at your destination on time and relaxed. Pioneering for performance also went hand in hand with sustainability. BMW has been providing services to their customers since 1996 when they equipped cars with an emergency call function.

Ultimate driving experience

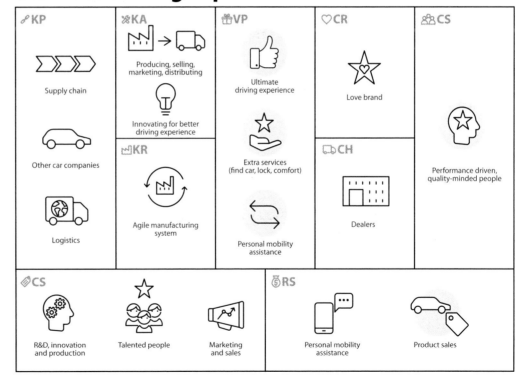

2001
UN Environment

Committed itself to the United Nations Environment Programme, the UN Global Compact and the Cleaner Production Declaration. 26 years earlier (1973), it was also the first company in the automotive industry to appoint an Environmental Officer.

2004
1 Series

Driving pleasure for the compact class. First plant opened in Shenyang, China. Plant Leipzig begins production in 2005.

2007
Strategy Number One

The mission statement up to the year 2020 is clearly defined: "To become the world's leading provider of premium products and premium services for individual mobility."

2011
Drive Now

Launch of a car sharing service in Münich, established under the sub brand BMW i. ActiveE testing started with companies and individuals around the world.

BMW is generally thought of as an innovator in the automobile industry. It invests a lot of resources in understanding the context in which the future car will be driven and how customer needs may change. BMW designers and strategists are informed by internal sources, such as their concept cars, as well as external sources, such as visionaries and domain experts in other fields.

In 2009, BMW began its journey to explore the future through BMW i's Future Thought series. This series of events was designed to ask questions around the biggest trends reshaping people's lives in the years to come. How will cities develop when more and more people are concentrating there? What problems will arise when two-thirds of all people on Earth live in cities by 2050?

Through this questioning, BMW realized that urbanization is one of the most significant social shifts in modern society, leading to new problems but also new opportunities.

Cities are becoming increasingly flooded with cars, which has led to a lack of parking space and pollution as a result. What's more, many urbanites, especially young urbanites,

no longer want to deal with owning their own vehicles; they'd rather simply have access to mobility services when they need to travel. This has helped to lead to new forms of transportation, such as services operated by Uber. At the apex of this, BMW also sees this as an opportunity to design smaller cars, electric vehicles, and even car sharing services, like BMW DriveNow.

Our ability to decode the signs and shifts that are occurring around us is key to understanding business and society as we negotiate the uncertain waters of the twenty-first century."

Future Cities. BMW i Future Thought Series - Part 1

2012
San Francisco launch

DriveNow launched with an all-electric fleet of
ActiveE cars in San Francisco.

2013
BMW i3

Designed from top to bottom with
sustainability in mind, perfect for urban
adventures. This marked the start of a new era
of electric mobility.

2015
Shutdown San Francisco

BMW DriveNow in San Francisco was
shutdown. Strict parking regulations
hampered the ability to scale BMW DriveNow.

BMW Drive Now offered hassle-free mobility.
And, true to BMW's promise, people could get
the ultimate, electric, driving experience by the
minute. Through an app, a nearby vehicle could
be located to start your trip. Parking was included in the service, through the ParkNow app.

The service was initially validated in San Francisco, in large part because the mayor welcomed
mobility services that would reduce emissions.
The promise was that customers could pick
up and drop their cars anywhere (called a *free
floating* parking arrangement), but this was in
direct conflict with local parking and car-sharing
regulations. In 2015, the service in San Francisco
was terminated.

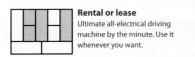

Rental or lease
Ultimate all-electrical driving
machine by the minute. Use it
whenever you want.

BMW DriveNow (San Francisco)

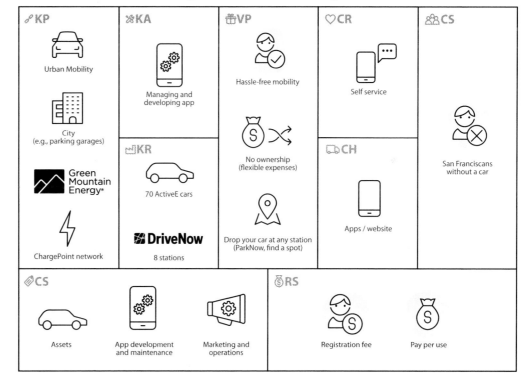

2016
RideCell

2016
Reach Now

2017
1m customers

BMW's capital arm iVenture leads a Series A round, raising $11.7m for further development of transportation software that enables multi-modal transportation

A new attempt to gain traction with car sharing in the US, planning to expand to 10 other US cities.

DriveNow has 1 million customers across 13 cities and 8 countries.

Creating the future together

"BMW i exists to generate creative, pioneering ideas which transform the way we think about mobility."

Adrian van Hooydonk,
Senior Vice President BMW Group Design

It's clear that the future of mobility is about convenience. This implies the availability of options to get from A to B; immediate access to services; and no hassle, on-time arrival. These objectives must be attained without increasing the impact to the environment.

Creating such a future is not easy. Although cities want to facilitate such services, existing regulations effectively hamper implementation of the flexibility people demand. The competition is fierce, coming from Uber, Lyft, public services, and micro-mobility providers. It is really the customer that decides which option is most relevant at any given time. So, instead of having another rival to deal with, BMW joined forces with Daimler AG, for the first time in history.

Both companies share a vision of a seamless future in which everyone can instantly, easily, and freely move around. They want to give people their freedom back and give cities room to breathe again. By combining their knowledge, experience, and technologies, better solutions can be found that create value for both users and society. In such a future, they state "Our own set of wheels has never mattered less. Because it's not really about the car we drive, it's about the freedom to get where we're going." For their ride hailing service, FreeNow, BMW and Daimler AG are augmenting their fleet with vehicles from Tesla because neither BMW nor Daimler AG has an electric car on the market that is suitable for taxi services.

2018
Joint venture

BMW Group & Daimler AG announce that they are going to work together for the first time in history on creating the future of mobility.

Launch of YourNow

Launch of YourNow, a group of 5 subsidiaries bringing together 14 services to reinvent mobility. Investing €1 billion to establish these new mobility services with 4m customers, 20.000 vehicles within 31 cities.

YourNow promises on-demand mobility at your fingertips. It is a service that goes well beyond the car. The ultimate plan is a wider mobility app focused on electrification with more electric vehicles, e-scooters, electric bikes, car sharing, and public transport.

It is still an umbrella company that comprises five subsidiaries offering a whole range of services. ShareNow is a car rental service that combines Car2Go and DriveNow. FreeNow is a ride-hailing service. ReachNow helps you find the easiest way to arrive at your destination and buy tickets on the go. ParkNow is mobile cashless parking. ChargeNow is a service to easily charge your vehicle.

Managed services
Use whatever you want, when you need it. The ultimate freedom.

BMW/Daimler YourNow

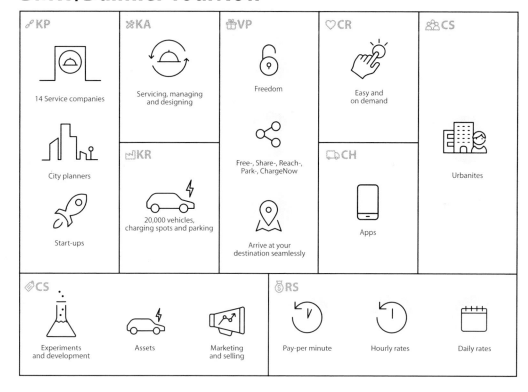

⚲ KP	✳ KA	🎁 VP	♡ CR	👥 CS
14 Service companies	Servicing, managing and designing	Freedom	Easy and on demand	
City planners	Free-, Share-, Reach-, Park-, ChargeNow		Urbanites	
KR		📱 CH		
Start-ups	20,000 vehicles, charging spots and parking	Arrive at your destination seamlessly	Apps	

✎ CS			⛽ RS		
Experiments and development	Assets	Marketing and selling	Pay-per minute	Hourly rates	Daily rates

Driven by high-quality

BMW has always been innovating for a better driving experience, while at the same time improving the environmental performance of BMW Group as a whole. The company's drive for high-quality is reflected in everything it does. It is also clearly articulated with respect to the future of mobility that BMW wants to create, benefiting both users and society.

BMW i is a sub brand dedicated to creating the future for existing, but especially new, customer segments, with Daimler AG and start-ups like RideCell. BMW can build upon a vast pool of knowledge and experience yet is very open to internal and external triggers that challenge the status quo. BMW's mobility services may someday be powered by usage data and smart in-vehicle and cloud-based computers. The future BMW envisions can be developed from its high-quality products and the many existing services the company already offers—as long as BMW invests in the right experiments.

Aspiration			
Freedom	Cities that breathe	Create the future of mobility	Seamless and effortless

Energy			
Premium, Love Brand	BMW i (sub brand)	RideCell (and other start-ups)	Joint venture (with Daimler AG)

Information			
Knowledge and experience	Internal and external triggers	ICT	Usage data

Operations			
High-quality products	Services (Car2Go, DriveNow, Park Mobile)	iVentures	Experiments (BMW labs)

2019
Retreat

ShareNow exiting the US market early 2020. Also shut down of the service in London, Brussels, and Florence.

2020
Electrify

The goal is to electrify the YourNow fleet of cars and double revenues.

Future
Going electric

By 2025, BMW will have 25 electrified vehicle models. To be sold as products and used as building block for services. Hop on, hop off. Sit back and relax. Enjoy the ride. Arrive at your destination right on time.

BMW is slowly morphing into a full-service mobility provider. The tipping point is yet to be reached.

BMW has a clear vision about the future of mobility. More than ever, the company is aware that the customer is in the driver's seat. Customers favor seamless, easy, and instant access to products and services over anything else. People just want to get the job of moving from A to B done. YourNow has 5 services that will merge ever more closely to get that job done in the best way possible. The ultimate goal is to facilitate this with an all-electric, self-driving fleet of vehicles that charge and park autonomously and interconnect with other modes of transport.

Car sharing is gaining popularity among millennials and younger generations. As a result, car leases have also grown in popularity. People are slowly moving away from the hassle of owning a car. If this continues, urban life may change drastically as a single car-sharing vehicle can replace 8 to 20 private vehicles, reducing congestion and parking spaces.

At the same time, behavior change, on the grand scale, is rather slow. Because of this, both investors and automakers have increased their investments in electrification over mobility-as-a-service. In fact, YourNow pulled out of the US and some European cities to refocus. Digitization of transportation could further fuel demand for on-demand mobility services. Users of BMW's mobility services can already use a handful of apps to determine the best possible way to arrive at their destination, using their phone to guide them on their journey with real-time information, purchasing of tickets, and booking and unlocking vehicles. Driving is certainly evolving and, at BMW, evolving around the big question "How will we be moving around in the future?" At BMW, a car won't necessarily be a car for much longer. In the not so distant future, a car may be an electric vehicle that drives itself and is connected to everything. And, as part of the shift, what we know as the car may just end up being a service provider that provides way more than just taking people from A to B.

Medtronic

Medtronic started as a repair shop for electrical devices. Helping hospitals maintain their equipment led to the invention of a life-saving product, the pacemaker. Medtronic is now both a product and a services company, taking healthcare into the future.

Facts

Founder
Earl Bakken

Founded in 1949
Minneapolis, USA

Total revenue
$30.6 billion

Industry
Medical devices
Healthcare

Scale
150+ countries
78 manufacturing sites
90,000 employees
21 R&D sites

> We are restoring people by the millions to full life.
> That helps people feel positive about their efforts."

Earl Bakken, Founder Medtronic.

Earl Bakken founded Medtronic as a medical device repair shop with his brother-in-law, Palmer Hermundslie, in 1949. Working out of a garage, the two serviced and repaired open-heart surgery equipment, which made a lot of sense for hospitals as the service eliminated the need to have a maintenance department.

The first years were a struggle. Revenue for the first month was just $8; to get by, they resorted to doing other repairs. Because Bakken and Hermundslie traveled quite a bit to pick up devices needing repairs, they began to develop tight relationships with doctors in local university hospitals, including Walton Lillehei, a heart surgeon at the University of Minnesota Medical School, who pioneered open-heart surgery. This was a turning point.

In the 1950s, pacemakers were heavy and had to be connected to the wall to draw enough power to run. Not only was this cumbersome, it could be hazardous. Due to a power outage in 1957, one Dr. Lillehei's patients, who was just a child, passed away. Needless to say, this was devastating.

Given their relationship, and Bakken's intimate knowledge of medical devices, Dr. Lillehei asked Bakken to come up with a way to power a pacemaker with a battery. Bakken, who at this point had repaired hundreds of different kinds of electronics, looked beyond the apparent for ideas and solutions. It was in *Popular Electronics* magazine that he found a possible solution: a circuit diagram for a metronome. From this diagram Bakken created the first external,

wearable, battery-operated pacemaker, which was connected to a patient by Dr. Lillehei in 1958.

Bakken and Hermundslie shared a deep moral purpose and an inner drive to use their scientific knowledge and entrepreneurial skills to help others. Yet, even with their breakthrough pacemaker invention, they had to borrow money to grow. When lenders asked about Medtronic's mission, the founders stated the following: "To contribute to human welfare by application of biomedical engineering in the research, design, manufacture, and sale of instruments or appliances that alleviate pain, restore health, and extend life." Today, Medtronic is improving the lives of two people every second.

Alleviate pain, restore health, and extend life

The first implantable pacemaker was invented by scientists Wilson Greatbatch and William Chardack in 1960. Because of its vast knowledge in this area, Medtronic was granted the exclusive rights to manufacture and market this new device. Through this deal, Medtronic shifted from repairing heart devices to developing its own devices, always with patients in mind.

Product business model
Medtronic has a mission-driven product business model. The company develops, markets, and sells medical products and therapies to treat more than 30 chronic diseases.

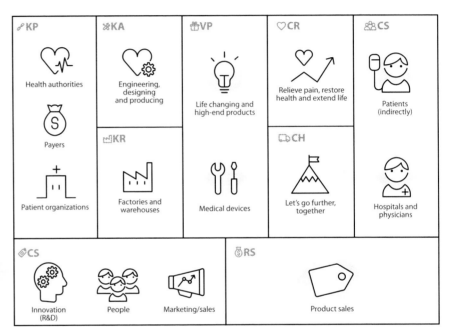

Even sophisticated devices such as pacemakers are at risk of becoming a commodity, however. This forced Medtronic to think beyond products, considering new shifts to its business model, specifically in the area of health care services. Medtronic has always put patients at the center of its business. This also meant that Medtronic staff came across the growing set of challenges that hospitals encounter every day. This triggered them to start Medtronic Integrated Health Solutions (IHS), a dedicated business unit for healthcare services.

The founding IHS team started by following Medtronic products through their journey. They visited customers who purchased Medtronic equipment to see how these high-tech devices were being used. In Russia, the team discovered that a fairly low number of patients were treated in heart centers because of a lack of monitoring equipment. At other sites, they found that too many supplies were being held in stock, some of them expiring before use. The team concluded that operational efficiency and effectiveness was low in many places.

Taking healthcare further, together

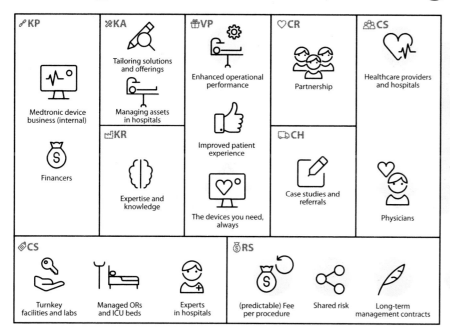

Job done!

The IHS team manages specific parts of a hospital so that doctors and care professionals can focus on their core jobs: treating patients, giving them the best experience possible, and making sure people are able to move on with their lives, healthy and active. Services offered range from material management inside the hospital to running an entire operating room or heart surgery lab.

Managed services
Offering a custom designed managed service that guarantees better outcomes for both patients and the business.

IHS began working with hospitals and other care providers to help them improve patient outcomes, enhance operational performance, and contain and manage costs. Through its IHS services, Medtronic now has partnerships with hundreds of hospitals and providers. And most unique about this business model is that it expanded the traditional supplier-customer relationship. Medtronic IHS teams take an active role in developing the healthcare system with their customers.

Though Medtronic has since its founding had a very successful product business model, the company has invested in a service business model in order to create new value. Former CEO Omar Ishrak noted that the company's service and solutions businesses are "long-term efforts" that will sustain growth in the long run (This quote come from "Further, Together 2015 Integrated Performance Report", page 7). These business models are all about the the shift to health care systems that reward value and patient outcomes over volume. Medtronic happens to be very strong in developing medical technology that can drive these new forms of value creation for the benefit of all people.

Rolls-Royce Aerospace

Since 1904, Rolls-Royce has been pioneering the power that matters, helping to ensure people arrive at their destinations on time. It's constantly innovating to come up with cutting-edge technologies that make air travel more efficient, reliable, and sustainable.

Facts

CEO Warren East	**Total revenue** $16.5 billion (2018)	**Other information** Second largest (after General Electric)	**Scale** 29,000+ airplane engines
Founded in 1904 C. Rolls & H. Royce	**Industry** Automotive and aviation		More than 100 million flying hours

Rolls-Royce Aerospace

 [. . .] to keep pace with with ever-changing, global demands, we know our future generation of engines need to be led by constant, thoughtful innovation."

Rolls-Royce

Since 1904, Rolls-Royce Aerospace has been designing, manufacturing, and distributing power systems for aviation and other industries. If you have ever been a passenger in a wide-body jet such as the Boeing 747 or Airbus A380, you have likely been carried through the air via Rolls-Royce jet engines. So even if you have never stepped foot in a Rolls-Royce luxury car, you may have "driven in a Rolls-Royce" without realizing it.

Since its very beginnings, the aviation industry has been a demanding (and competitive) industry. Airlines must ensure that they get passengers to their destinations safely, on time, and at reasonable costs, all while meeting strict environmental and air traffic regulations. Within the aviation industry,

Rolls-Royce is not only a frontrunner; for decades, the company has been developing breakthrough technologies, such as turbo-fan aircraft engines that power the global air transportation system. To date, Rolls-Royce engines have been used to power the fleets of more than 17 different airlines. It is expected that within a few years, over half of the world's wide-body fleet will be powered by Rolls-Royce engines. This is a huge leap, considering the company's market share was only 22% a decade ago.

It's no easy thing to design, manufacture, purchase, and maintain aircraft engines such as the ones produced by Rolls-Royce. Given how sophisticated these engines are, a single engine takes roughly 20 days to

manufacture. And, of course, these same engines require careful maintenance, relying on specialized knowledge and tools, to keep them in excellent working condition.

It's incumbent on the airlines and business aviation companies to keep their fleets in tip-top shape. Until recently, this responsibility meant maintaining complex aircraft engines, which can directly impact business and customers when they fail.

"So, isn't that the job of the airlines?" you might ask. In fact, this is a huge distraction for airlines. After all, airlines are in the transportation business, not in the engine maintenance, repair, and overhaul business. And Rolls-Royce knows this.

A high-performance product

Selling engines is a cumbersome process, that requires a dedicated direct salesforce. Many technical aspects related to engines need to be considered in making a deal. Besides all the aspects of engine performance, an airline also wants to know everything about warranties, guarantees, maintenance, and support. The manufacturer might sell additional maintenance and support services, but this is no guarantee for a long-term relationship.

Product business model
A high-performance product is sold to customers through a bargaining process. The product is sold, with a warranty and some maintenance and support services. The customer is responsible for the correct and efficient use of the product.

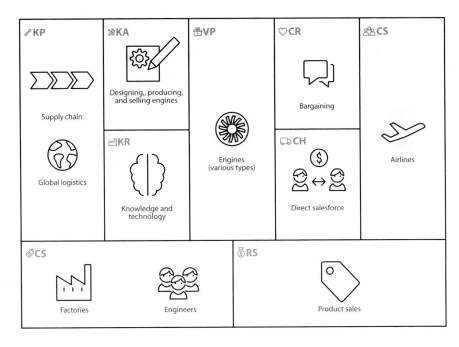

KP
Supply chain
Global logistics

KA
Designing,, producing, and selling engines

KR
Knowledge and technology

VP
Engines (various types)

CR
Bargaining

CH
Direct salesforce

CS
Airlines

CS
Factories
Engineers

RS
Product sales

In 1962, Bristol Siddeley, another British manufacturer of airplane engines, launched a service it coined "Power by the Hour." This service provided complete engine and accessory replacement for the Viper engine, typically installed on business jets, for a fixed fee per flying hour. The operator was now able to accurately forecast cost based on the number of hours flown by any plane in their fleet. What's more, operators no longer needed to focus on repairs or purchasing new stocks of engines and accessories. Everything engine related was managed by Bristol Siddeley's "Power by the Hour" contract. Due to its popularity, Rolls-Royce began to offer the same service in the 1980s, providing airlines with a fixed engine maintenance cost over an extended period of time, quickly becoming the market leader in this product-to-services shift. And although Rolls-Royce trademarked the "Power by the Hour" term, today it's the common name for this business model, which is also offered by General Electric and Pratt & Whitney.

Keep the world flying

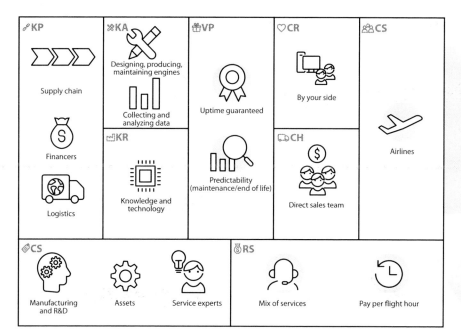

Job Done!

The focus of airlines is to make sure that passengers and freight arrive at their destinations on time, every time. It is all about focusing on efficiency and not having to worry about the technical aspects. The CareStore is the gateway for Rolls-Royce's innovative services providing different customers with the right mix of services they need to keep their engines turning.

Managed services
Engine Health Management (EHM) provides the transfer of data from an engine on an aircraft to an operational centre on the ground. EHM guarantees uptime and performance.

Today, more than 50% of Rolls-Royce's revenue comes from its service-oriented business model, which also happens to be the best way to help customer's get their jobs done. For airlines, this means they can now predict costs and reliability and receive guaranteed performance from their engine partner, Rolls-Royce.

Moreover, the "Power by the Hour" business model eliminates the need to stockpile engines and parts, thereby aligning the objectives of the customer with those of the supplier. Together, Rolls-Royce and its customers focus on minimizing downtime and controlling cost.

From Rolls-Royce 's perspective, via this business model, the company has been able to change the relationship it has with its customers, from transactional to something more akin to a true partnership. If an engine malfunctions, it's in the best interest of Rolls-Royce and the airline to get that airplane back in the sky as soon as possible.

Snackable cases

You stay in their house, while they stay in yours.

Instead of having to rent a hotel or an apartment at your holiday destination, **LoveHomeSwap** is connecting you with people who are making the opposite trip. You stay in their house, while they stay in yours.

Do you fly more often in Europe? Then **KLM** Flight Bundle is something for you. KLM is offering a **service** via which you can **pre-book tickets** and go **whenever you want**. If you already know you will fly more than 3 times this year, you can book a bundle and save a lot of money.

HelloFresh helps solving the problem of having to go to the supermarket to buy dinner. In their service, you can choose what you want

to eat out of a selection of dinners that week, and have it delivered to your home.

Zilok allows you to rent anything you can think of . . .

From individual rentals to business rentals, **Zilok** has it all. Online, you can rent tools, electronics, and luxury goods for an hour, day, week, or even a month. Because of this, you don't need to buy these goods anymore.

Paying for **car insurance is often an expensive cost**. Especially for people that don't drive their car so often. **Metromile** believes it is only fair if users **pay for what they use** and therefore disrupted the industry with its **pay-per-mile car insurance.** Customers only pay based on the miles they drive, allowing its customers to **save $741** on average per person a year.

Maternity clothing as a service

Le Tote, the f**ashion subscription service** launched a **new service** helping women in their maternity providing them **the right clothes**. The rental clothes are designed to evolve and fit your changing body during maternity.

1 Subscription 30,000 gyms

Instead of doing the same workout in the same gym over and over again, **ClassPass** is offering its customers the opportunity to visit 30,000 fitness studios in 2,500 cities around the world. Via the subscription service, you can **choose** what kind of experience you want to attend **instead of being stuck with separate subscription services** for all kind of different activities.

3 Short case studies

Short. Crisp. Fast. Clear.

	Founders	Total revenue	Founded	Scale
1 Dollar Shave Club	Dubin & Levine	$200 million+	2011 in USA	3.2m subscribers
2 SwapFiets	Burger, Uitentuis, Obers & de Bruijn	€20 million	2014 in Delft, NL	124,000 subscribers
3 Rent the Runway	Hyman & Fleiss	$1 billion (2019) *(Total valuation)*	2009 in New York	9m customers

Dollar Shave Club: Fixing a broken experience

Michael Dubin had been frustrated with razors for quite some time. They're used almost every day and should be replaced as often as every few days. Yet, since their invention, there had never been a good way to purchase new razors, outside of going to the convenience or drug store and purchasing them over the counter. Not to mention, due to their pocketable size and high prices, many stores keep razors behind locked doors.

Collective frustrations are great subjects to discuss at parties. So, when Dubin, at a party with one of his family friends, Mark Levin, learned that Levin had a couple of boxes of razors lying around in a warehouse, the two decided to turn their frustrations into Dollar Shave Club. Using their own money and investments from start-up incubator, Science Inc., Dubin and Levin launched Dollar Shave Club in beta mode to learn what customers really wanted.

In March 2012, the founders launched the "Our Blades Are F***ing Great" video on YouTube, which went viral. Dollar Shave Club's promise was simple: "For $1 a month, we send high-quality razors right to your door." In the video, Michael clearly differentiated their proposition, calling out all the extras (10 blades, a flashlight, etc.) that you don't actually need to get a good shave. Shave time, shave money. It was a clear hit from that moment forward.

In turn, using new razors afforded customers the ability to get better shaves and generally feel better. They also s(h)ave time because they don't have to go the store and wait for a cashier to get them razors from behind locked doors. No hassle, saving money, and always looking good are pretty compelling reasons to switch from a bloated, expensive, and hard to get product. What's more, razor subscriptions help to condition customers to change blades every week, which directly enhances customer experience.

"We're here to innovate, disrupt, and remake industries. To do it, we'll need diverse, killer talent from anywhere and everywhere. Join us. It'll be fun."

Slogan on job openings page

Pay for quality and convenience, not marketing

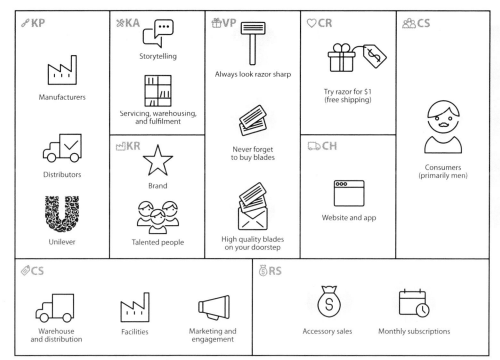

Job Done!
Dollar Shave Club helps their customers accomplish an important and frequent task: ensuring they start the day as the best version of themselves.

Dollar Shave Club expanded and is now offering more than just razors. The company provides a personalized top-shelf grooming routine for over 4 million subscribers. Making sure men look, smell, and feel their best.

Consumables
From needing to intentionally think about and go to the store to buy grooming products to a service that delivers everything you need straight to your doorstep.

Dollar Shave Club's YouTube video was so effective that the very first day it launched, 12,000 people subscribed and joined "the Club." Dollar Shave Club expanded quickly, funded by several rounds of venture capital. During its third round of fundraising in 2014, the company announced the expansion of its product line to include a dozen other men's products, pursuing the founders' ambition to "own" the men's bathroom.

On July 19, 2016, Dollar Shave Club was acquired by Unilever for $1 billion in cash. Unilever, a personal care company, did not have a direct channel to customers and believed in the Dollar Shave Club construct. For Dollar Shave Club, the acquisition provided access to global knowledge and experience in the male grooming sector as well as financial backing to help achieve its global ambitions.

Swapfiets:
Never late again

When a few students in Delft, The Netherlands, saw a fellow student ride by on a worn-out bicycle that could break down any minute, they saw an opportunity. What if you could have a bike that always worked? The answer: a subscription business model that provides and services bikes to riders who need them. "We experienced the hassle of buying a bike and maintaining it so that it keeps working. You are always in so much trouble when it breaks down." So, they went ahead and fixed this problem.

Delft Blue in the streets
In January 2015, they launched Swapfiets, offering city dwellers a bike for €15 per month. If it breaks down, the Swapfiets team meets you at your location, repairs it on the spot if possible, or trades it out for a new bike within a day. If the Swapfiets bike is stolen, customers pay €40 and get a new one right away.

When Swapfiets was launched, the student entrepreneurs bought secondhand bikes and parts on Marktplaats (the Dutch eBay) and refurbished them into the first editions of Swapfiets, painting the front tire Delft Blue. Today you can see Delft Blue spinning in the streets in many cities in the Netherlands, Belgium, Germany, and Denmark.

The customer in the loop
Swapfiets is a service company that is closely connected to its customers. The company goes the extra mile to ensure its customers always have a safe, working bike. The swap teams see customers every day, ensuring that bike swaps are painless. This daily connection with customers also provides a direct feedback loop for the teams that design the customer experience and the bike. Having the customer in the loop has enabled the Swapfiets design team to continuously improve the service and the bike as well.

> For a fixed monthly fee you get a Swapfiets. We make sure your Swapfiets always works."

Promise on the Swapfiets website

Cycling without worries

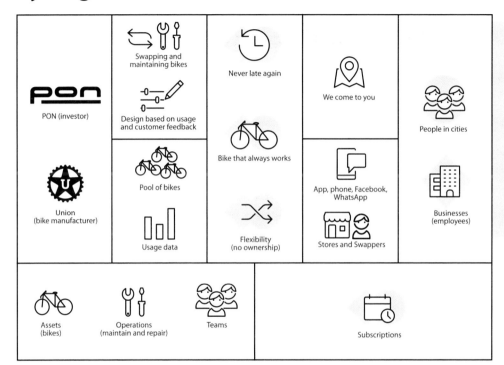

PON (investor)

Swapping and maintaining bikes

Design based on usage and customer feedback

Pool of bikes

Usage data

Union (bike manufacturer)

Never late again

Bike that always works

Flexibility (no ownership)

We come to you

App, phone, Facebook, WhatsApp

Stores and Swappers

People in cities

Businesses (employees)

Assets (bikes)

Operations (maintain and repair)

Teams

Subscriptions

Job done!

Fifteen euros a month is quite something compared to a 100 euros second-hand bike. Yet, lots of people are willing to pay this monthly fee. In return they get flexibility and no maintenance hassle or big upfront costs. With a Swapfiets that always works, you're never late again for a lecture, date, or beer. For Swapfiets, the company, it's a different picture. In order to make the bike service available to customers, the company had to invest a lot of money upfront.

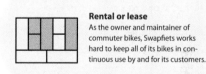

Rental or lease
As the owner and maintainer of commuter bikes, Swapfiets works hard to keep all of its bikes in continuous use by and for its customers.

Keeping bikes in use

Travel to any city where bikes are used for commuting and you'll likely find lots of forgotten, broken, and stolen bikes. Unlike other bike sharing services, Swapfiets customers have a shared sense of "ownership," because they use Swapfiets bikes every day, traveling door-to-door. And as with other service business models, such as Rolls-Royce's "Power by the Hour," it's incumbent on Swapfiets to keep their bikes in good, working condition. Moreover, Swapfiets works with their design and manufacturing partner, Union, to better serve their customers by continually updating bike designs to be more durable and user-friendly.

And it shows! With its customer-focused service business model, Swapfiets has grown way beyond its student roots. From its humble beginnings, serving 150 students, the company has grown to service more than 124,000 customers and operates in more than 60 cities in 4 countries. The future looks bright for Swapfiets.

Rent the Runway: Only pay for what you wear

You've been invited to attend an amazing party . . . yay! This also raises an internal alarm: *What should I wear?!* Many people know the anxiety of "a closet full of clothes, but nothing to wear." Seeing this problem firsthand was the reason Jenny Hyman and Jennifer Fleiss started Rent the Runway in 2008. Rent the Runway is a service focused on renting out party dresses. The need that Hyman and Fleiss sought to fill turned out to be much bigger than they thought. Rent the Runway now offers a dream closet for various occasions. The company even rents out party dresses for kids and has a partnership with West Elm to rent out home décor.

A smart closet

Rent the Runway offers a smart closet, ensuring women are dressed in style and can go out feeling confident. This closet changes with how women want to lead their lives, easily accommodating changes in life stage, taste, and mood. Rent the Runway has a sophisticated process for inbound logistics in order to achieve the highest usage possible. Clothes that are returned by customers are checked for stains and damage and are cleaned and repaired so that they can be rented out to another customer. Everything the company does is focused on making renting easier and more affordable than purchasing clothes. Rent the Runway has return boxes at WeWork and Nordstrom, making it convenient for customers to return items on the go. The company has also opened stores as an extension of their customers' closets. Just browse, pick what you like, and go.

Design for the real user

High profile designers like Jason Wu and Derek Lam work with Rent the Runway. By leveraging the insights collected from data, designs can be customized to its users in terms of fit and style. A traditional retailer does not have information about how clothes are used after they leave the store. Is this why more retailers are starting subscription services?

Always a dress to impress

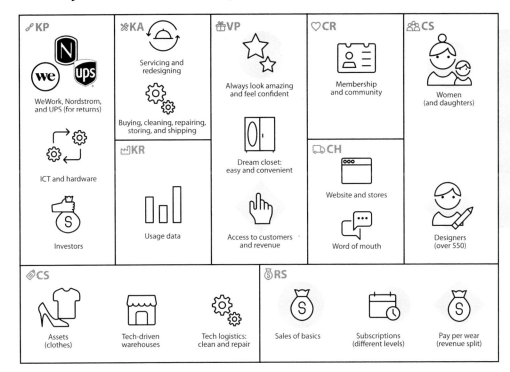

Job done!

Having all the clothes of your liking at your disposal for every occasion, without breaking the bank. What's more: no more shopping required. That is also a big problem solved for many men too, giving them more time left to enjoy life. The value proposition for designers is that they get to test the newest styles, allowing them to optimize them for fit, finish, and price.

Rental or lease
A platform to connect designer brands directly to consumers, driven by data to provide brands and consumers a next level experience.

The sharing economy in action

Instead of owning clothes, women have access to all the designers' clothes they like for a flat fee per month. Women have a closet in the cloud that helps them look amazing and feel good for every occasion, which also helps to ensure clothes are actually worn more.

With women serving as walking billboards, the company has grown organically and exponentially. With all of this growth, Rent the Runway has worked hard to streamline its operations, ensuring it always has the freshest outfits to meet the ever-growing demand of its customers. In many ways, Rent the Runway is changing the fashion

industry. Whereas most fashion brands have focused on high-end retail stores for decades, today many of these same brands supply clothes to Rent the Runway at zero upfront cost, adopting a pay-per-wear model, splitting the revenue. In the end, all that matters is that every woman is able to look amazing in each designer's clothes.

What kind of premium service provider will you be, before your products become a commodity?

BMW sees itself as a mobility provider delivering premium services. Historically, BMW already offered many car-related services to help its customers get the most out of their cars. YourNow is the mobility brand from BMW and Daimler AG with over 60 million customers.

Ask yourself the following questions . . .

Where do you see an opportunity in starting a dedicated service business model that makes customers successful?

Medtronic is the technology company that is famous for its pacemakers with annual sales of about $30 billion. Earl Bakken founded the company with the mission to alleviate pain, restore health, and extend life. The company has a dedicated business unit Integrated Health Solutions that is fulfilling the mission with a range of services.

How can you become embedded into the operations of your customers, keeping their business spinning?

Rolls-Royce truly understands customer needs and what jobs their customers must accomplish. In the aviation industry, product and service have become so closely connected that they are now inseparable. Advancements in digital capabilities now make serving a single customer at a time possible, while continuously improving the business model and performance based on data coming from all customers.

What products could you be providing from the cloud, removing the headache customers have from choosing what to buy?

Rent the Runway is the rental company for designer's clothes, making sure its 9 million members are dressed in style. Some of its customers have even stopped buying clothes.

What Club could you start that would fix a terrible broken consumer experience?

Dollar Shave Club started from personal frustration and saw an opportunity to own the men's bathroom. Remember, this service is not about shipping products to customers; it is all about making sure its "Club members" have what they need to look, smell, and feel good.

What product can you think of that customers would prefer to swap instead of being the owner of it?

Swapfiets started from a simple observation. Students have big problems when their bikes break down. They may be late for class or a visit to the bar with friends. As it turns out, renting a bike that is swapped the moment it breaks down is what many people (not just students) are more than willing to pay for on a monthly basis.

High level strategic choices

1   2   3

 **Adopt a services mindset**

Customers expect more from a service company. You must therefore (dare to) re-think the end-to-end experience.

Really be of service. Do everything you need to do to make your service work for customers and live up to your promise.

 Focus on the job to be done

Make sure that customers can focus on their core business. You are hired to get one of their other important jobs done.

Focus on the job that your customers need done and do it very well. Communicate about what you are getting done for them.

 Finance your assets

You won't have capital sales anymore. Your company makes the capital investments and customers profit from using your services.

Do not use a product perspective to look at financials. Use the right metrics and find a way to finance service delivery long term.

to drive this shift.

4 ——— 5 ——— 6 ———

 Engage

 Partner with providers

 Renew

A close relationship is crucial when selling and delivering services. It is how you get to deeply understand a customer's business and organization.

Don't just deliver the service. Make the experience human and engaging. Interact with customers frequently. You just might discover another job they need to get done.

There are many moving parts in a service business model. You need to make sure that everything comes together and that the agreed service levels are achieved.

Figure out what is core and non-core. Work with partners that take care of the non-core parts. Focus everything on delivering a great outcome.

Service contracts have an end date or can be canceled. It's important to stay connected to your customers during the entire contract period.

Regularly evaluate the service delivered. This is your feedback loop for renewing the service offer and staying relevant. Use those insights to innovate your services.

From shareholder to stakeholder

Generating revenue and making a profit is a result, not a goal. In the long term, a company will destroy shareholder value if it neglects its stakeholders by creating declining or inconsistent value for its customers.

shareholder →

The stakeholder shift is a business model strategy that seeks to **ensure that value is created for all stakeholders—customers, employees, partners, society, and investors—simultaneously.** It's a business model that **actively engages each and every stakeholder to make sure they achieve their goals as well.** As a result, customers are much more satisfied; employees are more dedicated to serving customers and innovating to meet future needs of customers; partners invest in collaboration because it drives growth of their business; society welcomes companies that embrace this shift because of the positive impact they have on communities; and last but not least, investors love companies that make the stakeholder shift because **they outperform profit-seeking companies by a factor of 5 to 8 in the long term** (according to the book Firms of Endearment). Shifting from prioritizing short-term profits for shareholders to prioritizing long-term value for all stakeholders requires ongoing effort, as demonstrated by the companies highlighted in this chapter.

Shift stories

Large
↗ Unilever

Medium
↗ BlackRock
↗ TOMS Shoes

Short
↗ Cipla
↗ WE.org
↗ Tony's Chocolonely
↗ Starbucks

stakeholder

The Long-Term Stock Exchange is more than a platform for trading shares. It's a chance to build a new relationship between companies that are built to last and the stakeholders who believe in them. (. . .) Today's companies deserve a public market where they are rewarded for making smart choices that embrace their futures—choices to innovate, to invest in their employees, to seed future growth."

Source: longtermstockexchange.com

Short-termism

Most public companies cater to their shareholders to the exclusion of almost any other goals. Most shareholders want to see results and return on their investment today or at least next quarter. These narrowly defined financial demands are not supportive of growing your business in a value-driven way.

Short-termism does not provide a solid foundation for anyone to make decisions that are beneficial for customers and the value the company could be creating for them. Short-termism also tends to kill innovation that goes beyond incremental improvements of your current business (model). Not to mention, short-term thinking (and actions) often come with external costs, like environmental damage, that are paid by society.

On the other side, quite a few public companies have bravely abandoned quarterly reporting to create the conditions to innovate and thrive in the long term. Are you bold enough to tell your shareholders, "If you do not like this, please invest your money elsewhere"?

Strategic questions
Do you as a board or management team member favor shareholder interests over the interests of customers, employees, partners, and society? Do you think that such a narrow view allows you to keep your license to operate? What do you think is the effect of this viewpoint on how customers are treated and how employees feel about their work? How can you turn this around? Who are your stakeholders and how might you create value for all of them? What about enlarging the (business) pie for the benefit of all stakeholders instead of leaving your stakeholders out of the equation? What can you learn and apply from companies that are making this shift or that have made this shift already?

From shareholder

The shareholder business model is designed to maximize returns to shareholders. It's the job of the management team to ensure efficient operations so that as much product as possible can be sold to customers at the best margins, often irrespective of the external costs.

Selling at good margins

Customers have a general or specific need, and the product they buy satisfies that need. The relationship with customers lacks loyalty. In the shareholder business model, selling product is more important than knowing who's buying it. This business model is all about sales, sales, sales, at good margins. Profit is returned to shareholders and partially invested in push marketing to reach more and more customers.

Maximizing profits

The key activity in the shareholder business model is setting quarterly targets and ensuring they are met each and every time. The company is obsessed with chasing customers and deals just to make sure it achieves its revenue goals. If financial goals cannot be met through sales-driven revenue, cost-cutting programs are initiated to sanitize the financial health of the company. Another way companies working with this business model achieve targets is to acquire another company and its revenue, just to make the balance sheet look good.

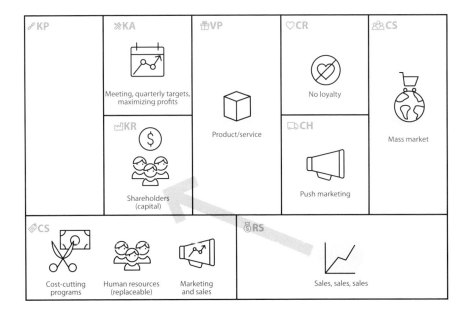

to stakeholder

Serving customers and beyond

A stakeholder business model offers customers a product or service that serves functional and social/emotional needs at the same time. The customer relationship is characterized by empathy, resulting in customers being emotionally attached to the company (often referred to as a company's *lovemark*). Sales are often recurring, and customer acquisition is mostly through word of mouth.

Engage all stakeholders

A key activity in this business model is delighting customers. In order to accomplish this, employees are consistently trained and coached on the job ensuring that they empathize with customers and have everything they need to make customers happy. Employees receive above average wages and love working together and with partners. Partners are fully engaged in the value creation and delivery process and are able to grow their business as a result. Investors are patient and confident that investing in innovation and community projects results in the greatest return on capital in the long term.

The stakeholder business model is designed to create as much value as possible for every stakeholder of the company (and society at large). The job of the management team is to ensure each and every stakeholder is fully engaged.

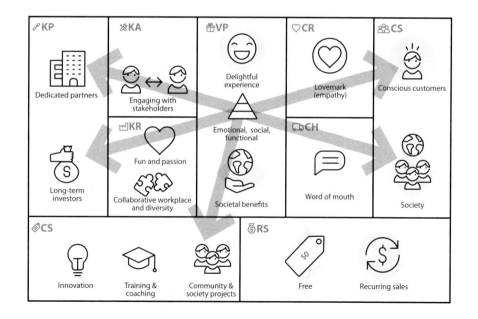

Serve
the ones
in real need

Boost
emerging
economies

---

①

The Serve the Ones in Real Need pattern addresses an unmet need for people that are not served by the market. This pattern serves a customer segment that is ignored by other companies or government by using an innovative approach to creating and delivering value.

Examples

Cipla

②

The Boost Emerging Economies pattern offers consumers and communities in emerging economies a better future. Companies that work with this pattern provide consumers access to affordable and quality products and services. These companies provide people within communities a good income opportunity and access to markets.

Examples

Unilever, Hilnet, Sustainable South Bronx

Patterns

One for One™

Force to do good

The One for One pattern is about embedding giving at the heart of the business model. One customer segment (often wealthy) buys goods. The value of the purchased item is given away to another customer segment, people who are in need.

Examples

TOMS Shoes, Lemonade, Warby Parker

The Force to Do Good pattern is about activating people for a common cause. This pattern presents a value proposition that gets people motivated to join the mission of the social enterprise. Funding of the value proposition comes from donors, philanthropists, or companies. These are also companies with a mission to change society.

Examples

BlackRock, WE.org, Starbucks, Tony Chocolonely, The BodyShop, Brownies and Downies

Unilever

Unilever was founded based on the value of shared prosperity. Throughout its history, Unilever has introduced many products that provide social benefits. Over the past decade, by fearlessly developing its multi-stakeholder business model, Unilever has become a leader in sustainability.

Facts

Founding companies
Margarine Unie and Lever Brothers

Founded in 1929
in United Kingdom

Total revenue
$52 billion (2019)

Industry
Consumer goods

Scale
400 brands
190 countries
155,000 employees
(2019)

Timeline

1929
Founded

Unilever is formed by a merger of the operations of Dutch Margarine Unie and British soap maker Lever Brothers.

1930-2000
Global expansion

Unilever diversifies and expands the portfolio of brands, while also divesting of some. In 2000, Unilever acquires Ben & Jerry's, a social enterprise.

2004
Vitality

The brand identity is developed around the idea of "adding vitality to life," showing 25 distinct symbols representing sub brands or corporate values. The Dove brand launches its Real Beauty campaign, which focuses on women of all shapes and color.

> Unless we change direction, models show that the profit of the entire consumer goods sector could be wiped out by 2050."

Source: Paul Polman at Rio+20.

Shared prosperity

Unilever brought together Margarine Unie, a merger of four margarine companies, and Lever Brothers, a company that introduced soaps meant to help prevent disease and promote personal hygiene; all these companies were driven by an ambition to create societal benefits. In fact, The Lever brothers believed social benefit started with their own workers. In 1887, they built them Port Sunlight, a village providing a high quality of living, even before the factory was running. They also fought for a 6-day workweek and introduced pensions in the UK. In 1929, Margarine Unie and Lever Brothers merged to become Unilever.

In 1996, the World Wide Fund for Nature (WWF) and Unilever founded the Marine Stewardship Council to address the problem of overfishing and declining fish stock. The Marine Stewardship Council works with farmers and suppliers to create sustainable agriculture plans. The Council also partners with Greenpeace to develop ice cream freezers that use natural refrigerants. Through such partnerships and its own initiatives, Unilever remains on the leading edge of stewardship.

Even as a company founded on stewardship and giving back, by the mid-2000s, Unilever fell into a standard quarterly rhythm and short-term focus, rather than long-term value creation. In 2009, with a new CEO, Paul Polman, at the helm, this ceased. Polman put a stop to quarterly reports, which he believed led to short-termism. Through clear-sighted leadership, Polman gave Unilever permission to change.

Unilever

2007
Rainforest Alliance

Partnership to sustainably source all its tea for Lipton and PG Tips by 2015. This contributed to more than 38,000 smallholder farmers gaining Rainforest Alliance certification, providing good working conditions for 175,000 tea growers.

2008
Green Palm

Unilever makes decision to source all palm oil from sustainable sources by 2015.

2009
Paul Polman

Paul Polman becomes the first CEO from outside the company.

Sustainable Living Plan

In November 2010, the Sustainable Living Plan is launched. This plan has three big sustainability goals to be achieved in 2020:
1) improve health and well-being for more than 1 billion people,
2) reduce the environmental impact by half,
3) enhance livelihoods for millions.

Shareholder business model

Shareholder business model
In the 2000s, the overall Unilever business model was driven by financial performance, completing many mergers, acquisitions, and divestments attempting to achieve maximum shareholder return.

Unilever was founded on the idea of shared prosperity by introducing many products with social benefits, all managed under a brand portfolio business model. Separately branded goods are developed and sold to consumers through Unilever's other customer segments, retailers, and other points of sale.

Unilever's main activity is managing a huge portfolio of brands in food, personal care, and home care. For each brand, key activities are branding, selling, and distribution on the one hand, and manufacturing and developing quality products on the other hand.

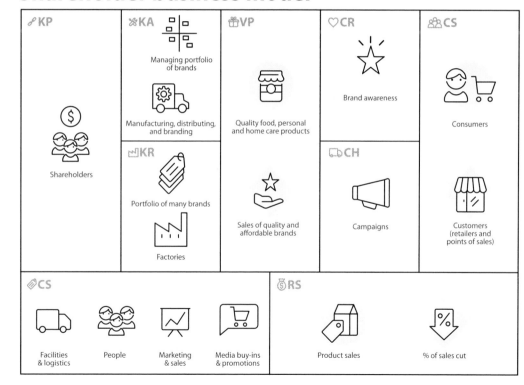

- **KP** Shareholders
- **KA** Managing portfolio of brands / Manufacturing, distributing, and branding
- **KR** Portfolio of many brands / Factories
- **VP** Quality food, personal and home care products / Sales of quality and affordable brands
- **CR** Brand awareness
- **CH** Campaigns
- **CS** Consumers / Customers (retailers and points of sales)
- **CS** Facilities & logistics / People / Marketing & sales / Media buy-ins & promotions
- **RS** Product sales / % of sales cut

<footer>From shareholder to stakeholder 61</footer>

2010
Fairtrade

Ben & Jerry's commits to sourcing only Fairtrade certified ingredients by 2013.

2011
Cage-free eggs

Unilever commits to move to 100% cage-free eggs for all products, including mayonnaise and Ben & Jerry's ice cream brands. This causes a ripple effect across the industry, leading to increased use of cage-free eggs.

2012
Plastics

Unilever makes decision to phase out micro-plastics in personal care products by 2015.

Sustainable living plan

Under Polman's leadership, Unilever publicly committed to aggressive social, environmental, and financial goals in order to drive innovation across its entire portfolio of businesses. These goals reach beyond products such as soap, toothpaste, and safe drinking water. Polman believes Unilever can help trigger people to change their habits, such as brushing teeth twice a day, eating healthier, and exercising. In many ways, Polman's ideals harken to Unilever's early beginnings with soap, which was developed to bring health and hygiene to the entire world simply by making it easier for people to wash their hands.

Emerging markets

Product development at Unilever always starts by seeking to understand consumer needs. Unilever product managers discovered that women living in rural India, for example, are interested in beauty products, just as are their counterparts in many other parts of the world. However, in many cases, rural communities lack access to these products. At the same time, rural markets work differently than developed ones in that products are sold by individuals and not necessarily by stores.

Being on the ground in these communities, Unilever product managers trained local women as rural sales agents who sell door-to-door in their communities. This is no small undertaking or market. In 2015, the number of sales agents had grown to 70,000 serving 165,000 Indian villages. Equipped with smartphone apps provided by Unilever to help them manage inventory and other aspects of their business, women are provided with new opportunities to make money and boost the local economy. Variations of this concept have been created in Bangladesh, Vietnam, Sri Lanka, Egypt, and other countries.

 The problems our society faces [. . .] are urgent and complex. Change in our own business is not enough."

Paul Polman, Unilever CEO (2009-2018)

Unilever

2015
UN SDGs

Publication of the United Nations Sustainable Development Goals. 15 of the 17 Sustainable Development Goals as set by the United Nations are covered by the Sustainable Living Plan, setting the bold target for Unilever and its subsidiaries to be carbon positive by 2030.

Sustainable Living brands

Sustainable Living brands account for half of Unilever's growth. These brands grew faster than the rest of the business. An oral health campaign created by children to get people to brush their teeth twice a day reached 71 million people. Millions of consumers engaged through campaigns to see how food is sustainably sourced (Hellmann's mayonnaise, Breyer's ice cream) and to save billions of liters of water (OMO laundry products)

This business model focuses on consumers in emerging markets who need quality food, personal care, and home care products that are packaged and priced to suit their needs and budget.

Local women are a customer segment acting as a sales channel, distributing products door-to-door and earning a commission on every product sold. A key activity is innovating for local needs of consumers and rural communities. NGOs, partners in this model, help to boost local economies and spread the business model to other rural areas.

Boost emerging economy
Offering access to Unilever brands through enabling women to run a micro-business serving the local economy door-to-door.

Unilever rural consumers

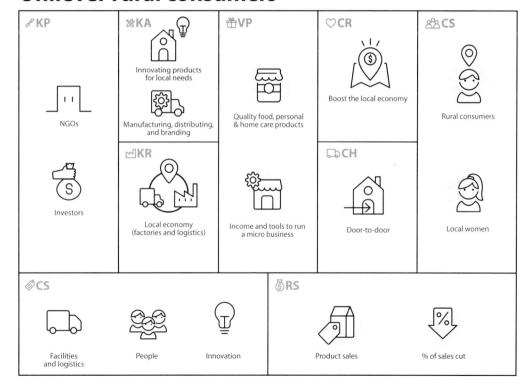

2016
Dollar Shave Club

Unilever acquires Dollar Shave Club for $1 billion, adding a brand to the portfolio with a direct channel and relationship to customers.

2017
Upgrade portfolio

Unilever acquires Pukka Herbs, a herbal tea company, and sells the margarine and spreads division to investment firm KKR for €6.8 billion.

We believe that sustainable business drives superior performance and that this is the only way to create long-term value for all our stakeholders."

Strategy page Unilever website.

Changing the industry

As one of the world's biggest food companies, about half of Unilever's raw materials comes from agriculture, making it among the largest buyers of certain crops, such as black tea, tomatoes, dried onion, and garlic. Unilever is also the biggest user of plastics. But Polman and Unilever don't believe the company exists in stasis, only achieving the status quo. The Unilever Sustainable Living Plan (USLP) is the bold ambition to achieve change within the company and the industry.

Changing consumer habits

Unilever also believes that it can help reduce environmental impact by creating better, more sustainable products that also encourage consumers to use them differently. For instance, whereas a large negative impact comes from products used for washing clothes, Unilever is developing products, such as Comfort One Rinse fabric conditioner, formulated for water-scarce regions. In such regions, hand-washing laundry is often the norm, and using Comfort One Rinse requires only one bucket of water per load of laundry, as opposed to the usual three buckets.

Circular economy

It is only logical that Unilever, with its stakeholder orientation and sustainable business model, is also driving the circular shift, as a Global Partner of Ellen Mac Arthur Foundation (EMF). Before Unilever can achieve its goal of reducing its environmental impact by half , the company must extend sustainability to circularity. Unilever plans to meet its sustainability goal by helping its 2.5 billion daily users live more sustainably while also working to shift its global supply chain to become more and more sustainable. Needless to say, this is a tall order.

Unilever

L

2017
Kraft-Heinz

Unilever declines a bid of $143 billion from much smaller Kraft-Heinz because Kraft-Heinz is a purely cost- and financially driven company, focused on maximizing return to shareholders, which is the exact opposite of everything Unilever stands for.

Purpose is growth

Brand purpose and economic growth are interlinked. The company's Sustainable Living brands account for 70% of turnover growth in 2018 and grow 46% faster than the rest of the business. 1.3 billion people reached with programs to increase health and wellness. Per consumer use, greenhouse gas impact increased by 6%, water use slightly decreased by 2%, and waste impact reduced by 31%. Opportunities created for 1.85 million women and 2.5 million smallholders and small retailers.

Multi-stakeholder business model

The multi-stakeholder business model has two customer segments. The first is the conscious consumer that is concerned about sustainability and making more deliberate choices about what they buy. The second is made up of the Unilever customers, which include retailers who sell Unilever products globally.

The left-hand side of the business model is focused on working with stakeholders to achieve the goals of the Sustainable Living Plan.

Force to do good
The new sustainable business model that has become an inspiration for global social enterprises seeking profit with a wider economic, social, and environmental impact.

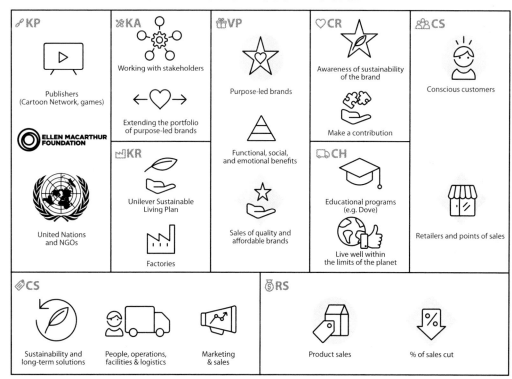

No more short-termism

Businesses can be driven by purpose or by profit. According to Paul Polman, a business that is driven only by shareholders' need to maximize profits won't be able to sustain itself and make a long-lasting difference. In an April 2019 conference call with more than 500 business leaders organized by YPO's Social Engagement Network, Polman states: "I have always felt that the reason that we, as businesses, are around is to help serve society. If after all, we cannot explain what we do positively for society, why should society keep us around? Business was invented first and foremost, to find solutions that would cater to the needs of the world's citizens."

To that end, Unilever has set ambitious goals to become the leader in sustainable business, manifesting itself in its multi-stakeholder business model. Throughout the years, Unilever's brand portfolio has become increasingly purpose-led, removing brands from the portfolios that don't support its sustainability ambitions. Being clear about its plan and progress, Unilever leads by example, continuously sharing its story to a variety of audiences.

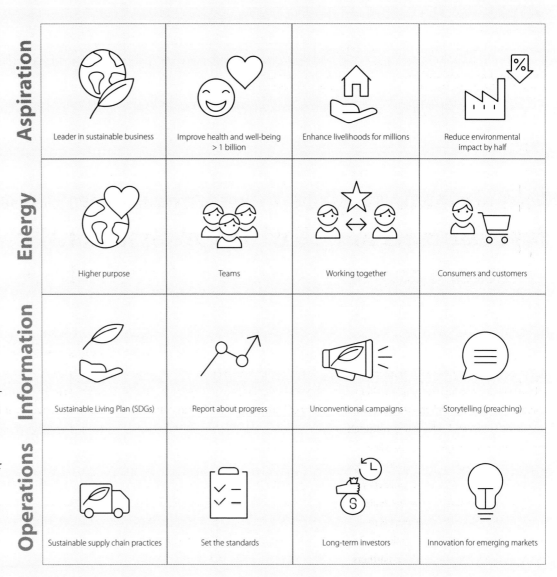

Aspiration
- Leader in sustainable business
- Improve health and well-being > 1 billion
- Enhance livelihoods for millions
- Reduce environmental impact by half

Energy
- Higher purpose
- Teams
- Working together
- Consumers and customers

Information
- Sustainable Living Plan (SDGs)
- Report about progress
- Unconventional campaigns
- Storytelling (preaching)

Operations
- Sustainable supply chain practices
- Set the standards
- Long-term investors
- Innovation for emerging markets

Unilever

L

2019
100% Renewable

Unilever sites across 5 continents are powered by 100% renewable grid electricity, ahead of their 2020 target.

2020
Compass strategy

Sustainability and stakeholder-focus are embedded into every part of Unilever's business.

Future
Carbon-neutral

Unilever's aim and vision is to become carbon-neutral in all operations by 2030

The ultimate purpose of a company is to create amazing value for customers and all of its stakeholders. With so much value created, a company is way more profitable in the long term.

Make purpose pay

About one-third of the world's population uses a Unilever product every day. To help continue to drive the stakeholder-first vision within the company, Unilever has instituted the slogan "make purpose pay" as a key part of board-level discussions, which helps to further the development of Unilever's multi-stakeholder business model. It also turns out that making that change is rewarding in other ways. Not only do employees, consumers, and supply chain partners receive more value, investors receive better returns (5-8 times higher than the average S&P 500 company , according to the book Firms of Endearment) on their investments.

Compass strategy

Paul Polman, set the course toward a global company that behaves responsibly and is a frontrunner in developing sustainable business models. The goals of the Sustainable Living Plan have more or less been achieved. Yet, Unilever's job is hardly finished in a world in the middle of health, climate, and equality crises. Embedding sustainability and stakeholder-focus into every part of its business is ongoing, using a stakeholder orientation as the compass for their strategy.

BlackRock

Financial return and social well-being are interrelated. Companies cannot turn a blind eye to the negative effects they generate on everyone and everything around them for the sake of profit. BlackRock demands corporations work to build a more sustainable business model that creates value for all stakeholders.

Facts

Founders
Fink, Kapito, Wagner,
Novick, Golub, Frater,
Schlosstein, and Anderson

Founded
in 1988

Total revenue
$14.5 billion (2019)

Industry
Investment management

Scale
70 offices in 30 countries.
Largest (shadow) bank
in the world

> *Purpose is not a mere tagline or marketing campaign; it is a company's fundamental reason for being—what it does every day to create value for its stakeholders. Purpose is not the sole pursuit of profits but the animating force for achieving them."*

Larry Fink's annual letter to CEOs, 2019.

Purpose is the reason for being

BlackRock was started by eight people determined to put clients' needs and interests first. They believed they could manage their clients' assets in a more holistic way by deeply understanding and managing risk. At the time, as with most investment management firms, BlackRock could only scale its services and risk-based approach by hiring more people. This changed in 1999.

A decade after launching BlackRock, the company developed and began to sell an innovative risk management software, called Aladdin. This not only helped BlackRock to scale beyond its walls, it put the company in a great position to IPO, which it did the same year Aladdin was launched. By the end of that year, BlackRock's assets under management grew to $165 billion.

The transparency BlackRock offered combined with industry leading software attracted more clients. And, in 2000, the company spun off BlackRock Solutions, based on Aladdin, turning BlackRock into a technology provider. The company continued its tremendous growth path into the 2000s, acquiring Merrill Lynch Investment Management and Barclay's Global Investors.

Crisis or opportunity?

When the economy crashed, it took down companies—and in some cases, countries—with it. As a fiduciary agent to thousands of institutions, BlackRock advised many how to navigate their way through the tough times ahead. In fact, BlackRock was so well trusted as an asset manager, the US government contracted with the company to help the largest economy in the world resolve the fallout. Coming out of the crash, BlackRock became the largest asset manager in the world, with $4.3 trillion under management.

BlackRock old model

BlackRock promises its clients control of their financial security and financial well-being. BlackRock's clients are investors of all types, subdivided into individuals, institutions, and finance professionals. The key activities are managing risk, advising clients, and developing software for risk management. The focus in this model is on profit and doing whatever is needed to keep customers with smiles on their faces and money in their pockets.

Shareholder business model
Managing assets and returning investments to its paying customers for a handsome fee.

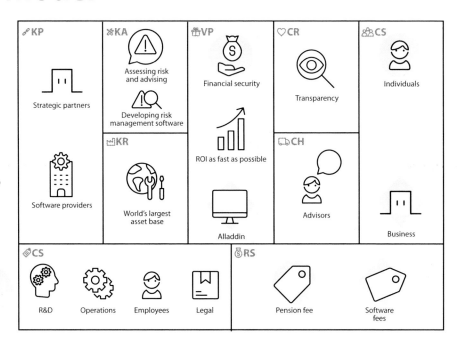

Being the largest asset manager on the planet isn't necessarily a good thing . . . at least not to everyone. Money hoarding is often criticized as a leading cause of many of the world's socio-economic problems. And when you're a company as large as BlackRock, which has a massive sway on the stock market, it's not easy to go unnoticed.

Long-term value, not profit
Upon being labeled "extremely dangerous" by some of its biggest critics, BlackRock's management decided that they needed to do more to help the world, and not just the companies in it. This led to what's called Investment Stewardship, a way to engage with companies to ensure they adhere to

sound corporate governance and business practices, emphasizing direct dialogue with other companies on governance issues affecting sustainable long-term financial performance.

Blackrock new model

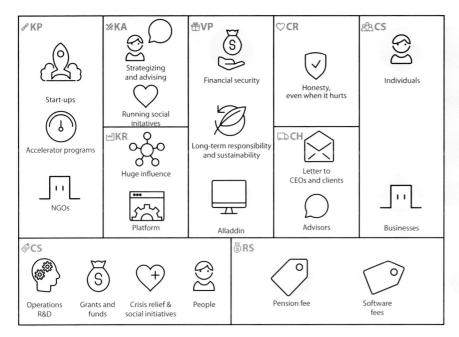

Shared value!

BlackRock didn't change its entire business model when it shifted towards focusing on all stakeholders. The promise today is no different than it was when the company started: help people to invest in their financial well-being.

Force to do good
Actively serving all stakeholders with state-of-the-art technology and leading industry knowledge.

BlackRock has also set its own goals to contribute positively to all of its stakeholders. Through accelerator programs, such as Echoing Green, the company hopes to help catalyze innovations that help advance social, economic, and environmental progress. BlackRock also partners with nonprofit organizations to help communities all over the

world through grants and skills trainings, even going so far as to set up a $50 million fund to help underserved people build emergency savings for times of crisis. To that end, BlackRock has grown to become a propagator of the notion of "long-term prosperity" and has become a model for a stakeholder-oriented company.

However, it was the realization that companies that lack purpose are also lousy investments that changed how BlackRock thinks about risk and long-term value creation. To that end, BlackRock has become an ambassador for purpose-based and stakeholder-oriented companies.

TOMS Shoes

Start something that matters. Create a business model that sells a product and gives one away to a person in need. Focus on maximizing the purpose first and profit second.

Facts

Founders
Blake Mycoskie
& Alejo Nittie

Founded in 2006
in United States

Total revenue
$330 million (2018)

Industry
Shoes, eyewear, and apparel

Scale
Donated over 60 million pairs of shoes, as well as eyewear, water, and birth kits

> # We're in business to improve lives.
> # For every $3 we make, we give $1 away"

Source: website of TOMS Company Mission Statement

Maximize purpose, not profit

In 2006, Blake Mycoskie was traveling through Argentina. What he saw gave him pause. Many of the children he encountered were growing up without a good pair of shoes. This was a journey that inspired Mycoskie and his friend, Alejo Nittie, to design the One for One™ business model: sell a retail product and give one product away to someone in need. Using this business model, Mycoskie and Nittie launched TOMS Shoes, which featured a simple canvas shoe inspired by the Alpargata slipper from Argentina. TOMS became an immediate hit. In the first year the company received orders for more than 10,000 pairs of shoes, for which it distributed an equal amount to Argentine children, for free.

Expanding the impact

TOMS saw its success with shoes as validation that given the choice, consumers would choose to purchase some items over others if those items did more than deliver quality. In essence, right out of the gates, TOMS cracked the code of breaking into the consumer goods market with a purpose-based business model.

Having cracked this code, in order to create even more impact, TOMS decided to expand this formula to other products. In 2011, the company launched TOMS Eyewear, providing sight restoration for over 400,000 people. With each purchase of TOMS Eyewear, TOMS provides everything from prescription glasses, medical treatment, to surgery for those in need. The company also launched TOMS Roasting Co., a consumer coffee bean company, which has provided millions of liters of safe water supply in six countries. Soon after, TOMS launched TOMS Bag Collection, selling canvas bags and totes to consumers and providing safe birth kits and training to tens of thousands of skilled birth attendants. With this growth in giving, TOMS also had to shift its business model to utilize grants for many of the donations the company makes. Whereas the company started with a simple one-for-one shoe business model, today for every $3 made from products TOMS gives away $1 to causes customers care about.

Customers on a mission

In addition to giving, TOMS inspires people to actively join the movement. For example, the company organizes the One Day Without Shoes event, where millions of people join in spending a full day without shoes. The company has done so well proving to the world that a business model that sells fashion and compassion is viable, that in 2014 Bain Capital acquired 50% of TOMS with the goal of helping it to grow faster.

Traditional shoe brand

Valued at hundreds of billions of dollars and continuing to expand, the global footwear market is huge. Traditional shoe brands target consumers with shoes and associated apparel, differentiating on brand, quality, technology, or price. Shoes are sold through on- and offline retail channels. These business models are all about maximizing profits.

Shareholder business model
Selling shoes and related apparel to as many consumers as possible through online and retail channels, at a good margin.

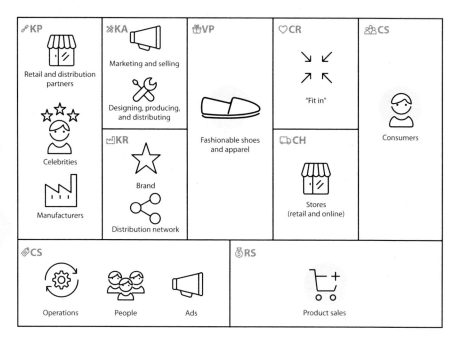

Effective enough

As with all businesses and their associated business models, there has also been a healthy amount of criticism on the One for One business model. Some believe that more people would benefit in the long term from money and education rather than a pair of shoes. To that end, along with its shift toward a grant-giving model, TOMS partners with NGOs to run its programs. The TOMS team is aware that in the end no single organization (company, NGO, government, or institution) has the ability to solve all social problems; it's the collaboration of all these parties and the sharing of value that makes the biggest difference.

Customer centric co-creation

One thing TOMS has been able to do very well is inspire a sense of ownership among its customers. The company has experienced a somewhat fierce loyalty and genuine desire of its customers to help their favorite shoe brand contribute to a better world. Tapping into this loyalty—and creating a stronger customer relationship in its business model   TOMS has made user-generated content a core part of its online presence, giving customers more than just a pair of shoes; they feel like part of TOMS's mission.

TOMS Shoes

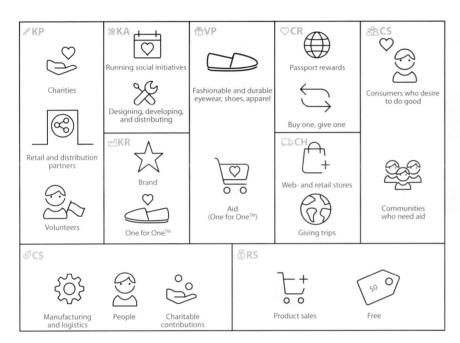

Shared value!

TOMS leaders realize that it doesn't have all the answers to the world's problems, but it does want to contribute to solving social issues. To do that, TOMS has further invested its expertise and capital into the TOMS Social Entrepreneur Fund. Through this fund, TOMS has invested in more than a dozen start-ups, like Change.org and Ava, to help them grow.

One for One™
Offering fashion and compassion. Customers buy a pair of shoes, eyewear, coffee, or a bag. Their purchase is used to help a person in need.

Less is more

There is nothing very fancy about TOMS's business model. The company developed a great value proposition, which it popularized by giving consumers a way to look good while helping people in need.

What began as a simple idea has evolved into a powerful business model that helps

people in need and advances health, education, and economic opportunity for children and their communities around the world. Of course, everything changes.

In the fast-changing world of consumer goods, TOMS is struggling to stay relevant among all the competition and has fallen victim to its own success. By popularizing

the idea of a socially conscious business model, the novelty of TOMS seems to be wearing off. In 2019, the company was taken over by its debtors. Where will it shift next?

Snackable cases

Animal testing . . .

With their **Forever Against Animals campaign,** The Body Shop advocates for change. **The Body Shop** is making sure that their beauty products, accessories, and packaging are all sourced from ingredients from high-quality natural sources.

"Forget everything you know about insurance"

Instead of making insurances a real pain in the ass, **Lemonade** is using AI to deliver insurance policies and handle claims in seconds. They remove the conflict of interest by charging a flat fee and giving the unused money to your choice of charity.

"Any penny we save, we pass on to you"

Costco is a membership-only warehouse, on a mission to bring you goods at the lowest possible prices. They believe that they are in charge of doing everything to save you money, forcing them to operate in the most efficient way possible.

Everyone should have a chance

Everyone that is denied a chance on the labour market should deserve a chance to work. **Sustainable South Bronx** was founded to green the ghetto and create new jobs in the area of green city development and sustainability.

In order to help start-ups in the biopharma industry, pharmaceutical company **Johnson & Johnson** is opening **JLABS** around the world, which is an open innovation ecosystem that gives start-ups the resources to innovate. This all comes without any strings attached, meaning that these start-ups don't need to share information or IP.

Everything online

In today's world, almost everything can be found online. Access to the internet can transform lives. However, not everyone has access to the internet. Therefore, **Hilnet** is building community hubs that provide access to people that don't have access to the online world.

Brownies & Downies

is a restaurant that brings the best quality food to you. However, they do things differently. Their employees are people with disabilities. Brownies & downies **employs almost 1200 people with disabilities.**

4 Short case studies

Short. Crisp. Fast. Clear.

1 Cipla

CEO	Total revenue	Founded in 1935	Scale
Umang Vohra	$2.3 billion	Khwaja Abdul Hamied	25,000 employees

2 WE.org

CEO	Total revenue	Founded in 1995	Scale
Roxanne Joyal	$14m fundraised	Craig and Marc Kielburger	1m ppl water access

3 Tony's

CEO	Total revenue	Founded in 2005	Scale
Henk Jan Beltman	$70 million (2019)	Teun van der Keuken	8 countries

4 Starbucks

CEO	Total revenue	Founded in 1971	Scale
Kevin Johnson	$26.5 billion (2019)	Jerry Baldwin, Zev Siegl, and Gordon	28,218 locations

Cipla:
Providing medicines

> "
>
> Our work is not just making medicines. It is about making a difference."
>
> Dr. Y K Hamied. Chairman Cipla.

Back in 1935, India was not able to produce medicines quickly enough to serve its fast-growing population. This is a recipe for disaster. Wanting to lift India up and bring it into the twentieth century, especially where essential pharmaceuticals are concerned, Dr K.A. Hamied founded The Chemical, Industrial & Pharmaceutical Laboratories, today simply known as Cipla.

Caring for life

Cipla's purpose is Caring for Life, and it is this purpose that guided its expansion to over 80 countries, providing over 1,500 products across various therapeutic categories. Just as when it was founded, Cipla's aim is to make healthcare more affordable globally. The entire company, from the top to the bottom, continually strives to uphold its values.

In fact, internally, Cipla uses a credo that ensures these core values guide internal conversations and conversations with clients, inform organizational decisions, and anchor the actions of its employees. The company revisits and calibrates its strategies based on these values to stay relevant to all its stakeholders.

Innovation driven

The average cost of bringing a pharmaceutical product to the market is around $1.2 billion. As a result, medicines are often very expensive, which means many people aren't able to afford the medicine they need. The innovation and shift that Cipla brings to the market is in the way medicines are manufactured. Focusing on medicines whose patents have expired, Cipla reverse engineers the production process used to create these medicines.

This means that Cipla avoids many of the costs associated with bringing new pharmaceuticals to market, such as research, development, and trials. Cipla continues to drive innovation and simplify healthcare, utilizing 46 state-of-the-art-manufacturing facilities, 6 research and development facilities, and over 1,300 scientists working to make medicines even cheaper and more available to more people.

Cipla

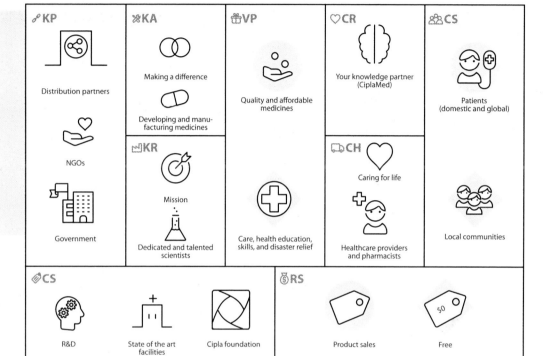

Shared value!

Cipla has played an important role in fighting AIDS, offering Doctors without Borders an AIDS cocktail for only $350 per year per patient with an agreement to distribute it to patients for free. Employing Cipla's values, company leaders believed providing medicine to those in need was more important than making money. This also forced other pharmaceutical companies to reduce prices.

Serve the real ones in need
Focus on people in real need that would otherwise lack access to medicines because traditional medicines are too expensive.

Expand the impact

Today, Cipla is one of the largest generic pharmaceutical companies in the world. Yet Cipla continues to focus on making a difference for people. Through the Cipla Foundation, the company is leading the way bringing its socially conscious legacy forward through initiatives in health, skills attainment, education, and disaster response. And, in 1997, Cipla started the Palliative Care & Training Centre to support patients and their families coping with serious illness beyond medicine and treatment. So far, this free-of-cost care has been delivered to over 15,500 patients. And, if that's not enough, the company runs several educational programs, making education accessible in remote communities through Mobile Science Labs, which supports pre-schools and primary schools near the company's facilities, and individual students.

WE.org:
Doing more good together

> "
> I won't give up until the exploitation of all children has ended and all children have their rights."
>
> Craig Kielburger, founder of WE.org

In 1995, 12-year-old Craig Kielburger was struck by the newspaper story of Iqbal Masih, a Pakistani child of the same age who was murdered after he tried to escape from child labor. Inspired by this story, Craig vowed to fight this problem. Together with his friends and older brother Marc, they founded WE Charity. For the last 24 years, WE has been on a mission to free children and their families from poverty and exploitation.

Addressing the root cause

Instead of raiding establishments that employ child labor, which seldom works due to systemic issues, WE created WE Villages, which provide a community access to education, water, health, food, and opportunity—the five key pillars that empower a community to lift itself out of poverty. WE Villages actively build assets within communities instead of using a traditional needs-based approach where communities are passive recipients of aid.

By partnering with a developing community, solutions are co-created using the strengths and talents of that community. The community acquires new knowledge and skills that enable them to successfully run projects long after they're started. This development model is not a handout or a single solution, but a hand-up, empowering people to create a brighter future together. Throughout the years this model has been built, tested, and rebuilt using a fail fast, learn fast innovation approach.

Youth for youth

WE has also expanded beyond developing countries. With WE Schools, WE engages educators and youth, teaching the skills and knowledge, and fostering the motivation needed, to bring positive change in themselves and the world. So far, 18,000 schools have participated in WE Schools, and the program has proven to increase academic and civic engagement as well as college and workplace readiness. In many ways, this has created a movement for young people by young people.

WE.org

Shared value!

WE brings people together to change the world. WE's business model is designed to connect and unite people to drive positive change. Communities are empowered to create a brighter future themselves, tapping into their strengths and talents. By purchasing a product or experience from ME to WE, consumers directly support change in the world that they can actually see for themselves through Track Your Impact.

Boost emerging economies
WE is a family of organizations: WE Charity and ME to WE. WE makes doing good, doable for them, benefiting rural communities in nine developing countries.

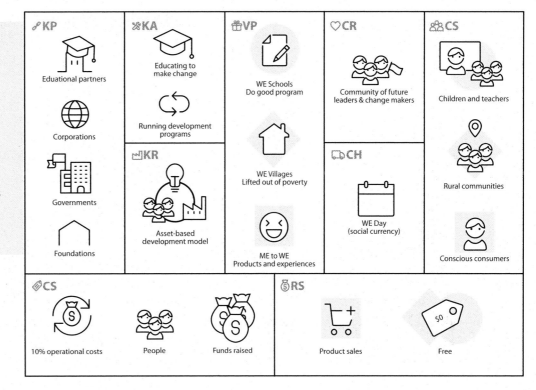

🔗 KP

Eduational partners

Corporations

Governments

Foundations

✂ KA

Educating to make change

Running development programs

✎ KR

Asset-based development model

🎁 VP

WE Schools
Do good program

WE Villages
Lifted out of poverty

ME to WE
Products and experiences

♡ CR

Community of future leaders & change makers

🚚 CH

WE Day
(social currency)

👥 CS

Children and teachers

Rural communities

Conscious consumers

🖊 CS

10% operational costs

People

Funds raised

💰 RS

Product sales

Free

Purchases that drive change

In 2009, along with Roxanne Joyal, WE's founders founded ME to WE, a social enterprise, that offers socially conscious products and experiences created by 1,800 makers from Kenya and Ecuador. Fifty percent of the net profit from this business funds WE Villages, which has brought in $20 million in cash and in-kind donations since 2017. Customers can track the impact of their purchases through stories about the people and places behind every purchase. To date, WE Villages has provided 30,000 women with the opportunity to create a steady income, access to clean water for 1 million people, $25 million worth of medical supplies, 200,000 children the opportunity to go to school, and 15 million nutritious meals served by farmers to people in need. The WE Schools program created $265 million of social value (money raised, food collected, and volunteer hours).

Tony's Chocolonely: Slave-free as a new norm

"

Right now there is slavery on cocoa farms in West Africa. Many of them are children. Tony's Chocolonely exists to change that."

Homepage website

In 2002, investigative reporter Teun van de Keuken was shocked to find that, despite industry agreements, West-Africa cocoa farms still used child slaves. Nobody at the largest chocolate brands wanted to address this disturbing issue with him.

After eating chocolate live on TV, van de Keuken turned himself in as a chocolate criminal to the Dutch authorities, collecting witness statements from four former child slaves. The judge refused to prosecute van de Keuken on the grounds that he would also have to prosecute everyone else who ate chocolate. Though van de Keuken failed in getting himself thrown in prison, he succeeded in raising awareness.

As his attempt to change this equation, in 2005, Teun van de Keuken officially launched Tony's Chocolonely. His vision was (and still is) to create the first 100% slave-free chocolate bar to the market. As part of this, Tony's Chocolonely traces every cocoa bean to its source and pays farmers 25% more for every lot.

Tony's Chocolonely provides a recipe for change with five ingredients: traceable beans, a higher price for products, farmers who have been lifted out of poverty, a long-term relationship with everyone in the supply chain, and better quality and productivity in every phase of production. All these ingredients together ensure that rural villages producing for the global food supply chain become stable economies.

With 1 million cocoa bean farmers in the world—Tony's Chocolonely is only sourcing from 7,000 of them—there is still a long way to go to change the entire chocolate ecosystem. To help move the fight forward, Tony's Chocolonely's uses storytelling and word-of-mouth advertising. To date, Tony's Chocolonely's story has been featured in the *Washington Post* and the Netflix documentary, *Rotten*, which highlights the injustices of the cocoa industry.

Tony's Chocolonely

Shared value!

Tony's Chocolonely aims to change an entire industry, all the way to the consumers who purchase chocolate. In fact, the company has done so well creating a great product and message, Tony's Chocolonely market share has surpassed that of multinational brands like Verkade, Mars, and Nestlé.

Force to do good
The company has also helped to establish The Living Income Reference Price, a standard price for cocoa beans that ensures farmers can earn a living wage.

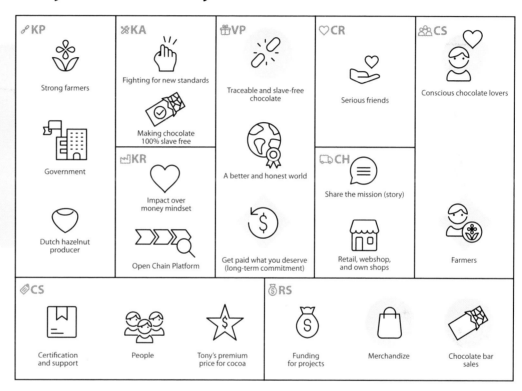

✎ KP	✂ KA	🎁 VP	♡ CR	♨ CS
Strong farmers	Fighting for new standards	Traceable and slave-free chocolate	Serious friends	Conscious chocolate lovers
Government	Making chocolate 100% slave free	A better and honest world	🚚 CH	
Dutch hazelnut producer	**📈 KR** Impact over money mindset		Share the mission (story)	
	Open Chain Platform	Get paid what you deserve (long-term commitment)	Retail, webshop, and own shops	Farmers

✐ CS			💰 RS		
Certification and support	People	Tony's premium price for cocoa	Funding for projects	Merchandize	Chocolate bar sales

Tony's Chocolonely also continues to create new chocolate bars with interesting flavors, which helps the company pass on its mission to its customers.

One of the best way to get consumers involved is to take them along on the journey of how chocolate is made, slave-free of course. Tony's Chocolonely is doing just this. In Tony's SuperStore, customers can make their own chocolate bar.

And in 2021, the company plans to open Tony's Chocolate Circus, turning a renovated warehouse into an Open Chain chocolate factory that puts on display how chocolate is made for everyone to see.

Starbucks:
Expect more than coffee

"

To inspire and nurture the human spirit— one person, one cup and one neighbourhood at a time."

Mission statement from website

At the height of the 2008 financial collapse, not only was the world feeling the pinch, Starbucks was as well. That morning double half-caf caramel macchiato that became the ritual of so many people, was traded for a simple cup of homebrewed coffee.

Prior to the crash, Starbucks had seen huge expansion globally and had even created new business models in music and entertainment. With this expansion came what was perceived as a lack of focus, which compounded Starbucks's problems. Consumers felt disconnected from the lifestyle brand they once loved. As a result, hundreds of stores were closed, and Starbucks's share price dropped to half of what it had been only 18-months prior.

This was the wakeup call Starbucks management needed. Within the turbulence of the downturn, Starbucks decided to completely redesign its value proposition, going back to its roots and focussing on the customer and the community.

Steady impact

Although Starbucks had managed to scale to become the largest coffee-house chain in the world, most people working at Starbucks had lost touch with the needs of their customers. Rather than hiring expensive market research firms to do the legwork to better understand customers' needs and wants, the company launched the "My Starbucks Idea" initiative, which enabled customers to provide valuable feedback and ideas to its headquarters. Using this direct link between the consumer and the company's decision makers, Starbucks tested and incorporated 100 ideas back into its core business model. What's more, a set of ambitious goals was formulated around using the company's "scale for the greatest good in the areas of ethical sourcing, environmental impact, and community improvement".

Starbucks

Shared value!

Starbucks has gone even further in its shift as well, referring to its 200,000 employees as partners, paying them better than the average employee in similar positions, and even supporting those who want to earn bachelor's degrees. What's more, Starbucks sets stakeholder-oriented goals that are constantly adapted each year to be more ambitious, whether it's fighting climate change, building a transparent supply chain, or nurturing the local communities around their stores.

Force to do good

Starbucks prioritizes purpose over profit. They leverage their position as a global leader to really show companies the power of compassion and just how much impact can be made.

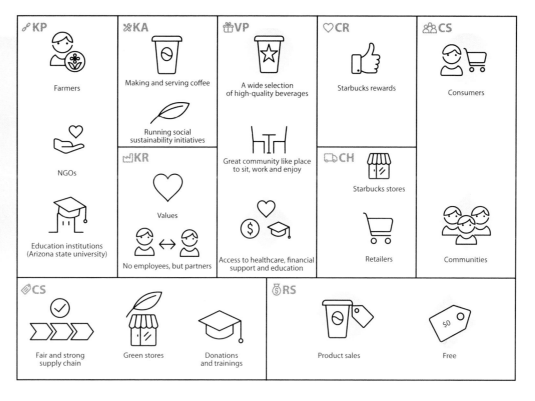

KP
- Farmers
- NGOs
- Education institutions (Arizona state university)

KA
- Making and serving coffee
- Running social sustainability initiatives

KR
- Values
- No employees, but partners

VP
- A wide selection of high-quality beverages
- Great community like place to sit, work and enjoy
- Access to healthcare, financial support and education

CR
- Starbucks rewards

CH
- Starbucks stores
- Retailers

CS
- Consumers
- Communities

CS
- Fair and strong supply chain
- Green stores
- Donations and trainings

RS
- Product sales
- Free

Starbucks didn't start with a grand vision to change the world, but as it grew in popularity so did the desire to empower communities to grow with it. As a leader of industry, Starbucks grew to understand its role in leading the way in responsible business. Through combining its customer-centric approach with its massive efforts to change the world, Starbucks is flourishing again. No simple task, Starbucks has rethought the way it does business. With initiatives like C.A.F.E. (Coffee and Farmer Equity), Starbucks aims to make ethical sourcing the standard in the industry, which certainly speaks to its customers as well. In many ways, Starbucks leads by example, demonstrating to other businesses how they also can orient toward their stakeholders.

Ask yourself the following questions . . .

What product would you give away and how would that make a difference in people's lives?

TOMS Shoes was founded to do something about the hardship experienced by people who cannot afford to buy shoes. They designed the One for One™ business model that gives a product away to a person in need when a wealthy consumer buys a product.

Where can you infuse purpose into your business making sure your products make a real difference in the lives of people?

Unilever got rid of quarterly reporting because it hampered innovation and creating value in the long term. Their portfolio of purpose-led brands and the positive impact of their businesses on people, environment, and communities is growing fast.

What needs to change in your company to maximize value for all stakeholders, making your shares rock-solid for the next decades?

BlackRock wants to provide financial security to their clients through clever investing. They realized that investing in companies that maximize profits is not that clever. A much higher return on investment is achieved by investing in companies that have a purpose and create value for all stakeholders.

Lessons learned

What can you do to co-create long-lasting commitment to change someone's life?

WE.org tapped into the intrinsic motivation of children to do good and change the world for the better. It turned into a global movement creating socially conscious leaders and change makers for whom doing good is the default behavior.

What unaddressed social problem could you be fighting for?

Tony's Chocolonely was founded to increase awareness about child labor and slavery in the cocoa industry. Because none of the chocolate brands took responsibility, Tony's decided to make awesome chocolate bars itself. They are now expanding globally until the whole industry is slave free.

How can you tighten the connection to each and every stakeholder, extending from the amazing customer experience you offer?

Starbucks is the Third Place (between home and work) people go to enjoy coffee and connection to other humans. Yet, for a moment it lost their customer orientation. The 2008 crises pushed Starbuck to reorient on all stakeholders again. It has seen remarkable growth as a result of supporting their employees (partners), farmers, and local communities.

How could your business unlock value for people in real need so that a global problem can finally be eliminated?

Cipla figured out a way to manufacture medicine at much lower cost so that India would never be starved of essential medicine again. They also made sure that people in Africa and other parts of the world got access to medicine for HIV/AIDS. Cipla valued providing access to these medicines as much more important than making money from it.

High-level strategic choices

1

 Create value for all

Value creation should be inclusive, instead of being focused on capturing value for just shareholders. If every stakeholder profits, more and more value will be created overall.

Deeply understand the goals of your stakeholders. Work with them to ensure that they are able to achieve them.

2

 Invest in others

A company can be seen as an organized effort to be of service to others. A company brings people and resources together in an efficient way.

Use your profits to invest in the success of others, making your company an engine for growth of employees, partners, and society.

3

 Engage everyone

A stakeholder business model is all about collaboration. Collaboration needs to be actively pursued by leaders and teams within organizations.

Engage with all your stakeholder on a frequent basis to align on common goals. Focus energy on those collaborative activities that move everybody closer to those goals.

to drive this shift.

4

 Tell stories

Collaboration is what makes humans unique. It is the story of our enduring success as a species.

Tell stories about what you and your stakeholders want to achieve in the long-term. Show the purpose of your company, explain why working together is a must, and communicate intermediate results.

5

 Measure impact

Revenues are just the result of value being created and lack meaning by itself. Value created for stakeholders makes the difference in one way of another.

Measure the impact generated by your company in relation to the goals of your stakeholders.

6

 Learn continuously

Each stakeholder has a different perspective, expectation, and need. It is important to find common ground that unites all the stakeholders.

Be open to the perspectives of your stakeholders. Ask them questions and engage in dialogue to learn from their worldview. Learn together.

From physical to digital

Humans are physical, tactile creatures. The physicality of objects makes them more tangible to us. Yet every day we take one step closer to a hybrid version of ourselves as we merge the online and offline worlds we live in.

physical →

The shift from physical to digital is nuanced. In some cases, we may still require physical goods and assets that are made more "connected." In other cases, business models shift to leverage information and communications technology (ICT) and related domains, such as data science, in order to engage and connect customers to the company and the products or services they use, tailoring value propositions to match each customer's individual taste. To that end, the digital shift is a business model strategy that **uses digital technology to create and deliver great customer experiences unencumbered by physical-only value propositions, resources, and activities.** Technology is the enabler in this case, and not the value proposition. This strategy may use existing and/or new technologies to enable organizations to create relevancy with and for customers. At its core, the digital shift is about figuring out **how to use digital technologies to drive value creation** as well as deliver that value to current and new customer segments.

digital

Shift stories

Large
↗ Salesforce

Medium
↗ Warby Parker
↗ The Times

Short
↗ Fortnite
↗ Duolingo
↗ Connecterra
↗ Disney Parks

Business models will reach their sell-by dates more quickly [. . .] The onus is on leaders to stay ahead of the curve for their industries' evolving business models. 'By the time it's obvious you need to change, it's usually too late.'

John T. Chambers, former executive chairman and CEO of Cisco Systems.

Shiny technology

Digital business models are not necessarily about digital technologies or using the newest, shiniest technologies in existence. Rather, a digital business model should ultimately be designed to enhance interaction and increase engagement with customers, making it easier to create value that is also easily consumed.

Organizations benefit when they can simplify the delivery of value by using a digital approach. Having a well-designed digital business model also enables an organization to make well-informed, data-driven decisions with regard to growing its business.

Too much digital technology

You've probably heard all the buzzwords by now — digital transformation, big data, growth hacking, digital channels, leveraging social media, and so many more. You may even find yourself asking what this all means and how these buzz-worthy terms and the ideas they represent might impact your business. Sure, you may have a bunch of information technology (IT) infrastructure for running internal operations. However, inasmuch as your IT infrastructure may help your company perform efficiently, countless ways may exist to leverage some of the same infrastructure along with new tools to create better connections with your customers. After all, your customers are likely demanding more and more in terms of easy ordering, smooth payments, fast delivery, and responsive customer service. What if you focused on making their lives easier?

Strategic questions

What does digital mean? Where is the opportunity to connect to customers in a digital way? Which new customer segments can you reach by immersing yourselves in the digital world? How might you be like those digitally native companies that have ICT infrastructure that enables their business, instead of working against it? What might you do about the legacy systems that hamper your ability to create and deliver new value? How might you get rid of those legacy systems? Do you build, buy, or partner where new ICT systems are concerned? What additional value can be created and delivered if you go digital? What can you learn and apply from companies that are making this shift or have made this shift already?

From physical

Physical business models are still dominant in almost every industry. Companies develop and deliver tangible products, which requires creating distribution processes to move things around from one place to another.

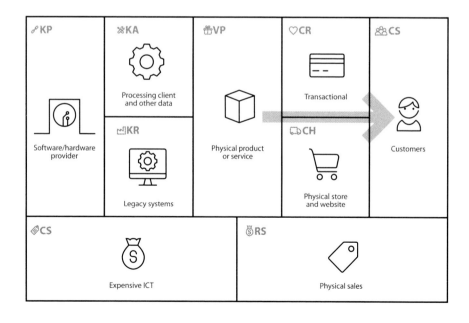

Physical products

A physical business model provides customers with some kind of tangible, physical product. These products find their way to customers through direct or indirect (retail) channels, and are usually paid for per unit, wherein the relationship is fairly transactional. Over time, customers might come back because they need more of the physical product, though this is not guaranteed and much effort is made to market new products and features to entice customers to buy the next version.

Moving things around

The key activity in a physical business model is the physical supply chain. This may be a traditional supply chain, optimized to satisfy customer demand and get physical products out the door. Production and operations may also be streamlined to improve efficiency and maintain healthy profit margins. Typically, internal IT systems are in place to maintain efficiency . . . at least internally. Keeping these systems running and upgrading them can be resource intensive.

to digital

At your fingertips

Digital business models focus on creating and delivering value seamlessly, whether through digital or physical channels. A digital business model sometimes offers some part of the value proposition for free, charging after a trial period or for some premium experience. Once customers are converted, there is a relationship to be maintained to keep customers connected and engaged.

Keeping connected

The key activities in a digital business model are to design customer experiences and track customer behavior and engagement. It's important to analyze data about the experience delivered to customers in order to ensure customers are fully engaged and satisfied. Companies can monitor customer engagement and satisfaction by using algorithms or initiating ongoing digital conversations. A digital proposition must be continuously developed, given that customer expectations are higher. That said, with digital business models, companies can more easily "experiment" to find the right balance of value proposition to revenue stream.

A digital business model is designed to provide a smooth and seamless customer experience, whether online or offline. It's optimized for frequent interactions, not a single transaction. Additionally, digital business models enable mass personalization and the ability to enhance value propositions on the fly.

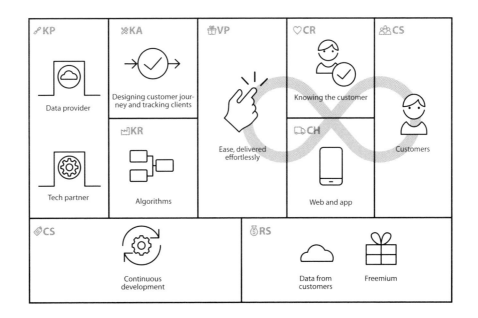

Digital first

 Digital proposition

---

❶

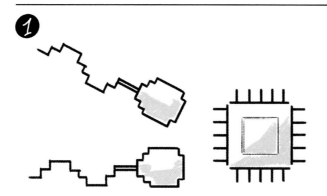

❷

An organization uses digital technologies to offer an entirely new customer experience. Technologies are developed and used to engage customers, enable business goals, and drive growth. A digitally first business model does not exclude physical interactions or assets. It fully integrates physical with digital and vice versa. Distinctions no longer exist between offline and online. Customers and the organizations serving them are always connected.

Examples: Salesforce, Warby Parker, Fortnite, Duolingo, Venmo, Bumble

This pattern is about offering a fully digital value proposition, i.e., a product, service, and/or customer experience. This digital proposition co-exists next to a proposition based on a physical product and/or service. A digital product, such as a piece of software, a movie, or song, is easy to distribute since it does not occupy any physical shelf space and the same product can be sold numerous times.

Examples: New York Times, Porsche, Under Armour, Connecterra

Patterns

 Digital connection

 Bolted on

This pattern focuses on using digital technologies to enhance, streamline, or innovate the way to connect to customers. The digital connection can be about providing online access to physical products and services being offered—a webshop for ordering physical products or a webpage for booking physical services. The digital connection can also be used to provide customer service and support, and even personalization of the main value proposition.

Examples: Disney Parks, Domino's Pizza, OpenTable

This pattern is about digital elements being added to a physical business. These digital elements are literally bolted-on to an existing physical business model. As a result, these elements are not connected to core business processes or interactions with customers. Often, substantial investments are made into digital elements, such as websites and apps, without considering whether doing so improves value creation and/or delivery.

Examples: "We also have an app", "You can go to our website", or "We're also on Twitter."

Salesforce

Salesforce set out on a mission to help companies connect with their customers in entirely new ways. It was this mission that drove the company to leverage the power of digital technology to humanize the way we do business.

Facts

Founders
Marc Benioff, Frank
Dominguez, Parker Harris,
and Dave Moellenhoff

Founded in 1999
in USA

Total revenue
$17.1 billion (2020)

Industry
Internet, cloud computing,
computer software, artificial
intelligence, B2B

Scale
150,000+ customers.
49,000 employees (2020)

Timeline

1999
Founded

Salesforce is founded by Marc Benioff—a former Oracle executive; Parker Harris; Dave Moellenhoff; and Frank Dominguez.

2000
Launch

Salesforce launches its first product, a CRM in the cloud, accompanied by the "The End of Software" campaign. Salesforce also publicly launches the Salesforce Foundation, integrating philanthropy into its business model by following the 1-1-1 model.

2003
Dreamforce

Their first annual user conference, which later became one of the biggest business festivals of its time, brings people together to share ideas and build a community. The company has its first profitable quarter.

We offer a complete architecture that empowers every business to experience the benefits of on-demand throughout its entire organization."

Salesforce website

Power your business

For any organization that exchanges value with customers (i.e., every company), managing relationships with those customers is paramount. Plenty of companies throughout history kept customer information in a ledger or Rolodex, and as companies scaled, these early solutions became unmanageable.

In the late 1990s, companies like Siebel, SAP, and Oracle developed on-premises customer relationship management (CRM) software to help companies manage their customer data by storing it all in one place and on site. Although using CRM worked well in most cases, the software itself was often expensive, complicated, and required extensive maintenance and patching. Further, should

something go awry, the company would have to employ its own resources to bring the software back up.

Marc Benioff, a Vice President at Oracle, saw an opportunity to do this differently. He quit his job at Oracle and, using his own knowledge and resources, recruited three consultants he knew from another start-up— Frank Dominguez, Parker Harris, and Dave Moellenhoff—and began to work on Salesforce, a CRM based in the cloud that would be set up and used a simple per user subscription business model. And just like that, Rolodexes were out, and Salesforce's cloud-based CRM system became accessible for every organization.

2004
IPO

Salesforce raises $110 million at a valuation of $1.1 billion. Their shares increase in value by 55% on the first day of trading. Salesforce Ohana is introduced to embed the shared values and the pursuit of a shared mission.

2005
AppExchange

Salesforce creates AppExchange, a marketplace for third parties, acting as an e-commerce website for apps that run on the Salesforce platform or connect to it. Later, entire companies form around the platform

Open innovation

In 2006, Salesforce announces Apex, an on-demand programming language allowing third parties to write and run code on Salesforce's multi-tenant, shared architecture. Visualforce was launched as well, which allowed users to build any user interface they wanted.

Digitally fit

Salesforce's core business is to break down the traditional boundaries between departments (marketing, sales, and service) in an organization, creating a single, shared perspective on customers. This seemingly simple but brilliant concept changed the way businesses connect with their customers by bringing companies and customers closer together.

Digital first
The Salesforce online CRM eliminated the need to develop, install, and maintain software on premises.

Salesforce CRM

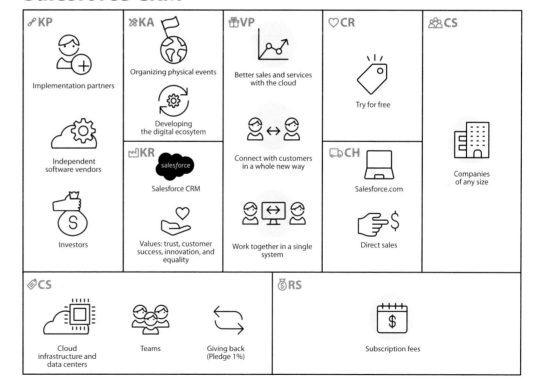

KP
- Implementation partners
- Independent software vendors
- Investors

KA
- Organizing physical events
- Developing the digital ecosytem

KR
- Salesforce CRM
- Values: trust, customer success, innovation, and equality

VP
- Better sales and services with the cloud
- Connect with customers in a whole new way
- Work together in a single system

CR
- Try for free

CH
- Salesforce.com
- Direct sales

CS
- Companies of any size

CS
- Cloud infrastructure and data centers
- Teams
- Giving back (Pledge 1%)

RS
- Subscription fees

2008
Force.com

Salesforce releases Force.com at Dreamforce, enabling customers to build their own custom applications, four times faster than previously.

2009
Ventures

As a result of the financial crisis, Salesforce Ventures is launched to invest in digital companies that help build the Salesforce platform, strengthening their value proposition. In 2009, Ventures creates $1 billion dollars in revenue.

2011
Most innovative

Salesforce is named the world's most innovative company by *Forbes* magazine. Salesforce keeps steadily growing and reaches the milestone of 100,000 customers.

2012
Marketing cloud

Salesforce creates Marketing cloud by acquiring the following companies: Radian 6, a social listening tool; Buddy Media, a company that publishes and analyzes social media content; and ExactTarget, a company that provides a variety of media tools.

Creating connections

The small company, once called an ant at the picnic because of its "No software" marketing stunts, quickly became the industry leader in the $250 billion global market it created. Whereas on-premises software required huge investments just to deploy, running Salesforce's cloud-based software required much less setup time for customers. And scaling became a no-brainer.

And this didn't stop with CRM. Using the revenue from the core product as well as venture capital, the company developed an ever-expanding lineup up of value propositions tied to its vision of helping any company create connections between people, processes, data, and functions. In this, every value proposition was (and is) organized around the customer.

Platform as a Service

A big part of Salesforce's early expansion was tied to its AppExchange, now the biggest digital B2B marketplace where companies can develop and sell specific enterprise applications to other Salesforce customers. AppExchange was built on Force.com, a Platform as a Service (PaaS), enabling customers and partners to deploy apps directly on Salesforce's system.

It was at this point that Salesforce also began acquiring other SaaS companies, rebranding and repurposing them into its own suite of services, expanding further into other business functions such as service, marketing, and more. This included industry-specific solutions—marketing, artificial intelligence (AI), analytics, integration, new social, and mobile.

We want to create the future. So you better be ready to disrupt yourself and constantly change the game."

Marc Benioff. Co-founder and CEO of Salesforce.

2013
Mobile

Salesforce releases the Salesforce 1 platform, enabling customers to access all their Force.com information by smartphone.

2014
Trailhead

Salesforce releases Trailhead, a fun and free way to learn Salesforce's technology and acquire the skills needed for a job in the industry. Available online.

2015
Lighting

Lighting unifies the user experience across web, mobile, tablet, and wearables. Lighting is a service that was created to simplify the programming process for business users.

AI for everyone

Over 2 million apps are downloaded from the AppExchange. In 2016, Einstein is launched, offering AI for everyone across all functionalities of the Salesforce ecosystem. In 2018, Dreamforce attracts a crowd of 170,000 people and 15 million online viewers.

Boosting open innovation

Today, Salesforce serves just about every type of business imaginable, including government, with a vast array of services that enables organizations to become Customer Companies. As Salesforce has continued to grow, the company has invested about $4 billion acquiring over 2 dozen companies, mostly to infuse its core with new innovators, new ideas, and entrepreneurs. This has meant that Salesforce also had to continually reinvent itself.

Digital first
Provide a platform for developing, selling, and using apps that make it easier to connect to customers aligning sales, marketing, and service.

Salesforce Lighting Platform

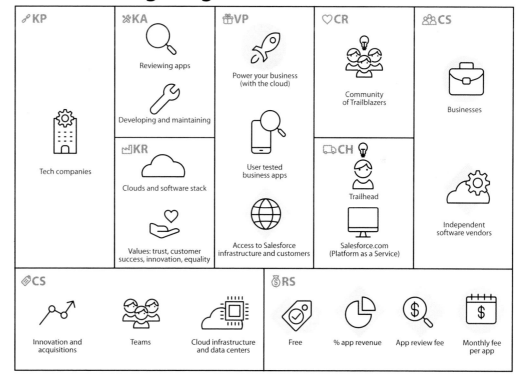

2016
Nonprofit Success Pack

Salesforce launches Nonprofit Starter Pack as Nonprofit Success Pack, ensuring that nonprofits have access to the best CRM for connecting to their audience.

2017
Rapid growth

Salesforce is named the world's most innovative company again by *Forbes*. Salesforce is an $8.3 billion company by the end of 2017.

2018
Dedicated clouds

Salesforce launches the Nonprofit and Education Cloud to better serve the nonprofit and education customer segments by providing them with their own cloud. In addition, the company announces, together with United Way, the Philanthropy Cloud, which connects companies and their employees to nonprofits at scale.

Changing the world is everybody's business."

Marc Benioff. Co-founder and CEO of Salesforce

Transforming together

Pledge 1%

From the start, Salesforce has been committed to social causes, seeing business as the greatest platform for change. As part of this, Salesforce created the 1-1-1 model, offering 1% of time, 1% of equity, and 1% of product to organizations and people that work on a social mission to improve the world.

Social impact center

In 1999, the company established Salesforce.org, a dedicated business unit acting as the social impact center of Salesforce, focusing on partnering with the global community of changemakers. Through Salesforce.org, the company helps nonprofits, educational institutions, and philanthropic organizations so that they can have a greater impact. As a

business unit within Salesforce, it can also innovate on top of the Salesforce platform, tap into the power of Salesforce's 45,000 employees, and inspire Salesforce customers to join its global movement for good.

Skill up for free

Salesforce not only focuses on providing social good to well-established organizations, but as the digital economy has continued to expand, it has been creating new professions along the way. Salesforce has included as part of its mission providing learning pathways for those endeavoring to start a new profession or grow their digital skills in their current profession. Everyone can close their skills gap, not just people in the tech world.

2018
Iconic home

Salesforce moves into Salesforce tower and offers the space to its partners and nonprofits as well.

Joining the pledge

Through the Pledge 1% program, Salesforce has donated 4.5 million hours, $310 million in grants, and 45,000 licenses to nonprofit partners. Also, 9,000 other companies have joined the program since 2000.

Giving back

Salesforce.org is a dedicated business model within Salesforce that serves nonprofits and educational institutions to better connect with their customers.

Besides giving away these free basic services, the Trailblazer learning management system is freely accessible for anyone who wants to learn Salesforce and other new digital skills. As such, people who are new to digital are supported to enter the digital world. No one is left behind in moving to the digital space.

Digital first
Salesforce believes the purpose of business is to improve the state of the world. All of their technology is therefore made available to nonprofits and educational institutions to amplify their impact.

Salesforce.org

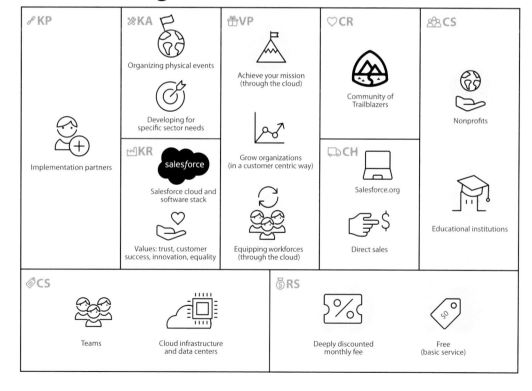

- **KP** Implementation partners
- **KA** Organizing physical events; Developing for specific sector needs
- **KR** Salesforce cloud and software stack; Values: trust, customer success, innovation, equality
- **VP** Achieve your mission (through the cloud); Grow organizations (in a customer centric way); Equipping workforces (through the cloud)
- **CR** Community of Trailblazers
- **CH** Salesforce.org; Direct sales
- **CS** Nonprofits; Educational institutions
- **CS** Teams; Cloud infrastructure and data centers
- **RS** Deeply discounted monthly fee; Free (basic service)

Ohana

The company uses Ohana, the Hawaiian word for family, to describe its family-oriented culture. Ohana shows up everywhere in the Salesforce strategy and actions, representing the bond between employees, partners, and customers. Every Salesforce building has Ohana floors, which are offered to nonprofits and foundations, further cementing Salesforce's culture of giving back.

Internally, Salesforce sees itself as a diverse family of commercial companies, nonprofits, educational organizations, war veterans, artists, technologists, software developers, and others. What keeps this family together is a set of shared values: trust, customer success, innovation, and equality.

Salesforce has been called a leader in innovation, philanthropy, and culture, proving that doing well and doing good go well together, especially in a digital world. In many ways, Salesforce's digital business models are simply a means to an end, connecting organizations and customers to create impact for all.

Aspiration	Trust	Improve the state of the world	Connecting everyone and everything	Customer centric
Energy	Ohana (family)	Partners (not competitors)	Physical events	Innovators
Information	Customer 360	Integration, APIs	Einstein (AI)	Analytics and visualization
Operations	Salesforce.com (Software as a service)	AppExchange	Trailhead (learning)	Connecting people and ideas

2018
MuleSoft

Salesforce acquires integration vendor, MuleSoft, for $6.5 billion.

2019
Tableau

Salesforce acquires Tableau, an analytics and visualization company, for $15.7 billion. All-time giving reached $300 million, including more than 4 million employees volunteer hours. Salesforce launches Customer 360 platform.

Future
New jobs, new revenue

It is estimated that by 2025, 4.2 million new jobs and $1.2 trillion in new revenue will be created by Salesforce customers.

Salesforce supports growth by closely and deeply connecting companies to customers, resulting in a thriving economy.

For any company or organization, being connected to customers is fundamental to success — not only success in creating profits, but success in creating value for its customers. Although Salesforce can help with this, in the end, it's not about the software.

In many respects, Salesforce has tried to humanize technology. Whether it's through the AppExchange, its artificial intelligence agent (called *Einstein*), its many philanthropic endeavors, or its acquisitions of other software platforms (like Tableau), the company consistently focuses its efforts on helping customers help their customers.

Digital does not kill physical
Perhaps what's most fascinating about the digital shift that Salesforce has helped create is that the company's own growth trajectory is not built on the philosophy of developing state-of-the-art technology first and thinking about customers last. Although Salesforce is a digital-first company, since its early beginnings, the company has organized physical events and its own office space to connect ideas and people. This has allowed the company to share its vision of customer centricity and cloud computing, while also bringing employees, customers, partners, and society along on the journey.

Warby Parker

The eyewear industry has been a monopoly for decades, resulting in little new value created for customers. Warby Parker wanted to make customers look good, leave money in their pockets, and donate a pair of glasses to a person in need. And it did so by starting with a digital strategy.

Facts

Founders
Neil Blumenthal, David Gilboa, Andrew Hunt, and Jeffrey Raider

Founded in 2010
in New York, New York

Total revenue
$250 million (2017)

Industry
Online eyewear

Scale
Almost 100 stores across the US and Canada, and 4 million glasses given away

Warby Parker

People who are passionate about Warby Parker are passionate about creating a company that can scale, be profitable, and do good in the world — without charging a premium for it."

Neil Blumental, founder
Warby Parker

Warby Parker was founded by four friends after Neil Blumenthal, one of the founders, lost his $500 Prada glasses on a flight and could not afford to buy new ones — which affected the rest of his semester at grad school. Facing an industry that was dominated by a single company, Luxottica, the founders set off to offer consumers a much better, more affordable alternative to the expensive frames and limited selection available throughout much of the eyeglasses market.

Warby Parker was built on the belief that buying glasses should be easy and fun. Customers should look good, feel happy about their purchase, and still have money in their pockets. To do this, the company circumvented traditional channels, designing all its glasses in-house, sourcing all materials, and selling directly to its customers, starting with an online-only channel strategy.

Buy a pair, give a pair
Warby Parker's founders also carry with them the belief that everyone has the right to see. Given that almost 1 billion people globally lack access to glasses, Warby Parker founded the Buy a Pair, Give a Pair program. For every pair of glasses sold, a pair is distributed to someone in need through the company's nonprofit partner VisionSpring. Moreover, Warby Parker also designed its business — which is set up as a B Corp — to be carbon neutral, focusing on reducing environmental impact and creating a greater societal impact.

Even though Warby Parker's founders share what sound like altruistic visions for the future, it's not all fluff. After selling 100 thousand pairs of glasses in 2011, hitting its annual sales target in the first three weeks, with 20,000 people still on the waiting list, it's clear that cheap and chic is what people had been waiting for. In 2015, the company reached a $1.2 billion valuation, becoming a real player in the eyeglasses market.

As the company continues to grow, it has also shown that it can do so without reverting to the business model its competitors have used for decades. For instance, in 2016, Warby Parker opened its own optical lab, shifting from external manufacturers to in-house production for lenses. Likewise, the company has expanded to both digital and physical channels, establishing a branded retail footprint in cities all over the US as well as a couple in Canada.

Big, horizontal, mostly physical

The physical business model of the eyewear industry is based on a traditional supply chain that is horizontally organized, meaning that all the different companies involved add to the price of the final product. Basically, Luxottica and Safilo (Gucci, Fendi, and Dior) control the industry. They set product prices however they want, without making a product that matches the taste and needs of consumers. Very expensive glasses, but no value added.

Physical business model
Consumers pay way too much for eyewear, because of the way the industry and supply chain has been organized, resulting in very expensive glasses, but no value added.

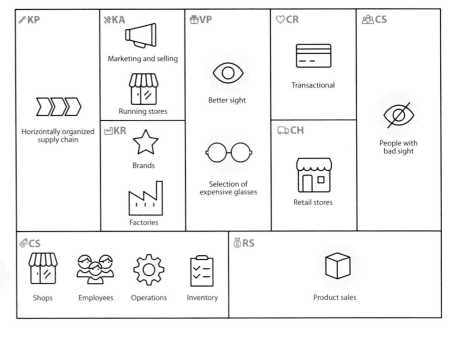

At about $140 billion in revenue, the eyewear industry is huge, and hugely inefficient. Over the last several decades, Luxottica, employing a horizontal supply chain, has more or less created a monopoly in eyewear. This Italian conglomerate owns nearly every designer brand, including Ray Ban, Oakley, Oliver Peoples, and Persol, and many of the physical retail chains, like Sunglass Hut, LensCrafters, Pearle Vision, Target Optical, and Sears Optical. Luxottica even owns EyeMed, the second largest vision insurance provider in the US. Suffice it to say, Luxottica is at the top of the food chain when it comes to glasses, for which it can set almost any price it finds reasonable.

In-house, for the benefit of the customer
To compete effectively, Warby Parker uses a vertical integration strategy that eliminates much of the outsourcing by putting everything under one roof, so to speak, enabling it to provide customers with stylish, affordable glasses starting at $95 as opposed to about $500.

Lean, vertical, integrating physical & digital

Innovate Point of Sale

Wanting to connect with and serve customers wherever they are, Warby Parker started its business model journey with a digital-first channel strategy. To do this, the company designed the entire experience around supporting customers in finding, trying, buying, and even returning glasses without ever needing to go to a physical store. Only after digital channels were dialed in did Warby Parker expand its physical presence.

Digital first
By observing what customers do online and offline, a better experience can be developed.

Warby Parker has proven that even in industries with heavily entrenched players, there's always an opportunity to disrupt the status quo with a new business model. Although focused on digital shifts, this chapter includes a case study about the eyewear company, Warby Parker, as sometimes it makes sense to link both physical and digital channels together such that customers are provided with a seamless, delightful online and offline experiences.

In this way, physical and digital must work together to enhance and facilitate the entire shopping journey. To that end, Warby Parker supports customers throughout their entire journey, irrespective of where they start their journey (online or offline). In fact, Warby Parker has done so well designing the physical and digital customer experience, Jeff Raider, one of the company's co-founders, took what he learned and started Harrys.com, another $1 billon direct-to-consumer business model, in men's grooming.

The New York Times

For quite some time it was clear that the traditional newspaper business model, based on cross-subsidising journalism by selling ads, was broken. However, shifting to a new kind of customer-focused value creation required quite a bit of heavy lifting and an entire new mindset to boot.

[. . .] without question we make more money on a print subscriber. But the point about digital is that we believe we can grow many, many more of them."

- Mark Thompson, CEO

The *New York Times* (the *Times*), nicknamed "The Gray Lady," was founded as a penny paper with the mission of seeking the truth and helping people understand the world — which it has done exceedingly well at by most accounts. Since its founding in 1851, The *Times* has won 127 Pulitzer Prizes, more than any other newspaper in existence.

Struggle between physical and digital

Though the *Times* continued to flourish as a paper-based news medium, in the late 1990s, as other companies set up their digital mastheads as websites, the *Times* followed suit, launching a website where articles from the printed paper were published and could be accessed for free. A decade later, the company launched a new website and mobile web companion. At the time, there was not much strategic thought behind the intitiative.

The world was moving online, and even though the *Times* had a web presence, the company had not made any strategic choices that would make it successful in this new world. In fact, even as other companies, like Google, were finding tremendous traction in the online content world, like at other periodicals, leadership at the *Times* went about cutting costs, like the actual size of the print edition, as their main strategic tool.

But this didn't last long. Although leadership struggled with going digital, in many respects they were ahead of their time in the decision to continue digitalizing the *Times*. After launching native apps for iPhones, Android, and Windows devices, the company began to see digital as a core strategy unto itself, and not simply a part of the paper-based strategy. As revenues continued to decline for print media, management realized that these revenues were never coming back, and launched a digital paywall, providing readers with some limited free access without a subscription.

Unlike many of its competitors, the *Times* had made the strategic choice to be a subscription-first business, just as it had with its original printed version. Instead of maximizing clicks and selling low-margin advertising, like many other news outlets continue to do today, the focus was on providing journalism so strong that millions of people would be willing to pay for it. Over time, substantial investments were made in the core offering, while continuously adding new online services and features, following a strategy similar to that used by other digital first businesses, such as Netflix, Spotify, and HBO.

Physical newspapers

Even as the *Times* doubled down on its digital strategy, readership remained spotty as readers shifted to other sources of news, such as social media. In fact, according to Thompson, Derek. 2016. "The Print Apocalypse Of American Newspapers". *The Atlantic* overall newspaper revenues declined 90% between 2000 to 2015. This wasn't just about moving online; newspapers and the news media industry were facing complete digital disruption as eyeballs shifted toward free digital news aggregators and social media.

Bolted on
In 1996, the physical business model was taken online, by publishing articles on a website. The look stayed the same for 10 years and pageviews were quite important.

What people really want

Rather than continuing to cut costs, the *Times* formed a new "Beta Group," which brought together different cross-disciplinary teams to develop new digital value propositions. As productive as the Beta Group was, it wasn't long before the leadership and staff admitted that their digital innovation efforts still weren't making up for the losses. As concluded in an internal document, "Innovation Report," it was the editors, most of whom were dyed-in-the-wool newspaper people, who too often said no to the Beta Group. In a culture that prided itself on having lengthy discussions about everything from headline styles to article specifics, it was the newsroom that had been slowing down digital innovation. But this also brought to the surface an important point: the *Times*'s customers care about readability, access, and visually engaging content, all things the *Times* prided itself on. The question was no longer "should we change?" but "how do we change?"

Content is king

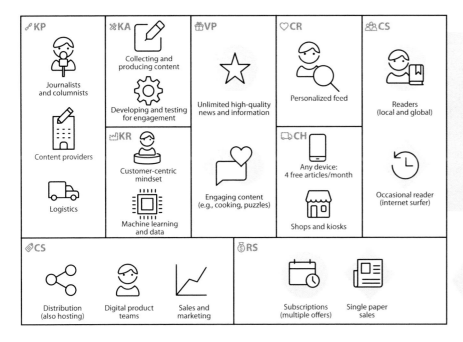

Digitally enabled

Using a two-week Agile sprint process, a tech standard, staff rapidly improved existing digital products like Cooking and Crosswords, focusing on customer experience rather than details unseen by users. As the *Times* got better at developing digital value propositions that resonated with its customers, it released new experiences, focusing on its bread-and-butter, content.

Digital proposition
Packaging a proven product i.e., high quality news and information, to make it easy to consume, anytime and anywhere.

After the publication of the "Innovation Report," the *Times* kicked off Project 2020. The goal of this project was to attract and retain subscribers by using innovative, high-quality, digital content. Leadership committed to doubling digital revenue to at least $800 million by the end of 2020. The company invested in more tech talent, and the entire organization began to work more iteratively, taking a page out of the Beta Group's book.

The *Times* has become a digital juggernaut in the 2020s, learning the hard way that old strategies for monetization don't make sense in the digital world. What customers really value, like high-quality news, coming from reliable sources, often needed to be rediscovered and designed to be consumed differently. By shifting to new digital value propositions and new ways of working, the *Times* actually beat its revenue goals a year earlier than expected and aims to double their current 5 million subscribers by 2025.

Snackable cases

"Just Venmo me"

Venmo was able to transform an awkward interaction between people, to make it something cool. If you need to split a bill, or ask money back from a friend, you can just send them a Venmo through the app, and the money will be transferred to you.

Using data for sportswear

With the investment of a billion dollars **Under Armour** showcases that it takes digital transformation seriously. Under Armour purchased three fitness apps, and is using the data to optimize their sportswear to provide you with ultimate performance clothes.

Chatbots to order your pizza

Domino's pizza is using **chatbots** to make the **user experienc**e easier and more fun. Via **whatever channel** you want to use, you can get in contact with Dom the pizza bot, and order the pizza you want.

Ring's mission is to make neighbourhoods simple. By their video doorbell, they can see who is ringing the door, as well as watch the footage when somebody is close to your home. Not only does it help with security, it is also convenient.

Bumble is taking the dating process online by connecting people that like each other. Via a **swipe to the right,** you can be matched with the person you like. However, Bumble is **breaking the traditional stigma.**

Women need to take the first step to contact the other person.

Better driving

The **Porsche** Digital lab is the so to say digital manufacture of Porsche. In this lab, Porsche is working on creating innovative solutions for their drivers by using the latest technology available. With new digital products and services, Porsche wants to make the experience of driving a Porsche car even better.

You'll never have to wait on the phone to reserve a table for a restaurant. With just a few clicks, you could book a table at one of the 54.000 restaurants worldwide that **OpenTable** has in their network, which is taking away both the hassle for visitors and restaurants having to deal with reservations and administration.

4 Short case studies

Short. Crisp. Fast. Clear.

1 Fortnite

Founded by	**Total revenue**	**Founded**	**Scale**
EPIC Games	$1.8 billion (2019)	July 25th, 2017	250 million active gamers

2 Duolingo

Founder	**Total revenue**	**Founded**	**Scale**
Luis Von Ahn	$86 million (2019)	2011 in Pittsburgh, PA	300 million users

3 Connecterra

Founders	**Total funding**	**Founded**	**Scale**
Ansari and Khokhar	$9.5 million	2012 in Amsterdam, Netherlands	10 countries

4 Disney Parks

Founder	**Total revenue**	**Founded**	**Scale**
Walt Disney	$26.2 billion (2019)	1971 in Orlando, Florida	6 parks worldwide

> Games like 'Fortnite' are way more fun to play with your real-world friends, and they're so accessible that anybody can play."

Tim Sweeney, CEO of Epic Games

Fortnite:
The last one standing

Epic Games was founded as Potomac Computer Systems by Tim Sweeney in 1991. His first game, ZZT, became quite popular, and for years he was taking orders through bulletin boards and shipping out the game by mail. In 1998, Epic Games released Unreal, a 3D first-person shooter game that evolved into a series of Unreal games. Later, it licensed the core technology, the Unreal Engine, to other game developers.

Shift away from publishers

In 2011, Epic Games announced Fortnite as a cooperative/survival mashup. The original idea was a game in which players could build structures, like Minecraft, and fight against zombies, like Call of Duty. At the same time, Epic also wanted to move away from publishers dictating game concepts to a games-as-a-service model (GaaS). Upon closing a big deal with Tencent, the Chinese tech conglomerate, Epic was able to offer the Unreal Engine 4 for free to all users to develop with, with Epic taking 5% royalties

on games developed using the engine. In 2014, this engine was named the "most successful videogame engine" by Guinness World Records.

Fortnite launched

In 2017, Epic finally launched its game, Fortnite, through a paid early access game mode it called *Save The World*. While working on the game, the company also observed the popularity of PlayerUnknown's Battlegrounds (PUBG), a battle royale game released earlier in 2017. Due to its popularity, Epic added Battle Royale to Fortnite as one of its game modes. But unlike the about $30 you had to pay for PUBG, Fortnite offered the game mode as a free-to-play title across computer, console, and mobile platforms. Fortnite Battle Royale quickly gained an audience of over 125 million players. This doubled again when Epic convinced Sony to allow players on any device to compete with each other.

Buying upgrades with V-Bucks

Digitally enabled

Although Epic's original game mode cost $50, Fortnite generates most revenue via micro-transactions. Through its own digital currency, called V-bucks, which players can use to buy features such as skins, dances, and other add-ons, Epic has totally shifted its business model. This customer-focused business model has caught on with gamers, as they get to customize who they are in the game, which further cements the customer relationship with Epic and Fortnite.

Digital first
Fortnite is 100% digital play across multiple devices. You are connected with friends wearing your favorite skin.

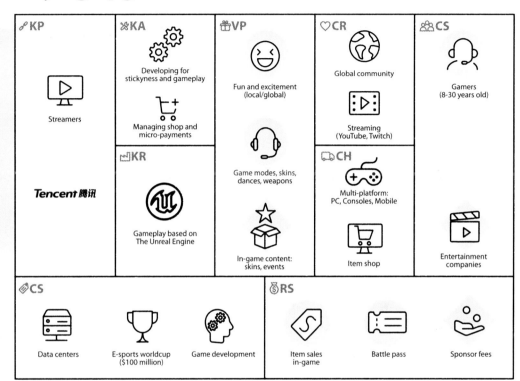

KP
Streamers

KA
Developing for stickyness and gameplay
Managing shop and micro-payments

KR
Tencent 腾讯
Gameplay based on The Unreal Engine

VP
Fun and excitement (local/global)
Game modes, skins, dances, weapons
In-game content: skins, events

CR
Global community
Streaming (YouTube, Twitch)

CH
Multi-platform: PC, Consoles, Mobile
Item shop

CS
Gamers (8-30 years old)
Entertainment companies

CS
Data centers
E-sports worldcup ($100 million)
Game development

RS
Item sales in-game
Battle pass
Sponsor fees

As players broadcast Fortnite on game streaming platforms such as Twitch and YouTube, Fortnite found a new customer segment in game watchers. And in 2019, Epic began to expand into Esports by organizing the Fortnite World Cup, investing $100 million of the $2.4 billion revenues generated the previous year.

A new season is coming

Fortnite is a constantly evolving, living game. With new seasons and features every 10 weeks, the game engages old players and attracts new players alike. Via its in-game revenue streams for all kinds of items as well as time restricted content, such as seasonal themed content, Epic has found a way to offer exclusivity and newness without necessarily reinventing Fortnite. What's more, Epic has succeeded in creating an experience that is as exciting for gamers as it is for fans.

Duolingo:
Help those who need it most

The current business model for language education is: the student pays—in particular, the student pays Rosetta Stone $500. The problem with this business model is that 95% of the world's population doesn't have $500."

Luis Von Ahn

Whether it's for travel, to get a job, for love, or simply to learn something new, learning a new language is something that more than one-eighth of the world's population is doing at this very moment; most are learning English. Yet, due to the lack of time and money, learning a language is not easy or inexpensive. Likewise, many immersive courses are offered only certain days of the week and require travel.

Luis Von Ahn, a professor at Carnegie Mellon University, realized that not only do vast differences in the quality of the education exist, especially in less developed countries, a lot of unequal access to education exists, especially where learning a new language is concerned. In many countries, new languages are only learned at institutional organizations, such as at well-funded schools, through private tutors, or via online courses, which can be expensive and costly in time and effort.

To address this inequality, Von Ahn, Severin Hacker (a graduate student), and several others, launched Duolingo, a platform that provides high-quality language education completely free to anyone and everyone.

Free, fun, and effective

Duolingo is an app that can be used on just about any mobile device and is designed to make learning a new language fun and effective. Over the years, Duolingo has changed its business model from business-to-business to a business-to-consumer model. In 2014, Duolingo began selling certifications and partnered up with schools to use the platform in classrooms. In 2015, Duolingo saw no other way to create a sustainable revenue stream than to sell ads on the platform. At first, the founders didn't want to do this, but the company saw selling ads as the only way to operate and scale while remaining true to their mission to enable people to learn new languages for free.

Duolingo

Digitally enabled!

Duolingo gamified the process of learning, making it fun and addictive for users to keep on learning a new language. This makes learning possible on your mobile phone, anytime, anywhere. Through the app, users are motivated and supported to learn every day. Duolingo has a lot of data allowing it to optimize the learning process for every individual by using machine learning. This makes it a personal tutoring experience.

Digital first
Duolingo has replaced the old, expensive way of learning new languages by making it accessible, fun, and free for everyone.

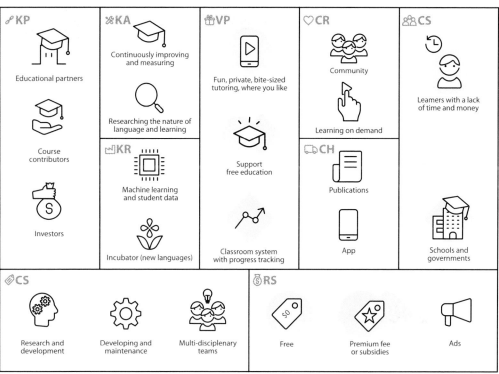

Since its launch, Duolingo has been used by more than 300 million people, making Duolingo the world's most downloaded education app. And, Duolingo doesn't want to stop there. In the coming years, the company plans to partner with more schools in order to help them use Duolingo in the classroom. Duolingo also wants to expand into different segments in education, stepping away from language education only.

Duolingo is already providing a personalized learning experience for free and continues to develop hy-per-personalized learning approaches for anyone. By becoming a paid user, you support free education, ads are removed, and offline access is provided. True to its mission, Duolingo continues to try to perfect how to teach everyone a new language.

> We imagine a future where livestock, land, water, even the atmosphere, are all connected by tools that help humans make sense of the biosphere's hidden internal language."

Yassir Khokhar, CEO Connecterra

Connecterra: Happy and healthy cows

Trying to feed the world is tough work, especially for the world's dairy farmers. People tend to think of dairy cows as an eternal fountain of milk, but just like any other animal, cows get sick. And sick cows don't produce a lot of milk. Dairy farmers are under a great deal of pressure to increase production and decrease costs. What's more, consumer demand for quality products has never been higher. Add to this societal trends pushing for increased sustainability and energy efficiency, and farmers are in the eye of a perfect storm with competing pressures on all sides.

Farming revolution

Yasir Khokhar, a technology entrepreneur, saw dairy farmers' challenges as an opportunity to start a farming revolution. Khokhar's vision is to use technology to gain a deep understanding of cows and their environment, and use this understanding to increase farming efficiency by focusing on the cows' well-being and fertility. To do this, Khokhar founded Connecterra to "connect farmers

and the value chain to identify issues on farm, recommend solutions and support farmers to make the transition to sustainable farming." https://www.connecterra.io/about/

In true revolutionary style, Khokhar aims to democratize the knowledge Connecterra gathers, in order to design the world's most efficient farm, sharing insights and recommendations with every farm and farmer. Ultimately, the Connecterra team wants to use the platform to solve inefficiencies in the food system, climate management, disease prevention, energy use, natural disaster response, and more.

To scale its solutions, Connecterra partners with regional resellers, who sell and install all of the necessary hardware. The company has also partnered with Lely, a global leader in robotics and data management for the dairy farm, to share and merge the data, better assisting farmers in their complex decision-making process.

Technology with a face

Digitally enabled

As the average farmer is getting older, Connecterra designed IDA, its "Moo-chine learning" platform, as a personal assistant, making technology more human. The company's digital system delivers actionable insights, rather than raw data, that farmers use to make better decisions.

Digital proposition

Data collected through sensors to deeply understand cow behavior to prevent diseases and keep cows happy and healthy. This increases efficiency and productivity.

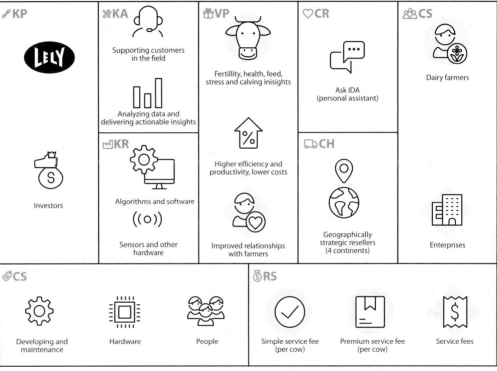

KP

LELY

Investors

KA

Supporting customers in the field

Analyzing data and delivering actionable insights

KR

Algorithms and software

Sensors and other hardware

VP

Fertillity, health, feed, stress and calving inisights

Higher efficiency and productivity, lower costs

Improved relationships with farmers

CR

Ask IDA (personal assistant)

CH

Geographically strategic resellers (4 continents)

CS

Dairy farmers

Enterprises

CS

Developing and maintenance

Hardware

People

RS

Simple service fee (per cow)

Premium service fee (per cow)

Service fees

Much better farming

The information most dairy farmers use today is largely institutional, passed on by other farmers via word of mouth. Connecterra is trying to change this. By using sensors, farmers can monitor the health of their cows and business.

IDA is also available for enterprises, such as dairy processors, as well as feed, genetics, and animal health companies, who can use IDA to make data-driven decisions to steer their production process and logistics. With IDA, Connecterra drives the transition to efficient, sustainable farming.

By leveraging digital technology such as sensors and artificial intelligence in the entire value chain, everybody is working together to bring the production of our food to the next level.

Disney Parks: It's a small world after all

> "Technology is lifting the limits of creativity and transforming the possibilities for entertainment and leisure."
>
> Bob Iger, CEO of The Walt Disney Company

If you've ever been to Disney World Resorts, you can probably remember the excitement you had for the magical experience. However, as the lines at Disney's theme parks have gotten ever longer for everything from attractions, restaurants, parking, and even bathrooms, Disney's lost quite a bit of its shine. If nothing else, though, Disney is about customer experience. So, when executives saw a drop in customer satisfaction, they knew they had to change something. Instead of bolting on technology to fix things, Disney set clear business goals for customer experience and operations to drive its digital transformation.

Setting clear business goals

Set as a strategic priority by the CEO, Disney embarked on a "digital transformation" journey to enhance the relationship with customers and transform the customer experience into something more magical (again). This meant becoming clear on how the business creates and delivers value and

identifying the bottlenecks that deteriorate the customer experience and satisfaction. Disney also reimagined how the business model would help to deliver a seamless and personalized customer experience . . . end-to-end.

MyMagic+

In 2011, Disney began to invest $1 billion in the development of MyMagic+, a combination of an updated website, app, and a wristband, equipped with built-in radio frequency identification (RFID) chips to identify customers and allow Disney to personalize every individual experience. Disney trained all its 70,000 employees and equipped all 28,000 hotel rooms, parks, shops, and attractions with the RFID chips. MyMagic+ officially launched in 2014 and has been a big success so far.

Seamless personalized experience

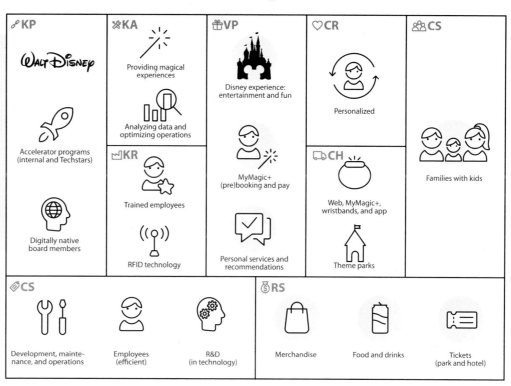

Digitally enabled!

With MyMagic+ in place, Disney was able to accommodate an extra 3,000 daily visitors. Not only do these people enjoy their experience more, they also spend more money on buying food, drinks, and merchandise because it is simply made easier and personalized to their wants and needs. In addition, Disney is able to decrease costs by optimizing operations using data to see where staff is needed most, as well as finding inefficiencies in park operations.

Digital connection
A Disney theme park is primarily a physical experience. Digital technologies ensure that it is magical and personal all the way.

With MyMagic+, Disney has proven that digital strategies are only as good as the value they produce and capture. For Disney, technology is used to create end-to-end magical experiences. Crowd management helps Disney deploy staff to where they are needed through wristbands that tell where customers are and what they're doing. What's more, enabling customers to use technology to make payments, manage reservations, access hotel rooms, and pre-book attractions without waiting in line, has not only decreased waiting times and streamlined logistics, people spend more time on entertainment and consuming. There's no reason to think that Disney will stop at MyMagic+ either. With new technological developments, such as machine learning, it's only a matter of time before Disney finds a way to create even more magic.

What about pioneering a vertically integrated supply chain in your industry that makes customers look good and save loads of money?

Warby Parker was born out of the frustration of the extremely high prices of eyewear because of the fragmented, horizontal way of organizing the supply chain. The customer ended up paying for all the inefficiencies in the way glasses are designed, manufactured, and sold. Warby Parker decided to flip this around, directly serving customers with designer glasses at a fraction of the usual prices. Customers visit their physical and digital store frequently because it just makes them look good.

Ask yourself the following questions . . .

What can you provide for free and make so exciting that people buy digital artifacts to enhance their online experience even more?

Fortnite is one of those rare innovations that became an overnight success. Within 2 years, over 250 million people were playing the game—for free. Playing Battle Royale on a digital island is exciting and addictive. Not only because of the cool digital items that are available in the item shop, but also the 99 unpredictable humans that are trying to take you down keep every game fresh.

What smart technology can you deploy and turn into actionable insights for your customers?

Connecterra helps farmers keep their cows healthy, their herds productive, and their businesses profitable. Using sensors to track the movements of every cow, their behavior can be derived from data, presented to the farmer as actionable insights by IDA, his/her personal assistant.

Lessons learned

What can you provide to make developing apps that move the needle of a business as easy as Point and Click?

Salesforce started with with an online CRM, a fairly simple product for companies of any size, making salespeople more effective. Customers could try the product for free, which lowered the barrier to adopt working from the cloud. Salesforce now offers support for virtually every business function from the cloud. And if a customer needs more, they can develop what they need on top of the Salesforce platform. Four times faster than what it used to be.

What if you run your business like Disney?

Disney Parks are fun every once in a while, apart from all the waiting in line to get your thrills. Disney understood that digital technologies can make the physical visit to their theme parks more attractive and engaging.

What about focusing on the core of your value proposition and make it so engaging that customer stay subscribed for a lifetime?

The *New York Times* still has the same mission as when they started in 1851, and that is to seek the truth and help people understand the world. The way they deliver this truth has however dramatically changed. Change did not come easy for them, but eventually they made bold strategic choices and invested heavily in engaging with customers in a digital way.

What can you gamify to make it more fun, addictive, and effective?

Duolingo makes learning a language fun, addictive, and universally accessible. Mining data of all those millions of students gives deep insights into language and learning, which is used to make Duolingo even more fun and effective.

High-level strategic choices

1

 Define business goals

Digital is a means to an end, not a goal itself. Digital technologies are just like any other technology. They are not a silver bullet for magically growing your business.

Be clear what you want to achieve by using digital means. Clarify your vision of future value creation and the role you play. Define your ambition in terms of digital revenues.

2

 Explore technology options

A single solution does not exist. There are many different digital technologies that you could use to achieve your business goals. New technologies are emerging all the time.

Make sure you don't fixate on one technology to achieve something. Create a big picture overview of existing and upcoming technologies you could use. Discuss pros and cons related to the value you want to create.

3

 Test small

Applying digital technologies across your entire organization in a big-bang approach never works. Plenty of digital tools are available for well-defined experiments.

Validate your digital value proposition or delivery on a small scale with just a bunch of customers. Capture data from those customer interactions, analyze, and draw conclusions. Expand what works and change what is not working.

to drive this shift.

4

 Make it personal

Digital is not the same as depersonalize. Digital technologies should be used to enhance value creation, while making delivery of that value more efficient.

Use the data and information you collect to make the experience personal and relevant for customers. Plus, digital technologies can enable you to personalize an experience or even ship products and provide the promised features at a later stage.

5

 Think beyond

Digital is not a replacement of what used to be physical. Digital is a way to achieve your vision and has to be considered from a strategy, not an operational, point of view.

Think deeply about the additional and new value (business models) that can be created with the newly acquired or implemented digital assets.

6

 Stay human

Yes, leverage the efficiency of digitizing and automating things, but don't hide behind your systems. Customers want to connect to humans if needed.

Make sure that your digital initiatives enrich the interaction and relationship between your company and your customers.

From
pipeline to platform

Throughout history, the biggest companies used pipeline business models to become what they are today. It took only a decade for new entrants, using platform business models, to eat their lunch. Why push when you can create pull?

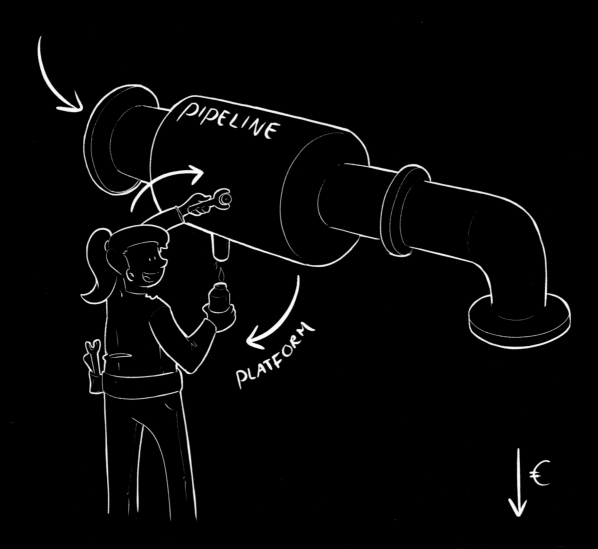

PIPELINE

PLATFORM

pipeline →

The Platform Shift is a business model strategy that aims to **connect people who need something with people who have something, for the benefit of both parties**. The company that operates a platform must be fully dedicated to delivering a unique value proposition for both the demand and supply sides of this equation. The ultimate goal of this strategy is to create strong network effects wherein **customers from both the demand and supply sides help to spread the word to others**. The platform is designed to grow such that new opportunities are presented on an ongoing basis, so that customers can continually exchange (better and more) value. More customers bring in more data and revenue, which is used to enhance the value provided to all participants on the platform. Of course, when a business has a thriving customer network, it often encounters other challenges, such as increased concerns about privacy and social equity.

platform

Shift stories
Large
↗ Alibaba Group

Medium
↗ Grab
↗ Apple

Short
↗ LinkedIn
↗ Kickstarter
↗ WeChat

"A platform is a plug-and-play business model that allows multiple participants (producers and consumers) to connect to it, interact with each other, and create and exchange value."

Sangeet Paul Choudary, co-author of "Platform Revolution: How Networked Markets Are Transforming the Economy and How to Make Them Work for You."

Too much friction

A platform business model is all about making the connection and facilitating the interaction between producers (or owner/ sharers) and consumers, as well as among customers. It's the responsibility of the platform owner to ensure that all customers can trust the value they receive from one another such that they might continue to exchange value on an ongoing basis.

The market your business model lives in may be highly intermediated. Without a lot of transparency (yet), most companies are involved in pushing value from producers to consumers, with each player wanting to capture a piece of that value creation. This landscape is filled with pipeline business models, i.e., complicated, obfuscated supply chains that benefit by maintaining high barriers to entry. This way of organizing the flow of value creates bottlenecks and causes a lack of transparency for both producers and consumers. Producers are often in the dark about what consumers really need because the direct feedback loop with customers is missing. Consumers end up confused about what's available in the market and waste a lot of time figuring out what to consume (or buy). Of course, even in these markets, the internet increases transparency and choice.

Strategic questions
Can you play a role in facilitating communication and value exchange between producers and users? How might you change from being just one of the cogs in a complicated value chain to a transparent and energetic marketplace where producers and customers (or in this context, *users*) thrive? Who are you connecting and what for? How might you attract both producers and users to this marketplace and what is your promise and offer to them? What role does data collection play for you, and how might you ensure trust and privacy? How can you start small and test the true value of your platform instead of building a technical platform in a big-bang approach?

From pipeline

Pipeline business models are the dominant business design for the industrial economy. Firms build products or craft services, push them out, and sell them to customers. Value is produced upstream and consumed downstream, creating a linear flow of value, much like water flowing through a pipe.

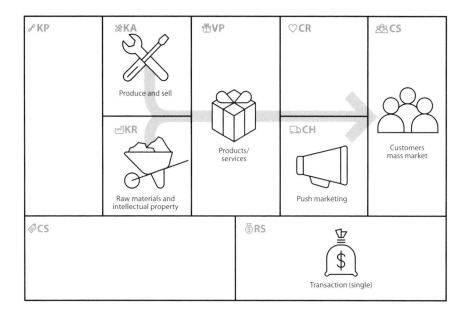

Pushing out products

Pipeline business models often focus on pushing out products or services to customers through *direct* (online ordering) or *indirect* (retail) channels. Customers pay for the product and/or service, creating a fairly transactional customer relationship. Over time, customers might come back because a company launches an improved version of a product or because customers need other things from the product assortment.

Streamlining marketing and production

The key activity in a pipeline business model is to streamline marketing and production. Marketing must target the right customer segment, ensuring the products and services are purchased by a fairly large (and often growing) group of customers.

For many products, a traditional (and often complex) manufacturing supply chain may exist that is optimized to satisfy customer demand. Companies working with a pipeline business model also often streamline production and operations to improve efficiency and maintain healthy profit margins.

to platform

Finding each other to exchange value

Platform business models rely on at least two interdependent customer segments. One segment is the demand side, which includes customers that have a specific need, called consumers, and the other is the supply side, which includes customers that have a product and/or service to offer, called producers. Consumers are drawn (pulled) to the platform due to the broad range of products and services. The supply side comes to the platform due to the effective access to large numbers of consumers. Trust and communication between both sides is paramount and is most often moderated. Search and peer reviews help to establish connections and keep everyone honest.

Facilitating connection, and interaction

The key activity is to connect customers from the supply and demand sides on an ongoing basis. This is done by designing for interaction between both sides and making sure openness and transparency exist in communication and transactions. The platform captures data, resulting in a rich dataset of all these interactions and transactions.

A platform is designed to connect demand and supply, facilitate and stimulate frequent interactions and transactions, and attract new people to participate in exchanging value. A platform is a vibrant ecosystem of value creation and consumption and can even be seen as an economy in itself.

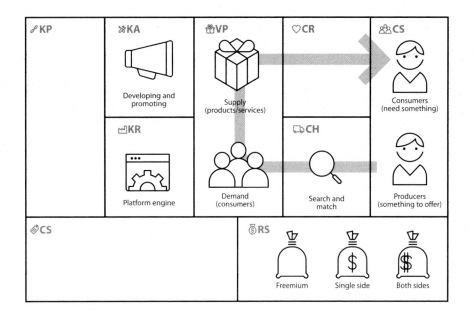

Efficient product trading

 Sharing the passion

 On-demand offline services

1 These marketplaces typically trade physical products—either commodities or standard products—among businesses (B2B) or consumers (C2C). Buyers go to the platform mainly for superior efficiency and prices. Sellers use the platform for access to a large market of buyers. Revenues come from commissions on the traded value and subscriptions for additional services for sellers. Facilitating search and negotiation is key for enabling fast and easy trading.

Examples: Alibaba.com, TMall

2 These marketplaces facilitate the exchange of physical products and create an emotional connection with a strong community aspect and shared passion for a certain product type. The seller side often pays a commission and/or enters into a subscription model. Sellers set fixed prices for the products they sell but have to accept fixed fees from the marketplace. Creating and curating the product listings is key.

Examples: TaoBao, Vinted, KickStarter

3 This marketplace matches service firms with consumers. The exchanged services are delivered through offline channels and therefore require some form of scheduling. The primary value for both the businesses offering the services and their customers relates to efficiency gains. Buyers mostly use the marketplace for free, while sellers pay commission fees. Given the location dependence, these marketplaces often focus on one geographic market and one segment.

Examples: Grab, uShip

Patterns

 Serviced by your peers

 Online products and services

 Ecosystems of platforms

These marketplaces involve peer-to-peer exchange of services in the physical world. Sellers are either individuals sharing physical resources or providing time and skills, for whom this provides a novel source of income. Buyers benefit from an increase in transaction efficiency. A review system to generate trust between the users must exist. Revenue streams are mainly generated from commission fees, with most platforms determining a fixed fee. Revenue is generated from both sides.

This is a marketplace offering digital services or products. Professional freelancers use it to earn additional income, selling services at fixed prices. Buyers get efficient access and are supported by an active community. Digital products and other content are offered by independent authors, musicians, and other creators. Content creation is facilitated and supported. Revenues come from commission fees.

This marketplace has evolved beyond connecting the original demand and supply sides. Through facilitating connections, new customer needs from one or both sides are discovered, spinning out new platforms. New platforms emerge by seizing opportunities to connect other customer segments. The infrastructure of the original platform becomes the foundational layer in terms of data and technology to support all platforms in the ecosystem.

Examples: LinkedIn, PatientsLikeMe, Turo, JustPark

Examples: Grab, LendingClub, FundersClub, Fiverr, Twitch, LinkedIn

Examples: Alibaba Group, Grab, Apple, WeChat

Alibaba Group

In 1999, Alibaba started connecting Chinese sellers and international buyers with the vision to build the future infrastructure of commerce. And this is only the start. Jack Ma, Alibaba's founder, also envisions Alibaba existing for 102 years. Even after 20 years of building one platform business model after another and becoming one of largest companies in the world, Alibaba is still in its infancy.

Facts

Founders
Jack Ma and 17 friends

CEO
Daniel Zhang

Founded in 1999
in China

Total revenue
$56.2 billion (2019)

Industry
Internet, cloud computing, artificial intelligence, retail, and media and entertainment.

Scale
Fourth largest internet company by revenue and largest retailer/e-commerce company in the world.

Timeline

1999
Founded

Alibaba Group is established by 18 founders, led by Jack Ma. Alibaba.com, a wholesale platform connecting Chinese sellers to international buyers, is launched.

2000
Softbank

$20 million raised from a group of investors, led by Softbank. Organized West Lake Summit, a gathering of internet business and thought leaders.

2001
Mission

"Making it easy to do business everywhere" is outlined as Alibaba Group's mission. The company's 6 values are made explicit, all centered on customers, collaboration, entrepreneurship, and innovation.

Our culture, business models and systems are built to last: achieving sustainability in the long run."

Vision story, Alibaba website

Grow your business

China's economy has shown remarkable growth (10%) over the last several decades. It's the largest manufacturing economy and exporter of goods, fastest-growing consumer market, and second-largest importer of goods in the world. At the same time, China is still a developing country; on average, the income level is still below the poverty line. Due to China's size, the country is finding that lifting its vast economy to the next level is not easy. Because of regional differences, and China's unique transportation system, it was hard for entrepreneurs to attract customers and grow small but flourishing businesses. Likewise, Chinese consumers have historically had fewer choices than the rest of the developed world. This, of course, is the power that

Alibaba brings, representing a kind, smart businessperson (Ali Baba) helping "villages." The Alibaba Group envisions a digital economy where all participants grow and prosper.

Connecting buyers and sellers

For every platform business model within the Alibaba ecosystem, ensuring trust and good communication between participants and handling disputes is a key activity. In addition, developing services to simplify doing business for both the supply and demand side is a crucial activity as well. This is what Alibaba Group has been doing on an ongoing basis for every platform business model the company has developed, making it easy for people to do business.

Alibaba Group

L

2002
Postive cashflow

Three years after its founding date, Alibaba Group is cashflow positive.

2003
Taobao

Alibaba Group launches a consumer to consumer marketplace, connecting very small businesses all over China with consumers.

Fund continued growth

Another $82 million was raised to further grow the ecosystem and build the future infrastructure of commerce.

Alibaba.com

Efficient product trading
Alibaba.com makes it easy for sellers to participate. Merchants can join for free and use the platform to grow their businesses. They pay for additional services to grow faster.

Alibaba.com is a wholesale B2B platform connecting over 1 million sellers and buyers from 240 countries. Sellers join for free. They are offered a global audience for their products, training to effectively trade, and tools to easily manage their businesses. Sellers can buy keyword advertising to boost sales and a Gold Supplier membership, providing a proof of authenticity, which helps to build trust with buyers. Buyers get an easy way to find suppliers quickly and easily together with the tools to buy from that supplier that best fits their needs. Buyers and sellers are both rewarded for bringing peers to the platform.

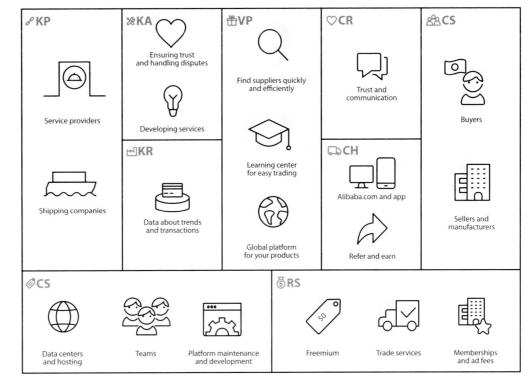

KP
Service providers
Shipping companies

KA
Ensuring trust and handling disputes
Developing services

KR
Data about trends and transactions

VP
Find suppliers quickly and efficiently
Learning center for easy trading
Global platform for your products

CR
Trust and communication

CH
Alibaba.com and app
Refer and earn

CS
Buyers
Sellers and manufacturers

CS
Data centers and hosting
Teams
Platform maintenance and development

RS
Freemium
Trade services
Memberships and ad fees

2004
AliPay

2005
Yahoo!

2007
IPO

Alibaba Group launches a third-party online payment platform, facilitating fast, safe, and easy transactions across all the marketplaces in the growing Alibaba ecosystem.

Alibaba Group creates a strategic partnership with Yahoo!, bringing in US$1 billion in cash and the Yahoo China assets valued at $700 million for a 40% stake.

Alibaba Group raises US$1.5 billion through an Initial Public Offering at the Hong Kong Stock Exchange, making it the biggest internet offering since Google in 2004.

Trade is about mutual trust

Given Alibaba Group's big 102-year vision, it should be no surprise that Alibaba Group's own dedicated entrepreneurial teams have continuously developed new business models to drive ever-increasing value creation within the Alibaba ecosystem. In 2003, Taobao.com was founded, again from Jack Ma's apartment, connecting Chinese consumers with each other. AliPay was founded a year later to facilitate transactions and payments in a seamless way for all the participants within the Alibaba ecosystem.

A partnership with Yahoo! in 2005 and Alibaba's IPO in 2007 at the Hong Kong Stock Exchange provided the company with the funds to take this approach to the next level. Energized by a bold vision and grounded in its company values—customers first, innovation, and entrepreneurship—Taobao

quickly became more valuable than eBay in the span of only three years. Although many reasons exist for Taobao's rapid success, one may be the *swift guanxi* concept employed by Alibaba, which is broadly defined as a close and pervasive interpersonal relationship, based on high-quality social interactions, whereby both parties benefit from an exchange. TaoBao facilitates swift quanxi as the core interaction, which is not necessarily something eBay does all that well.

True to Alibaba's goal to continuously develop the platform, teams constantly focus on the core interaction, developing streamlined approaches to make interacting and transacting easier for everyone. When the need for additional services increases, a service within a platform becomes a platform in and of itself, which led to Alimama (marketing platform) and Juhuasan (flash sales). Tmall, another Alibaba platform, started in the same way, as an extension of TaoBao.

Alibaba has brought to life one platform business model after another, satisfying the needs of many participants in the digital economy.

2008
Taobao Mall

Taobao is extended with a mall, enabling Chinese brands and companies to sell to consumers all over China.

2009
Alibaba cloud

At the 10th anniversary of Alibaba Group, Alibaba Cloud is launched. R&D and operations centers opened in Hangzhou, Beijing, and Silicon Valley. First Single's Day (11.11), Taobao's shopping festival, supported by the cloud in 2010.

Mission, vision, and values

In 2010, 0.3% of revenues is earmarked for environmental awareness and conservation initiatives. Alibaba Partnership is set up to ensure the sustainability of Alibaba Group's mission, vision, and values. Alibaba Group launches AliExpress, a platform that connects Chinese sellers directly to international consumers.

Shopping as a lifestyle

TMall.com connects local and international brands with Chinese consumers. Companies get access to the vast and growing market by means of their own online storefront. They can operate their Chinese store as if it were their own website. Consumers get a great shopping experience through easy searching and convenient purchasing and have a broad choice of branded products. TMall requires businesses to be on China's mainland so that expectations in terms of communication (fluent Chinese), customer service, and shipping are fully met.

Efficient product trading
Developing algorithms for facilitating the meaningful interaction between businesses and consumers is crucial.

TMall

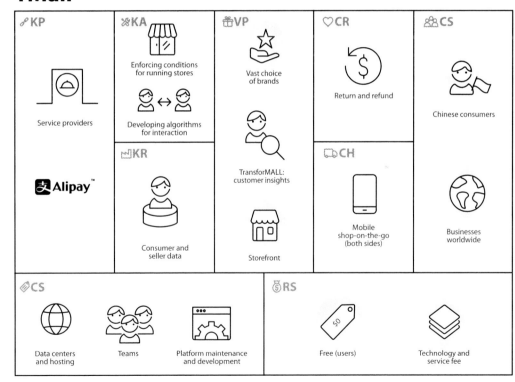

2011
TMall

Alibaba Group spins out Taobao Mall as TMall, a dedicated platform connecting Chinese brands and companies to consumers all over China.

2013
Cainiao

Alibaba Group launches the Cainiao network together with a consortium of logistics companies to relentlessly improve delivery times to buyers.

2014
IPO

Alibaba Group achieves a record-breaking IPO: US$25 billion raised at a market cap of US$231 billion. Earlier this year, TMall Global was launched.

The impact of Taobao villages extends far beyond the generation of wealth."

Wesley Wu-Yi Koo and Lizhi Liu, "E-commerce Can Ease social Ills in China's Villages"

Customers first, always

For the past 20 years, Alibaba Group has continually addressed the needs of sellers and consumers in China and abroad. In 2013 Alibaba launched Cainiao, a collaboration between all of the logistics companies throughout China meant to improve logistics across the entire supply chain. In addition, the company built 1,000 Taobao service centers at the county and 100,000 centers at the village level, improving the physical infrastructure for doing business. Alibaba's clear and compelling vision of the future infrastructure of commerce guided and energized entrepreneurial teams to create value in so many new ways for all these different customers. It's no wonder Alibaba's IPO was record-breaking. Even on Wall Street, the company stayed true to its values: customers first, employees second, shareholders third. On stage were eight customers, not Alibaba managers.

After its IPO, innovation initiatives and acquisitions exploded. Ant Financial Services launched MYbank in 2015, which uses an algorithm to grant loans to small companies within three minutes. Traditional banks neglect these customers because they often represent too much risk. So far, MYbank has borrowed US$290 billion to fuel growth of over 16 million small companies. As a result, small companies grow, more people are employed, and participants in this economy prosper, increasing the value of the ecosystem. In only five years, Alibaba Group's market capitalization doubled.

2015
Entrepreneurship

Alibaba Group takes on several initiatives to support entrepreneurship, like the Entrepreneurs Fund for Taiwan and Hong Kong and the first Global Conference on Women and Entrepreneurship.

Largest retail economy

In 2016, Alibaba Group exceeds US$0.4 trillion in gross merchandise volume (GMV) on its China retail marketplaces. The concept of an Electronic World Trade Platform (eWTP) is included in the official communiqué of the G20 summit.

An ecosystem adding value

The ecosystem business model enables connections between all participants in the economy. Value exchange in every imaginable way is facilitated: business to business with Alibaba.com and 1866.com (domestic), consumers to consumers with Taobao, and business to consumers with TMall (domestic) and TMall Global. Several service companies provide additional services to the participants within the ecosystem, like AliPay for payments and Cainiao for logistics, and Alibaba Cloud for cloud computing services, among others.

Ecosystem of platforms
Connection among all participants is facilitated by dedicated platform business models. Establishing and maintaining trust among users is crucial, and partners need to add value to the ecosystem for users.

The Alibaba ecosystem

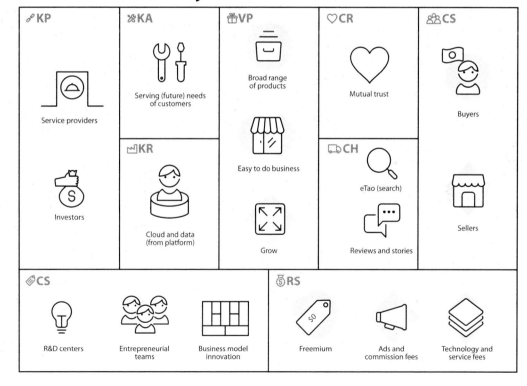

Everybody prospers

By pursuing a compelling vision, entrepreneurial teams at Alibaba Group have built an impressive ecosystem of platform business models. Obviously, this did not happen overnight. Innovation takes time, especially when working on platform business models.

Teams have had to figure out the real needs of customers on the demand and supply sides, test and develop unique value propositions for both sides, and build the business model around those propositions that constantly trigger and facilitate the core interaction. What's more, Alibaba Group's desire to exist for 102 years provides the patience needed to build such an ecosystem.

This stuctured approach to business model innovation, has resulted in a well-balanced portfolio of long-term value creation. And the company's vision and entrepreneurial teams keep growing this portfolio, ensuring that more and more value will be created for consumers, merchants, and society.

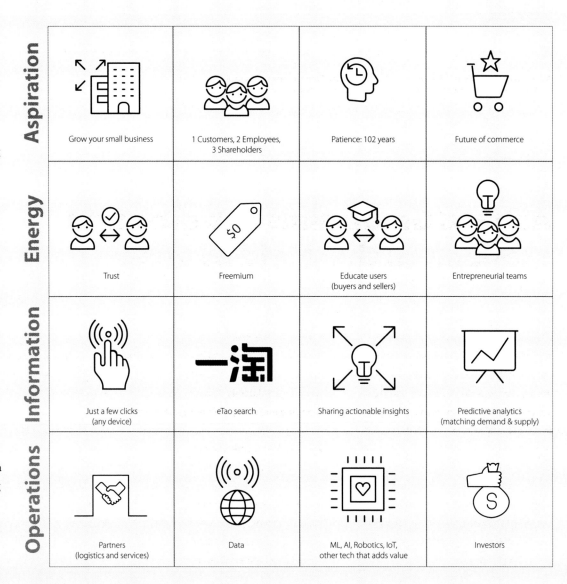

Aspiration

Grow your small business | 1 Customers, 2 Employees, 3 Shareholders | Patience: 102 years | Future of commerce

Energy

Trust | Freemium | Educate users (buyers and sellers) | Entrepreneurial teams

Information

Just a few clicks (any device) | eTao search | Sharing actionable insights | Predictive analytics (matching demand & supply)

Operations

Partners (logistics and services) | Data | ML, AI, Robotics, IoT, other tech that adds value | Investors

2018
New Retail

2019
Tech for Change

Future
2H strategy

Alibaba Group introduces HEMA and brick and mortar convenience stores powered by TMall.

Alibaba Group incorporates use of technologies like AI to solve real, complex, and urgent problems. Refresh of their 6 core values on their 20th anniversary.

"I think in the future technology has to be fun. Alibaba has the 2H strategy for our future: Happiness and Health. If the advent of technology cannot make people happier and healthier, there is no point doing it." Jack Ma in the *South China Morning Post*, April 2016.

Alibaba Group aims to be the fifth economy in the world by 2036

Alibaba Group fuels growth of their customers with fundamental infrastructure for commerce and new technology. Its customers are able to build businesses and create value that is shared among all participants in the Alibaba ecosystem. Alibaba Group's ecosystem of platforms is creating the future of commerce as we speak, write, and read. Keep in mind that Alibaba is just getting started. When Jack Ma retired in 2019, he reminded everyone that Alibaba wants to exist for at least 102 years. Hence, the company has a long way to go.

On a global level several hubs of the Electronic World Trade Platform (eWTP) have already been established in Rwanda, Belgium, and Malaysia. Alibaba Group is expanding into many different value spaces, including music, travel, movies, entertainment, and healthcare. The Alibaba Cloud Intelligence Brain offers an ultra-intelligent AI Platform for solving complex business and social problems for industry, cities, the environment, and healthcare; a similar "brain" for the aviation and financial sector is under development. The company's Tech for Change makes Alibaba's infrastructure, cloud tech, and other tools available for social entrepreneurs who want to give back to society.

Needless to say, Alibaba Group represents a giant ecosystem of platforms. Their long-term goal is to provide services for 2 billion customers, empowering 10 million profitable businesses, and creating 100 million jobs. At its current growth rate, Alibaba Group is on track to become the fifth largest economy in the world by the year 2036.

Grab

What started as a ride hailing company focusing on making life just a little bit easier, Grab has turned to become an everyday, everything app used by millions of consumers, driver-partners, and merchants. Using Grab, all these customer segments boost the economy for everyone's benefit.

Facts

Founders
Anthony Tan,
Tan Hooi Ling

Founded in 2012
in Malaysia

Total revenue
US $2.3 billion (2019)

Industry
Mobility
Food delivery
Finance
Entertainment

Scale
First Decacorn
in Southeast Asia
Active: Southeast Asia
(excluding Laos and Brunei)
and Japan

We're here to help you do it all, and more."

Grab homepage

Southeast Asia has long been a complex ecosystem of various ride hailing services. From unmarked livery vehicles, to taxis, to tuk-tuks, and everything in between, this ecosystem at best is overwhelming, and at worst it can be a scary cacophony of competing interests. Add on to that, just like in other countries that allow for unregulated, unmitigated capitalism where ride hailing is concerned, many proprietors (i.e., drivers) tend to follow incorrect routes and often overcharge for rides. Needless to say, many of the experiences in this part of the world were horrible.

Hearing this from a friend on a visit in Malaysia, Anthony Tan, a Harvard Business School student, was inspired to do something to fix the mess. Mirroring Uber's ridesharing concept, but focused on Southeast Asia, Tan entered a business plan contest in which he placed second

and was eventually selected as a finalist for Harvard's Minimum Viable Product Funding award. With the funding he received, Tan set out to develop an Uber-like platform for the Southeast Asian market.

In 2012, along with a group of friends, Tan launched My Teksi, an app for the Malaysian market, which promised to make ride hailing safer, provide taxi drivers with better working conditions, and make life just a little bit easier for everyone. Although most taxi companies at the time turned Tan down, one of the last ones he spoke with, who operated a fleet of only thirty taxis, decided to give him a chance. And with that, My Teksi gained the traction it needed to become something more than a dream.

With some success under its belt, My Teksi expanded into new countries, like the Philippines, Thailand, and Singapore, to

solve similar problems found in Malaysia. Uber's business model, is predicated on drivers having access to their own phones, but Tan and his team found that many taxi drivers simply couldn't afford to purchase their own phone outright. So, to help expand My Teksi in each new country it entered, the company handed out smartphones to drivers, allowing them to pay back the My Teksi phone through daily installments.

In 2014, My Teksi found its inflection point, partnering with HDT Holdings to form the largest e-taxi fleet in Singapore and the region. Like Uber, the My Teksi team realized that during peak hours, there was a lack of public transportation. To address this problem, they launched a rebranded service, called Grab, allowing anyone with a car to become a licensed partner, taking people where they need to go.

Grab transport

Grab has a range of services to meet people's transport needs, from ridesharing, shuttle services for groups, and services catering to people with pets and families with small children. Grab also caters to various kinds of drivers: taxi drivers looking for their next fare, car owners looking for additional income or to offset the cost of ownership, and other drivers wanting to help the community. All drivers are supported and are trained how to use their smartphone and Grab app.

On-demand offline services
Grab provides various transport services at your fingertips. Consumers can easily book and get transparent fees. Drivers are their own bosses and decide how they partner with Grab.

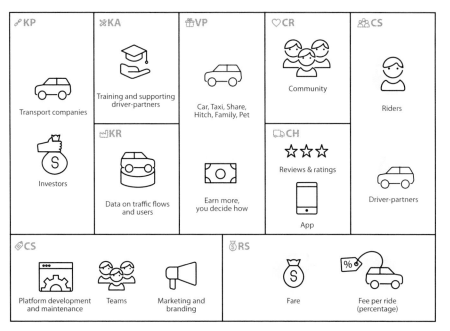

🔧 KP	⚒ KA	🏛 VP	♡ CR	👥 CS
Transport companies	Training and supporting driver-partners	Car, Taxi, Share, Hitch, Family, Pet	Community	Riders
Investors	📝 KR	Earn more, you decide how	🚚 CH	Driver-partners
	Data on traffic flows and users		⭐⭐☆ Reviews & ratings	
			App	
🏷 CS			💰 RS	
Platform development and maintenance / Teams / Marketing and branding			Fare	Fee per ride (percentage)

Grab has scaled in every way. WIth Grab, people can hire just about anything with wheels, from taxis, private cars, car-pooling, motorbikes, bicycles, luxury cars, shuttles, and bike taxis. In many respects, Grab is also seen as a way to transform public transport services to become more inclusive and expansive in Southeast Asia.

Similar to other platforms, Grab has launched payment and finance services, like GrabPay and GrabFinance. Not only do these services help to expand how people transact on the Grab platform, but for small businesses, Grab provides funding, tools, and insights helping these small businesses reach their goals. Unlike many huge platforms, Grab is building

for communities. Via its various "Grab for Good" initiatives, which include programs to bridge the tech skills gap in Southeast Asia as well as programs to create more opportunities for the deaf and hearing-impaired across the region, Grab estimates it will contribute $5.8 billion to the economy annually.

Grab for everything

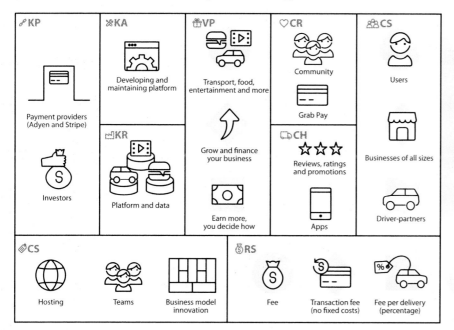

Core interaction

Grab is steadily expanding to provide everything people may need to make life easier, from transport, food, payments, delivery, tickets, hotels, rewards, subscription, insurance, and gifts. "From fast packages to faster payments. Streetside pick-ups to street food deliveries. Morning commutes to midnight food cravings." In many respects, Grab is reformulating some of the conveniences found in the US, Europe, and other parts of Asia, to fit the Southeast Asian markets.

Ecosystem of platforms
Grab evolved the connections it created through transport to connect ever more people and business of all sizes, lifting the whole economy to a higher level.

As of this writing, Grab is Southeast Asia's largest mobile technology company, connecting millions of consumers to millions of drivers, merchants, and businesses. To do this, Grab operates a multi-sided platform business model, taking on the largest challenges affecting the region, including access inequality, outdated infrastructure,

and income disparity. Southeast Asia has plenty of other ridesharing and ride hailing services, but what makes Grab unique is its hyperlocal, community-oriented focus. Whereas other services, including Uber, have attempted to expand into new regions by simply offering the same set of services that went gangbuster in another region,

Grab has changed its approach and respective offerings to meet the particular needs of the communities it serves. To do this, Grab tailors what it does to meet local requirements; it attempts to solve local problems; and it engages in hyperlocal outreach—all while continuously seeking out ways to improve its products.

Apple

So you think Apple is betting its continued growth into the future on iPhones?
Guess again. Behind the scenes, the company is building an ecosystem of services
(i.e., platform business models) the likes of which the world has never seen.

Apple

 You can focus on things that are barriers or you can focus on scaling the wall or redefining the problem."

Tim Cook, Apple CEO

Apple Inc. is known globally as the high-end, design-led hardware manufacturer of iPhones, Macs, and iPads. Even at its size and market reach, Apple has a growing fanbase that covets the sleek aesthetics and integrated experiences of its products. Apple releases new products to much fanfare. Even professional desktop products like the Mac Pro, some of which command prices well into the $10,000 range, were met with enormous applause. But what most people don't realize is that behind all Apple's shiny hardware lurks a giant platform ecosystem, which may soon eclipse everything else the company does.

Early in Apple's history, under John Scully's leadership, Apple found itself competing head-to-head with other PC manufacturers, like Dell. In this race to the bottom, Apple was forced to compete on price alone, manufacturing the same gray plastic boxes as its competitors. Needless to say, Apple's business model was, at this time, in life-support mode.

When Steve Jobs, Apple's co-founder and original CEO, came back to Apple in 1997, he went about restructuring the product line. His rationale: total focus on helping people achieve their goals at different moments in their lives. To help him do this, Jobs hand-picked Jonathan Ive, a talented industrial designer at Apple.

Throughout the early 2000s, Apple, under Jobs, continued to focus on well-designed computer hardware as well as Apple's operating system, Mac OS X, and accompanying software products for producing videos, audio, and the like. However, with human experience clearly at the center of just about every decision Jobs made, he and Ive began to expand beyond computers, releasing the first iPod in 2001. This elegant music device, along with its tight connection to iTunes, the software interface for the iPod, started what became a revolution in every sense of the word.

By 2003, not only had the Apple iPod cornered 70% of the portable music player market, Jobs made game-changing deals with the music companies to sell their music catalogs—song-by-song—on iTunes. It was this move to a platform business model for music that created what Apple is today. With iTunes, Apple opened a world of possibilities to both businesses and people to transact in a new way, with Apple facilitating every transaction. What's more, Apple created a platform ecosystem to deliver distinct and increasing value to its customers, both the creators and consumers.

Apple's walled garden

Apple's platform business models are varied, but are most often content services, wherein Apple's App Store enables application creators (developers) to host, market, and sell apps and content to consumers. What's unique about Apple's App Store is that it's accessed exclusively via Apple hardware, therein creating what's known as a *walled garden*.

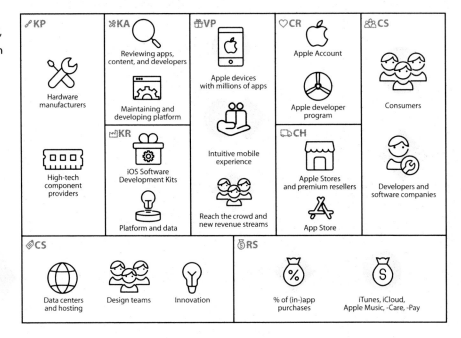

Online products or services
Apple services, like iTunes, Apple TV, Apple Arcade, the App Store, and Apple Pay, enable consumers to find, purchase, and/or subscribe to everything.

App Store

When Apple released the iPhone in 2007, iPhone's business model looked very similar to other mobile phone business models at the time. Though its sleek, full screen display was completely different from others on the market, the functionality was developed solely by Apple as a set of pre-installed applications. However, in 2008, Apple released the first version of its App Store, designed specifically to enable application developers to develop, market, host, and sell applications for consumers using iPhones.

Consumers could (and do) use the App Store to find applications that they want to install on their iPhones (or other Apple devices), providing them with new functionality as well as the ability to customize how they use their devices. Apple charges a fee to register as a developer for their App Store. Also, a commission is charged for every application sold and/or content delivered through an application. Though there were only about 500 applications when Apple launched the App Store, today there are more than 2 million.

Apple HealthKit

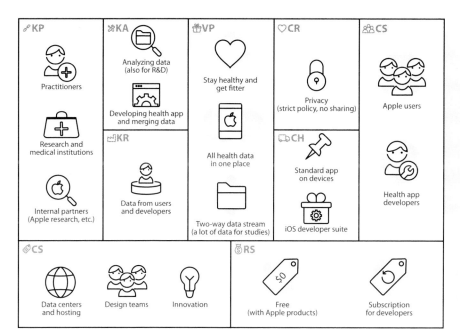

KP
- Practitioners
- Research and medical institutions
- Internal partners (Apple research, etc.)

KA
- Analyzing data (also for R&D)
- Developing health app and merging data

KR
- Data from users and developers

VP
- Stay healthy and get fitter
- All health data in one place
- Two-way data stream (a lot of data for studies)

CR
- Privacy (strict policy, no sharing)

CH
- Standard app on devices
- iOS developer suite

CS
- Apple users
- Health app developers

CS
- Data centers and hosting
- Design teams
- Innovation

RS
- Free (with Apple products)
- Subscription for developers

Core interaction

Though Apple's platform for health, called Apple Health, is in its early stages, Apple is already signing up both consumers and health businesses, including medical practitioners, to interact with each other using its service. In fact, as an intermediary—on the wrists of millions of Apple Watch wearers—Apple has already alerted emergency services when it's detected heart problems of some wearers. Apple relies on revenue for HealthKit coming from applications sold on the App Store.

Ecosystem of platforms
Through the Apple iPhone and Watch, users monitor their health and can call upon health services when required.

Apple, for a long time, has been well-known as a provider of productivity and entertainment, via its platforms, such as iTunes and the App Store. However, given that millions of people globally have integrated their devices, like iPhones, into their lives, even going so far as to wear their devices 24x7 (e.g., the Apple Watch), it may seem "natural" that Apple has begun the work to create yet

another set of platform business models, this time focused on health. Launched in 2014, Apple HealthKit is Apple's attempt to connect its consumers' health information with health practitioners and health applications such that Apple can facilitate the exchange of value between consumers and practitioners. What's unique about this burgeoning platform, is that it's built to provide

consumers with increasingly personalized healthcare offers, recommendations, and care, while providing detailed health information to practitioners who provide care. In the not-so-distant-future, Apple will likely capture value from players in the ecosystem of hospitals, practitioners, labs, devices, monitoring services, insurers, and analytics.

Snackable cases

Vinted is a platform that enables people to **sell, buy, and swap their secondhand clothes.** The growing community of 25 million people is trying to make secondhand clothing the first choice again.

Shippers, meet carriers. Carriers, meet shippers.

uShip is a marketplace on which trusted, feedback-rated carriers use their extra cargo space to earn money. You can list your item and let carriers such as small fleet, truck owners, or even travelers bid for your listing.

JustPark

Finding a parking spot has always been an issue. JustPark is making this easy by connecting people who want to rent out their driveway to people in need of a parking space.

Turo matches drivers who need a car with car owners. With over 350,000 vehicles listed, Turo is the world's largest peer-to-peer car sharing marketplace.

In need of money?

1. FundersClub is the world's first **online venture capital firm** enabling accredited investors to, within just minutes, invest in the most promising start-ups of the world.

2. LendingClub is the world's largest **peer-to-peer lending platform** that connects borrowers with investors. Borrowers can list a loan between $1,000 and $40,000 paired with the reason for the loan. Already, $50 billion has been borrowed through the platform.

PatientsLikeMe is a platform that connects you with people that are having the same conditions or diseases as you. With more than 43 million data points, PatientsLikeMe is also helping the health industry find new ways of treating these conditions and diseases.

Freelance marketplace

Fiverr is an online marketplace for freelance services for business. Via the platform, you can look for and post all kinds of freelance jobs and get work done fast by freelancers from all over the world.

Twitch is a platform that was built to enable gamers to watch their favorite games being played by other gamers. Viewers can interact with each other and the person they are watching in real-time. Anybody can start streaming and even start earning an income if they become popular enough.

3 Short case studies

Short. Crisp. Fast. Clear.

1 LinkedIn

CEO	Total revenue	Founded	Scale
Jeff Weiner	$5.3 billion (2018)	2002 in USA	300 million active users

2 Kickstarter

CEO	Total revenue	Founded	Scale
Aziz Hasan	$4.6 billion (since 2009)	2009 in USA	445,000 projects

3 WeChat

CEO	Total revenue	Founded	Scale
Ma Huateng	$22 billion (2018)	2011 in China	1.1 billion active users

LinkedIn: Revolutionizing networking

Landing a dream job has never been easy. Attracting the right talent is no easier. To help facilitate the needs of both employees and employers, Reid Hoffman launched LinkedIn, a professional networking platform which today connects more than 560 million users across all its customer segments, in more than 200 countries.

Fueled by humans' oldest instinct, to connect with one another and form communities, LinkedIn has made it easy to connect professionals from every industry imaginable, facilitating connections via requests, recommendations, and word-of-mouth. Where there used to be six degrees of separation when it comes to professional connections, LinkedIn in most cases has reduced this to less than three. In many respects, LinkedIn has modernized interactions that have been around for centuries.

Considering the oldest version of networking, a physical "networking" hour or meeting, LinkedIn has built something quite different, and markedly better in many ways. LinkedIn's forte is personal, professional, and business brand building. This is done mostly through virtual interactions and content sharing, which can be done for free on the platform. There are also premium options that provide people and businesses services with deeper access and more interactions.

Since part of networking is also about finding jobs and placing talent, LinkedIn has also brought another customer into its business model with professional recruiters. The game changer in this case is that recruiters can easily identify and target the right talent by access to rich profiles of 467 million professionals, many of whom aren't necessarily looking for jobs. In other words, given that LinkedIn is not just about job finding and placement and places most of its focus on networking, it has become a phenomenal place to spawn conversations about potential roles and hires.

> "Help the people in your network. And let them help you."
>
> Reid Hoffman, LinkedIn co-founder

The future of networking

Core interaction

Where in the old days you landed your dream job by asking for a referral from local people, now the whole world can become your local community in real time. LinkedIn is the perfect example of how a platform efficiently connects people who might never have been connected before. LinkedIn's Economic Graph is a digital representation of the global economy based on all the data on LinkedIn. Insights from this map help connect people to economic opportunity in new ways.

Online products or services

LinkedIn offers networking, connections, and job opportunities for free. More engagement is offered through a subscription. Recruiters and marketeers are offered tailored solutions.

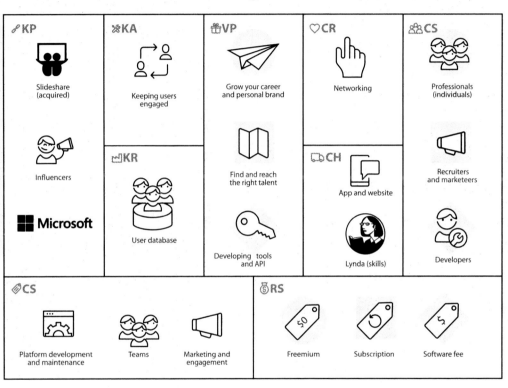

In December of 2016, Microsoft acquired LinkedIn in a heated round of offers and counter offers between Salesforce and others. At this point it's pretty clear what Microsoft and Salesforce were interested in. Today, LinkedIn represents not just a huge professional network, it's built on a fast-growing platform business model that taps into and caters to the needs of millions of professionals and countless businesses. For business-to-business software companies, like Microsoft, this offers myriad ways to create and foster new interactions between people and software solutions built for business. This includes developers in the broader ecosystem who wish to create and deliver value in new ways, via their own products and services. Imagine this all started when one person identified the need to modernize an age-old business model in professional networking.

> When I see Kickstarter, I don't see a company. Instead, I see a social movement. I see people doing things for people."
>
> Om Malik, partner at True Ventures

Kickstarter: Launch your idea

Crowdfunding, essentially getting a large amount of people to invest a small amount of money (each) in order to fund some venture, has been around for hundreds of years. From raising money using war bonds (in the 1730s) to arts endowments, people (i.e., funders) have been drawn to helping others when there is something useful (i.e., value) in it for the funders. Kickstarter, named for the act of helping to kick-start a project, was founded by Perry Chen, Yancey Strickler, and Charles Adler in 2009 for the same reason: helping others to get their projects off the ground through crowdfunding.

Kickstarter, as a platform, works like this: someone, or a business, with an idea can post their concept (art project, physical good, content, games, or other project) and related documentation, videos, and needs on Kickstarter.com. Others who endorse the project or want to have the product, can invest small amounts of money to help the concept owner develop it further. What's unique about Kickstarter as an investment platform—connecting investors with concept owners—is that Kickstarter does not own equity in any of the projects on its platform. Instead, it charges a 5% commission when a project has been funded.

Since its launch, Kickstarter has become something of a phenomenon. The *New York Times* called the company "the people's [National Endowment for the Arts]." What started out as a relatively simple construct, has turned into a common lexicon—a verb—describing the action of crowdfunding something. Due to its popularity in helping mostly small entrepreneurs launch their projects, Kickstarter has expanded rapidly, making its way into most of the Americas, Europe, and even Asia-Pacific.

Backing great ideas

Core interaction

Kickstarter directly connects creators and makers with their early adopters and customers. To date, the platform has been used to launch and scale numerous companies, such as Pebble (acquired by FitBit in 2016 . . . which was acquired by Alphabet in 2019). In many ways, Kickstarter has proven that people really do want to trust one another, especially when there is shared value to be exchanged. In most cases, it just takes a company like Kickstarter to facilitate that trust.

Sharing the passion

Kickstarter brings people together that love innovative products and experiences. Through sharing new ideas with many potential customers, customers become investors.

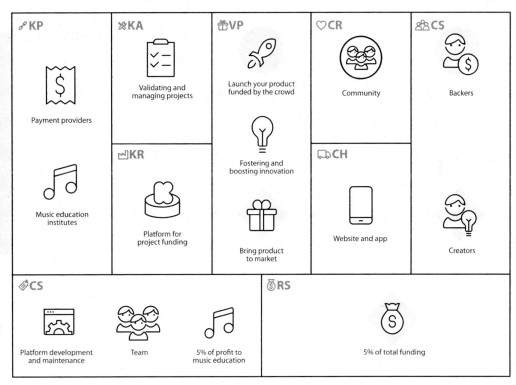

✈ KP	✂ KA	🎁 VP	♡ CR	👥 CS
Payment providers	Validating and managing projects	Launch your product funded by the crowd	Community	Backers
		Fostering and boosting innovation		
Music education institutes	◁ KR		🚚 CH	
	Platform for project funding	Bring product to market	Website and app	Creators

✎ CS			💰 RS	
Platform development and maintenance	Team	5% of profit to music education	5% of total funding	

Though crowdfunding and investment have been around for ages, the efforts have mostly focused on funding institutions, not individuals' personal projects. In this, Kickstarter has broken the mold. Given its mission, "to help bring creative projects to life," Kickstarter has come a long way. To date, the platform has brought together millions of creators and funders, helping to establish trust and create impact, while also providing useful feedback to creators. And Kickstarter is big. As of this writing, the company has facilitated the exchange of almost $5 billion in pledges to creative projects with 5% of its profits slated to fund music education. Needless to say, that's a lot connecting and facilitation of value exchange. Next time you have a creative project, perhaps rather than letting it linger in your brain or on paper, you'll publish a Kickstarter project. With almost 180 thousand successfully funded projects, and 18 million backers, your next big idea may become the next big success on Kickstarter.

> "Many observers rate WeChat as offering a superior user experience than its western counterparts today, and its innovative features are now being copied by others."
>
> Harvard Business Review

WeChat: Organize your life

WeChat, a Chinese app for, well . . . everything, started as a replacement for WhatsApp. But chat is where the similarities end. Developed by Tencent, the essence of the WeChat platform is providing services that make life easier and more enjoyable. Full stop. WeChat is used by more than 1 billion people for everything from messaging, to social media, to payments, to booking doctor's appointments, to ordering food. The list goes on and on. In essence, WeChat has become an app for life.

In many regards, like Alibaba, WeChat is an ecosystem of platforms. And, whereas companies like Apple and Google have created app stores full of single function apps, WeChat is an app of apps, providing its many capabilities within a single ecosystem. WeChat has effectively developed the equivalent of Apple's walled garden ecosystem, but within a single app that can be installed on many different kinds of devices. In this regard, WeChat focuses on groups of people and is designed as an Open Platform connecting businesses, websites, apps, and devices to its users. Within the WeChat platform ecosystem, businesses are provided with an official account, allowing them to interact with and provide practical services to users. WeChat provides support and Software Development Kits (SDK) to enable businesses to easily build functionality to bring value to their customers. In addition, WeChat's seamless payment service, WePay, links all its other services together, cementing the app within its customers' lives.

Although WeChat is known mostly as a super app, the real value that the company holds lies in its knowledge of how people interact and exchange value at almost every minute and stage in their lives. Because WeChat facilitates any transaction or interaction between both consumers and businesses, the company can use this information to develop new interactions and value exchanges, many of which may spur paradigm shifts.

The WeChat ecosystem

Core interaction

WeChat completely facilitates people's lives. The "super app" takes care of a great deal of chores, appointments, communication, bookings, and payments. WeChat helps users to get it done and move on, without having to switch to another app. The businesses on the platform are able to provide their services through the app by building their own customer interface right into the app. They can easily connect their own back-end systems to the WeChat ecosystem.

Ecosystem of platforms
WeChat is designed as an open platform allowing businesses to develop for direct customer interaction and leading to a single flow of value.

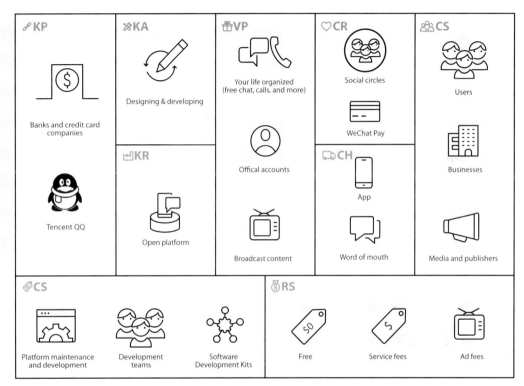

Given the size of WeChat's growing ecosystem, it's no wonder that WeChat and WePay have become synonymous with all kinds of transactions in just about every context. Today, WePay is helping to shift China into a cashless state, where anything and everything can be purchased using the WePay platform.

As one can imagine, although China is a huge market, WeChat has no plans to stop there. The company has set its sights on the rest of the world, with more and more functionalities being released into the international, multi-language version of the app. This, paired with the app's all-in-one suite of everything that people need to navigate through their lives with ease, is the reason why WeChat is taking the world by storm and has become the fifth most used app in existence. By connecting all parties via a platform ecosystem, WeChat is on course to change the way we live.

Ask yourself the following questions . . .

Where do you see an opportunity for connection because of a lack of infrastructure to trade?

Alibaba started with a simple website connecting buyers and sellers to make it easy to do business. By putting customers first, they developed multiple platform business models, each focused on easily connecting users, satisfying the needs of both sides. Alibaba is the ultimate platform builder, creating an ever-evolving ecosystem of value exchange that forms a thriving economy of its own.

What resources can you mobilize to get customers × with the tap of a button?

Grab launched a service on the back of other giants, like Uber; push a button, get a ride. However, Grab built its business model to serve local communities, helping to connect people with unique wants/needs with those who can fulfill those wants/needs . . . all at the push of a button. This has led to an entire economy orchestrated by a simple app.

Lessons learned

What connection can you facilitate around moments in the lives of consumers?

Apple started as a pipeline business model and found itself in a race to the bottom with other hardware manufacturers. They shifted towards designing for people and their lives. People don't need a shiny MP3 player, they desire to be connected to their favorite music or other favorite content. This eventually led to a whole app ecosystem where Apple streamlines and facilitates a mobile consumer experience with apps from others.

How would your super app make people's lives easier by connecting consumer needs to services directly?

WeChat started as a simple messaging app to stay connected to family and friends. It evolved into a super app that elegantly and unobtrusively connects its over a billion users to any service provider. WeChat makes sure that the lives of its users are smoothly organized. People are less occupied by taking care of chores and appointments and have more time to spend with their friends and family.

What basic need for connection can you fulfill with a platform that brings people together faster?

LinkedIn connects professionals to each other and their future career. It started as a simple networking site to link to colleagues, customers, and peers. Professionals adopted LinkedIn massively to link to each other and use it as a personal branding tool. Recruiters moved to the platform as well to find and recruit the right talent.

How can you use the crowd to judge and fund your product ideas?

Kickstarter changed the way we start developing products. Products used to be developed without really knowing if there was real customer demand. Many product launches therefore turned into disasters. Kickstarter prevents this from happening. Creators and makers are connected to their potential customers, who turn into real customers if enough people back their idea.

High-level strategic choices

1

 Envision the why

Platforms must be built to connect demand and supply. Volume is crucial; customer segments have to be large enough for a platform to be attractive for both sides and create so-called network effects.

Specify what the economic benefits of your platform are as a whole that make it relevant in the market. Define exactly what your platform offers to both sides. Quantify the size of both sides and explore how to achieve network effects.

2

 Facilitate interactions

A platform must facilitate (and govern) interactions among participants to ensure trust among all participants. Dedicated teams should work on the value proposition for each side.

Make sure you design to make the core interaction happen frequently. Design an easy way for the demand side to search for what they need and a clear and simple way for the supply side to present their offerings.

3

 Attract participants

Attracting customers from both sides is vital to ultimately drive network effects and economies of scale. More users on both sides increases the value of the platform; recurring customers will advocate using it among their peers.

Use reviews and ratings as a channel for attracting new users. Make it easy for participants to share their experience on the platform with others on social media.

Bold platform steps

to drive this shift.

4

 Develop for connectivity

Ongoing technology development is crucial for platforms. Platforms cannot simply be built and maintained. Platforms must be able to "talk" to other platforms, service providers, and companies.

Develop APIs to ensure that it's easy for customers and third parties to connect to your platform, exchange data, and extend or enhance the usability of the platform.

5

 Track the right metrics

A platform business requires a big vision, bold decision making, and rigorous validation of those choices.

Track metrics related to the core interaction. Stay away from vanity metrics like total users on your platform. It's not about the number of users. It's about what happens in their interactions. Measure and monitor that!

6

 Monetize interactions

Monetizing the interactions on your platform is a tough job. For most platforms, it takes years to monetize. Charging fees might discourage potential customers from using the platform.

Make it frictionless to join, offering access for free up front, and offer a premium for purchase later on.

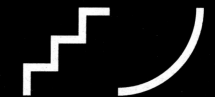

From incremental to exponential

Most business models begin with a short burst of exponential growth followed by a long period of linear growth, if they grow at all. What if you could inject your business model with some secret sauce that would take it from 10% improvement to 10X growth? That's what this chapter is all about . . .

incremental →

The exponential shift is focused on creating the "right" environment, with a balance of business model elements, to enable **exponential scale during the life of the business model.** To do this, most companies must **invest in exponential technologies,** like Artificial Intelligence, that enable the business model to continually adjust to customer needs and/ or other inputs and outputs. However, **exponential business models are not just about technology.** At their core, exponential business models are fostered, scaled, and continually shifted to do one thing: address some grand (perhaps unreachable) challenge. Although maintaining a healthy profit margin may already pose a grand enough challenge for most companies, when it comes to exponentiality, profits are often secondary to scale.

exponential

Exponential technologies are those which are rapidly accelerating and shaping major industries and all aspects of our lives. [. . .] We believe that the solutions to the world's most pressing challenges lie at the intersection of these exponential technologies."

The Exponential Primer of Singularity University

Challenges unsolved

An exponential business model applies two or more exponential technologies to solve a grand challenge for the many. Exponential businesses aim to eliminate a big problem by challenging industry assumptions through an exponential mindset.

Whether the grand challenge you plan to address is global in nature or affects only your industry, what's clear is this: if you don't address it, someone else will. And the companies that do so will create entire new categories that other businesses will end up living within. "But what is a grand challenge?" you might ask. Singularity University, a global learning and innovation community that uses exponential technologies to tackle the world's biggest challenges and build a better future for all, lists twelve global grand challenges to be solved for ensuring basic needs are met for all people, sustaining and improving quality of life, and mitigating future risks. That said, if you zoom out and look at your industry from space, you might also see that it has its own unique brand of grand challenges that might include tasks like removing barriers to information. In just about every case, to solve these grand challenges, you need to employ new (exponential) technologies that enable you to redefine how value is created and delivered by your business model.

Strategic questions

What is the global grand challenge you want to solve? Who has this challenge? What needs to be fundamentally different in the way you deal with this challenge? What is exponential about your mindset? Why is this and that technology needed to solve this challenge? How are two or more exponential technologies combined to provide the breakthrough you need? Who do you need to partner with to bring the right technologies into your business model? Or should you develop technology on your own? Can we build upon existing technologies? How do you start testing value creation with the first early adopters? What new skills and capabilities do you need?

From incremental

The incremental business model slightly improves how you create, deliver, and capture value, representing business-as-usual thinking. This is all about defending and maintaining the status quo in your business and growing by a few percentage points every year.

Product slightly improved

The customers served are consumers or businesses whose immediate needs you satisfy with a product you offer. Incremental models aren't typically based on big visionary thinking. Hence, these business models most often focus on immediate needs rather than systemic ones. The value proposition's promise may also be a slightly improved version of the product. Often there's only a shallow relationship with customers related to the product being offered (warranties or services). Products are pushed into the market.

Squeezing out growth

A key activity is to improve and optimize the product, processes, marketing efficiency, and costs . . . all by a few percentage points. Employees spend all their time working on incremental improvements in various parts of the business. The hope is that all these incremental improvements will lead to incremental growth of a few percentage points annually. An incremental business model can be given a boost, but only by applying "brute force," which requires significantly expanding the number of people and investing lots of money.

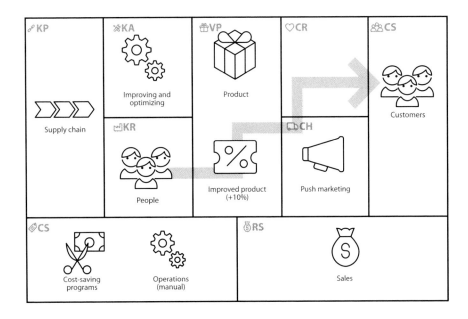

to exponential

Need fulfilled

The value proposition is to eliminate a big problem and solve the needs for as many people as possible in the long term. The relationship is a community of fans that share how they perceive and receive value and promote the value proposition (word of mouth). These customers are often self-organizing and self-servicing.

Driving impact

A key activity is to design for scale and impact, ensuring that additional input creates 10x more output. The design and delivery of the customer value is driven through experimentation. Delivering value is done by combining different exponential technologies to unlock new value creation. Resources are a combination of two or more exponential technologies. Algorithms are often used to connect customers, bring synergy, and fuel growth. Partners are other "crazy" companies and the Open-source community, since keeping pace with an ever faster changing world using closed source technologies won't work. Other partners may be start-ups working on specific applications of exponential technology.

The exponential business model is designed to transform an industry and change the world and typically targets a grand challenge affecting lots of people. This model is about solving a big problem for the masses at 10X the scale an incremental model would.

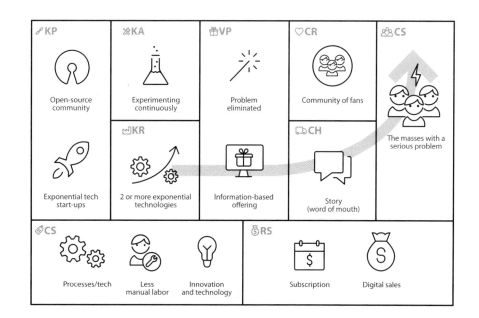

Energy

 Food

 Health

Elimate the need to rely on polluting energy sources such as kerosine. Offer new means of transportation, powered by the sun and even more powerful batteries. Provide affordable tech to generate energy locally using abundant sources such as the sun, wind, geothermal, and moving water. Facilitate people to exchange energy in marketplaces. Manage energy grids better with AI.

Examples: Alphabet, Local Motors, Shapeways

Offer global citizens affordable, high-quality, organic, and natural food. Make it available everywhere because food can be grown anywhere, even in urban and hostile environments. We can also do this using less resources and as such reduce the drain on our planet. Food production runs 24 hours a day with optimal and customized inputs, by combining robotics, sensors, biotech, and AI.

Examples: Netafim, Beyond Meat

Offer individuals and communities health, wellness, and treatments that are precise and personalized. By combining robotics, big data, machine learning, and bio- and nanotech, diseases can be better understood, diagnosed earlier or even prevented, and treated more effectively. Consumers are partners by sharing their anonymized health data to support data-driven healthcare.

Examples: Stellar Biotechnologies, Alphabet, Apple HealthKit

Patterns

 Water

 Learning

 Space

❹

❺

❻

Offer safe and plentiful water for various purposes. Extract water from the air or turn salt water into drinkable water without using chemicals or lots of energy—no more deaths because of polluted water or wars. Predicting water supply and demand and optimize water systems using AI. Use robotics and big data to use less water. Use 3D printing to create toilets that help provide basic sanitation.

Examples: WE.org, Netafim

Offer information and experiences that build knowledge and skills; not just for children, but for learners of all ages. Learning is lifelong and Massive Open Online Courses (MOOCs) provide a wide variety of interactive and sophisticated classes and content. The learning journey is guided and enhanced through gamification, AI, and VR/AR.

Examples: Khan Academy, Duolingo, Github, Reddit

Offer humanity a future that is multi-planetary. Everybody on the planet has internet access. An exoskeleton is provided for communications and monitoring. Besides this, there are spin-off applications that ultimately improve qualify of life. The private sector and governments work together to explore space and build settlements for the benefit of all.

Examples: SpaceX

L

Alphabet

Since its humble beginnings in a Stanford computer lab, Google has made its mission to organize the world's information and make that information universally accessible, thereby improving the lives of many. Today, Alphabet, Google's parent company, has expanded into hundreds of areas in its quest to improve the lives of as many people as it can—exponentially, of course.

Facts

Founders
Sergey Brin and Larry Page

CEO
Sundar Pichai

Founded in 1998
Menlo Park, CA

Total revenue
$161 billion (2019)

Industry
Internet, cloud computing, computer software and hardware, artificial intelligence, advertising

Scale
Offices in 50 countries
118,000 employees

Timeline ⟩

1998
Founded

Google is founded by Larry Page and Sergey Brin. In 1996, the initial version of Google was already available on the Stanford website.

2001
Eric Schmidt

In the first of over 200 acquisitions, Google acquires Deja (now Google Groups). Eric Schmidt is brought in as CEO to bring structure and execution power.

2004
IPO

Google launches GOOG stock and empowers people to be more creative and innovative by encouraging them to spend 20% of their time working on what they think will most benefit Google.

On a search mission

Larry Page and Sergey Brin met while they were both pursuing PhDs at Stanford University. Page's dissertation project, called "Backrub," was about an algorithm that checked all the backlinks attached to URLs in order to determine the importance of a webpage. They saw an opportunity to use what is now called the PageRank algorithm to power a search engine that would produce much more relevant results for users.

Google was born as a digitally native company offering fast and effective search to internet users. By the end of 1998, Google had an index of 60 million webpages—proof that Google indeed produced better search results than its competitors. Investors at that time still believed that overloaded portal sites like Yahoo!, MSN.com, and AOL.com were the future of the Web.

What the future really holds in terms of value creation is hard to predict. Therefore, exponential growth is quite deceptive and hard to spot in the early stages. In early 1999, Larry and Sergey even tried to sell Google for $1 million to Excite.com (AltaVista) but failed. As Google's usership continued to climb, due in part to its simple, easy-to-use design, Brin and Page received their first round of venture capital funding of $25 million in 1999.

By 2002, Google had grown so popular, Brin and Page turned down a $3 billion offer from Yahoo!. In 2004, Google went public, raising $1.9 billion at $84 per share. Google has since entirely disrupted advertising and other industries. Today, a Google share is worth around $1,300; the company's market cap hovers around $1 trillion.

Find what you need, instantly

Today virtually anyone and everyone is provided with unlimited indexed access to all publicly available online content via Google Search. Even offline content, like books, are often scanned by Google and made available via Google Books and Google Scholar. Google ranks search results on relevance, using their advanced algorithm. This search service is free of charge. Advertisers pay to display their content at the top of the search results. Purchasing of advertising space is done through dynamic, automated auctions. Advertisers also get much more in-depth insights into how effective their campaigns are because, unlike in offline advertising, every action, such as clicks and cursor movements, can be tracked online.

2005
Free maps

Google Maps & Google Earth are released, undercutting the market for navigation devices and software. Google acquires Android Inc. for about $50 million.

2006
YouTube

In the first of Google's mega-acquisitions of $1.6 billion, Google acquires YouTube, a revolutionary addition to its advertising arsenal. YouTube helps Google expand its advertising power as part of the Google Display Network.

Google it!

In March 2006, Alphabet obtains a listing in Standard & Poor's 500. The verb "google" is added to the Merriam Webster Collegiate Dictionary and the Oxford English Dictionary.

Search and advertising

Learning
Indexing all the information in the world and being able to access it through a few clicks or taps on a digital device empowers the masses with knowledge.

Search and more, for free

Everybody uses Google to find the information they need. Google not only provides a search service, it offers services like mail, navigation, cloud storage, news, and more. All these services are free to the end user. Advertisers buy online advertising space, reach, and visibility, and these funds help further the development of Google's vast array of services. The 20% Time rule mentioned in Google's IPO letter has indeed sparked creativity and innovation. This rule is how Google expanded their value proposition for both users and advertisers (AdSense).

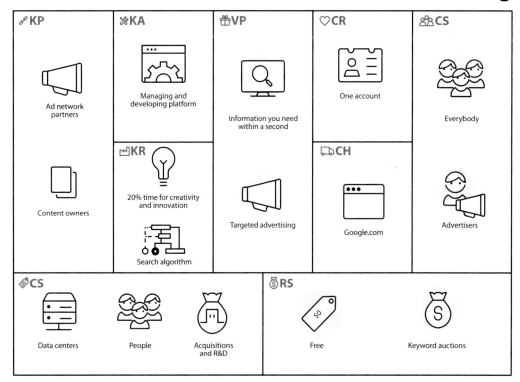

2007
DoubleClick

Google purchases DoubleClick, a huge online advertising service for $3.1 billion, enabling them to expand far beyond algorithm-driven ad auctions and into a relationship-based business with web publishers and advertisers.

2007
Open Handset Alliance

Consortium of Google, HTC, Motorola, Qualcomm, Samsung, Sprint, T-Mobile, and Texas Instruments to develop Android, "the first truly open and comprehensive platform for mobile devices."

2009
Google ventures

Start of a service-based venture fund, standing side by side with founders and their team to transform industries and create new ones.

2010
Hardware

A move into the hardware business with Nexus, a line of flagship Android devices. Experiments with Google Fiber, an offering of ultra-high-speed internet.

The 20% Time rule enabled employees to work on their own new ideas while at work, leading to new products creating new value for more users. Google has also digitized geographic information, such as maps and satellite images, offering access to that information for free through apps like Google Maps and Google Earth. These free products expanded Google's user base and relevance.

Google's search and advertising business relies on indexing content and selling online advertising space on those websites. The acquisitions of Blogger in 2003, YouTube in 2005, and DoubleClick in 2007 reinforced this core business. Blogs have become a mainstream medium, and people have shifted their media consumption from traditional to online content. As a result, large companies have shifted their advertising strategies to focus primarily on internet-based advertising. Through these acquisitions, Google positioned itself as a leader in advertising. In 2009, it surpassed 1 billion daily searches on its website and served 65% of the web search market. The Google Display Network reaches 90% of all internet users.

Betting on the future

Google Ventures, now GV, was born as a way for Google to share what it had learned about innovation with the companies that are creating the future. Corporate venturing enables Google to make many small bets, with a focus on enterprise, life sciences, consumer, and frontier technology. Today, GV manages a portfolio of 300 companies, with $4.5 billion under its management. So far this has resulted in 20 IPOs and over a hundred mergers and/or acquisitions.

A stable core business generating cashflow, while staying at the forefront of innovation. Spreading knowledge and experience on how to innovate by putting skin in the game.

2010
GoogleX

Google launches its secretive in-house research and development company, harnessing the company's resources to innovate and solve the world's hardest problems.

2011
Motorola

Google makes its biggest acquisition for $12.5 billion to defend and protect Android in a patent war against Microsoft, Apple, and Oracle. Google Drive launches in 2012.

Lots of revenue

In 2012, Google reaches the $50 billion revenue milestone. The company launches Google for Entrepreneurs, a largely nonprofit incubator providing start-ups with co-working spaces known as *Campuses*.

Google Ventures

All patterns
GV focuses on enterprise, life sciences, consumer, and frontier technology, tackling several problems covered by the Exponential Patterns.

It takes more than funding

Since the founding of Google, the company has gained a lot of expertise in many industries. Google saw this stockpile of industry knowledge as a resource it wasn't utilizing to the fullest. Google pumped all this knowledge into Google Ventures. They create value for start-ups with a service-based venturing model that provides funds, knowledge, expertise, and partnerships to increase a start-up's chance to succeed in the market. Start-ups that Google Ventures invested in include Fitbit, Medium, Nest, Slack, 23andMe, Impossible Foods, and many more.

2013
Calico

2014
More AI

2015
Alphabet

Google Ventures invests in a health and well-being company working on the challenge of aging and associated diseases, led by Arthur D. Levinson (also Chairman of Apple). Their mission is to "cure death."

Google acquires DeepMind, an artificial intelligence research and development company, for $500 million. Google also acquires Nest, a home automation company, for $3.2 billion.

Google restructures to increase its focus on developing extraordinary innovation while reinforcing its core competency. Sundar Pichai becomes CEO of Google, and Larry Page and Sergey Brin become CEO and president of Alphabet.

> In the technology industry, where revolutionary ideas drive the next big growth areas, you need to be a bit uncomfortable to stay relevant."
>
> Larry Page

Scaling the mindset

Until 2011, Google had been on an exponential growth path. During this growth phase, AI hadn't been used—or researched—to its fullest extent. Although Google's search algorithm was smart, machine learning in general had not yet delivered on its grand promise: machines able to make predictions or decisions without explicitly programming them to do so. Thinking machines still seemed like a long-term dream.

In 2012, Sundar Pichai, now the CEO of Google's parent company, Alphabet, was invited by engineer Jeff Dean, while working on the Google Brain team at GoogleX, to review a project they had been working on. The Google Brain team had wired up 16,000 processors in 1,000 computers, capable of making 1 billion connections. The machine spontaneously generated an image of a cat, after "watching" YouTube videos of cats for three days in a row. For the first time in (Google's) history, a machine had taught itself to think in a massive way. Google Brain graduated from X in 2012 to become Google AI, turning this technology into DistBelief, an internal framework to let machines think on a massive scale. Teams started to use it to make YouTube, Android, and Maps smarter.

When Sundar became CEO in 2015, he made Google an "AI First" company, making sure all the intelligence being developed in the company is used to constantly improve Google's products, such as Gmail's Smart Compose and Google Translate. DistBelief was redesigned into TensorFlow and was open-sourced in 2015. It is now used by a diverse community of developers, enterprises,

2016
Waxmo

Waymo, a self-driving technology company, graduated from Google X with the mission to make it safe and easy to move people and cargo. Google launches its own line of smart home speakers, powered by Google Assistant. AI enters the home.

2017
Criticized

Employees urge Pichai to cancel Project Maven, a military project to harness the power of artificial intelligence to improve drone strikes. In 2018, "Don't be evil" is removed from the code of conduct, but added again one month later.

Most valuable brand

Google is listed by *Forbes* as the second most valuable brand in the world of fiscal year 2019. Android becomes the best-selling OS, with 2 billion monthly users (2017). Google is fined by the EU for €4.3 billion because of forcing traffic on Android devices to go to the Google search engine. A year earlier, they were fined for €2.4 billion for promoting its own shopping comparison service at the top of search results.

Google X

and researchers to solve challenging, real-world problems with machine learning. It's inside millions of devices, including cars, drones, satellites, laptops, and phones, that use it to learn and think.

The Moonshot Factory

Google X is a business model focused on creating radically new technologies to solve some of the world's hardest problems. It aims to bring innovation to the world, much like a factory produces products. In order to do this, teams at Google X generate lots of crazy ideas with uncapped possibilities.

All patterns
GoogleX turns crazy ideas into projects and helps "graduate" them into businesses. Examples include Verily, which focuses on disease prevention, global health problems; Makani, which focuses on generating energy via kites; and many others.

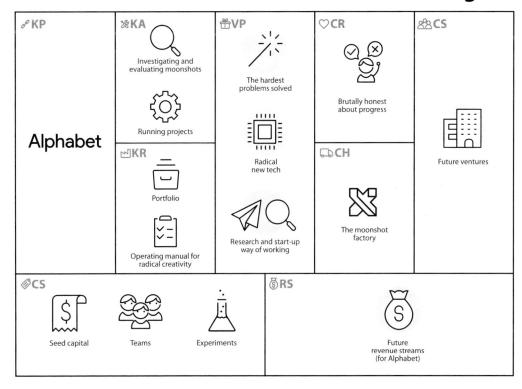

Alpha-bets

Alphabet is a company that organizes its resources to innovate at different levels and in many different fields. They expand and enhance their core products and services with an AI-First mindset, aiming to make life easier for people and augment human abilities so that we can accomplish more in less time.

The money they earn with their advertising business model is used to bet on the future. GV is a venture fund that invests in start-ups that transform industries or create new ones. Capital G is a private equity fund investing in later-stage companies, including Lyft, Airbnb, and more.

And finally, GoogleX is making long-term bets, trying to tackle the world's hardest problems. By creating a funnel of moonshot ideas, the probability that some actually work is increased. Their structured approach towards producing companies, enabled by exponential technologies that solve important real-world problems, could generate huge future revenue streams.

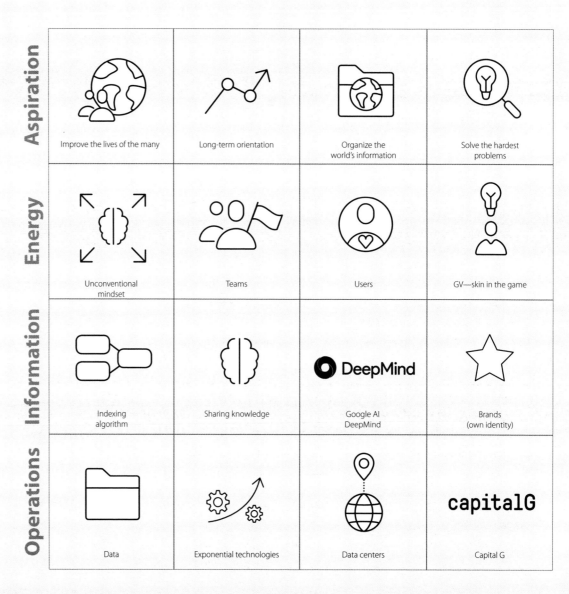

Aspiration	Improve the lives of the many	Long-term orientation	Organize the world's information	Solve the hardest problems
Energy	Unconventional mindset	Teams	Users	GV—skin in the game
Information	Indexing algorithm	Sharing knowledge	Google AI DeepMind	Brands (own identity)
Operations	Data	Exponential technologies	Data centers	Capital G

2018
Duplex

Google launches its AI-powered personal assistant Duplex, which makes appointments for you by calling small businesses as a living human being would do.

2019
Fitbit

Google acquires Fitbit for $2.1 billion in an attempt to break into the wearable device market. Larry Page and Sergey Brin both step down from the CEO and President roles, respectively. Sundar Pichai steps up to become the CEO of both Google and Alphabet.

Future
10% or 10x

Earn 10% more money from advertising or full focus on 10x impact, making life better for everyone? We'll see what the future holds.

Alphabet is making a lot of bets on the future with money earned from advertising. Is this still the right thing to do?

The exponential, 10x mindset has been fueling growth at Google since its beginning. What would the world look like if Larry Page and Sergey Brin had been successful in selling their one-year-old startup to Excite.com? Would Tensor Flow have been developed and open-sourced to power the world with AI?

Google has brought many innovations into the world, yet as the company has continued to grow, it also struggled to organize itself in order to get the return on innovation sought by leadership (and Wall Street). By restructuring and reorganizing into Alphabet, leaders at the company hope to get alpha-bets, i.e., above benchmark, returns.

Of course, because of its massive size and influence, Alphabet is constantly being investigated for breaking laws and abusing its power for its own gain. To date, the company has already been fined billions of dollars. What's more, even its own employees question how they behave as a company.

The question isn't anymore: "What would Google do?" The critical question right now is: "What is the right thing for Alphabet to do?" With so many people and organizations using Alphabet's products and services, is it the responsibility of the company to think beyond incremental change? After all, adding an additional 10% in revenues may not add more value or give a higher return. What if these billion users turn into engaged, and even subscribed and paying customers that see that Alphabet protects their privacy, makes their lives better, and solves the most pressing challenges of our time? Or would it be naïve to think that Alphabet could shift away from their hugely profitable advertising business model?

Beyond Meat

It's undeniable: the world's population continues to produce, purchase, and eat meat at a growing rate. With this growth comes a whole raft of systemic challenges, not the least which is running out of space needed to address demand. Beyond Meat was founded to address this challenge . . . and as the world reels due to the newest challenges that come by way of global pandemics, it just might get a shot.

Facts

Founder
Ethan Brown

Founded in 2009
Los Angeles, CA

Total revenue
$298 million (2019)

Industry
Food / meat (alternatives)

Other information
Company based on
university research

Scale
58,000 points
of distribution

> # I have a different question on my mind: 'Are animals the only way to produce meat?' "

Ethan Brown, founder Beyond Meat

A food production system favoring meat is often inefficient as it requires an enormous amount of land, water, and energy to produce one unit of meat; a lot of waste is embedded in this system as well. One of the people trying to find a solution to this big challenge—and opportunity—is Ethan Brown.

At an early age, Brown became interested in doing something about climate change, starting a career in Cleantech. As part of his research, he found that there are correlations between climate change and animal agriculture. Not to mention, he also believed that most people—at least those he knew—would do well to eat less meat. His desire to make a difference further intensified when he and his wife had kids.

What meat is and can be

Together with researchers from the University of Missouri and the University of Maryland, Brown began his quest researching alternatives to meat. He discovered that the five main building blocks of meat, i.e., protein, fat, minerals, carbohydrate, and water, are not exclusive to animals. In his mind, this meant that fundamentally he could produce meat-like alternatives without using animals. He received two grants for developing an initial product and sold his house to start Beyond Meat in 2009. The shift from animal to plant-based meat is not about coming up with vegetarian alternatives, but to fundamentally change the world's understanding of what meat is, and what meat can be. Beyond Meat targets meat lovers, creating a product that enables customers to eat what they love . . . even if it's not always animal-derived meat.

Backed by venture capital firm Kleiner Perkins, Bill Gates, and Leonardo DiCaprio, and even America's largest meat processor, Tyson Foods, Beyond Meat worked on formulating ways to create meat alternatives that would perform like the real thing. When Beyond Burgers were released, they not only attracted a lot of attention, this product had a lot of people wanting to try it (and buy it). Still, the food ecosystem is complex. Though supermarkets, like the giant US retailer Safeway, wanted to place the burgers in the vegetarian section, Beyond Meat was targeting meat lovers who rarely shop in the vegetarian section of the supermarket. Whole Foods Markets understood this, took the risk, and put the burgers in the meat section, resulting in massive demand for the product.

Growing animals for meat

The traditional meat production model targets the masses through various channels, selling as much meat as possible at fairly low prices. In order to do this, an industrialized system has been developed to efficiently raise, kill, and process animals. Animals are sourced from geographically dispersed farms which require a global logistics chain for transporting meat, as well as the feed, that is required to grow animals to a weight ready for slaughter.

Incremental business model
Factories that process live animals into packaged meat for consumption offer consumers a way to satisfy their dietary needs and taste preferences. This produces cheap protein yet requires a huge amount of inputs to produce 1 unit of meat.

🔗 KP	✂ KA	🎁 VP	♡ CR	🎎 CS
Farmers	Butchering and producing	Real Meat		Consumers (mass market)
🚚 KR			🚚 CH	
Transport	Meat factories		Butchers, grocery stores, and wholesale	

🖉 CS		💰 RS	
Animals	Production and logistics	Product sales	

Meat factories

The traditional system seems efficient only because the negative externalities are not factored into the price of the product. These include vast amounts of land, energy, and water needed to turn an animal into a piece of meat. Not to mention, in most places around the world, the ethics of meat pro-duction are also suspect. The real price we pay for industrialized meat is much higher than you might think.

Brown and the Beyond Meat team believe there is a better way to feed the planet. Beyond Meat's mission is to create The Future of Protein®—delicious plant-based burgers, beef, sausage, crumbles, and more. By shifting from animal to plant-based meat, the inefficiency and negative impact of the traditional meat production model can be addressed.

Growing plants to meet our needs

Beyond Meat focuses on Generation Z and Millennials, because the company believes these customers feel the need to do something different. The company has several high-profile ambassadors, such as basketball star Kyrie Irving, to drive consumers to think and act beyond the norms.

Beyond Meat searches for ways to make a difference not by changing customer behavior but by creating new options that did not exist before. To reach the masses, Beyond Meat still must find a way to undercut the price of animal protein. The company is doing this by expanding its selection to include meats such as chicken and sausage. The company also leverages partners, such as restaurant chains like Dunkin' (formerly Dunkin' Donuts), Subway, and McDonalds.

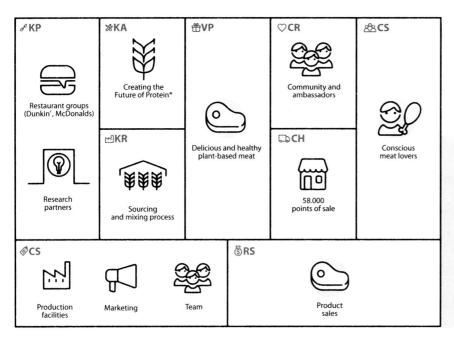

Food

Beyond Meat products are processed food but made from high-quality plant-based ingredients and therefore are better and healthier for people and planet.

10x effect

The Beyond Meat production system reduces the use of most resources by 10X or more:

- 99% less water
- 90% less greenhouse emissions
- 93% less land
- 46% less energy

Think about that, the next time you order a burger, if you want to contribute to exponential impact.

SpaceX

If humankind ever wants to become a self-sustaining multiplanetary species, access to space must become cheaper. Driven by this ambition, Elon Musk founded SpaceX in 2002.

Facts

CEO and founder
Elon Musk

Founded 2002
Hawthorne, CA

Total revenue
$2.5 billion (2019)

Industry
Aerospace

Scale
8,000 employees
3 launch sites

> # When something is important enough, you do it even if the odds are not in your favor."

-Elon Musk, CEO and founder SpaceX

After PayPal was sold to eBay, Elon Musk, one of PayPal's original founders, wanted to work on a BIG problem. He dabbled in a project called Mars Oasis, which focused on designing miniature greenhouses that could be sent to Mars to test and study plant growth in order to learn whether living on Mars is even possible. Upon reaching out to NASA, Musk was told that there were no Mars missions planned in the foreseeable future. Frustrated, Musk decided he would need to get involved directly. After a failed trip to Russia to purchase refurbished rockets, Musk pondered ways to make access to space much, much cheaper.

Upon doing some research, Musk found that the cost of the raw materials used to build a rocket was only 3% of the selling price of the actual rocket. The rest of the cost is in the rocket testing and fuel. Not to mention, at this point, most rockets were used only once, making their eventual commercial launches very expensive endeavors. Knowing this, Musk decided to revolutionize the costs of space travel forever, making it 10x less expensive (rather than 10% less). Musk challenged conventional methods and completely redesigned how rockets are built, doing most of the work in-house, rather than through another giant defense contractor.

Musk used money he (personally) earned from the sale of PayPal to found SpaceX and develop its first rocket, called Falcon 1, which was ready for launch by 2006. Of course, it goes without saying, space travel is hard: the first attempt to launch Falcon 1 failed miserably. The second and third launches also failed, putting SpaceX on the verge of bankruptcy. SpaceX only had money left for one more attempt. In 2008, the Falcon 1 launched for the fourth time, this time successfully, sending the rocket into Earth's orbit.

Launching customers

With this success, Musk gained a lot of interest from other parties earning SpaceX's first contracts. In 2008, SpaceX closed a $1.6 billion deal with NASA to transport cargo to the International Space Station (ISS). In 2010, SpaceX was able to successfully bring back a rocket to Earth and recover it, becoming the first private company to successfully launch and return a spacecraft from Earth's orbit. In 2011, SpaceX announced its reusable launch system development program to support further realization of the company's vision. In 2012, SpaceX was the first private company to dock with the ISS. In March 2017, Space X relaunched a used rocket and brought it back on a landing platform in the ocean.

From government funded

Traditional space programs

Traditional space programs as led by the US government are very expensive. For example, NASA's biggest program, SPACE Launch System, requires $2 billion each year to run. A multitude of different companies are involved as part of a multi-year program, requiring lots of coordination and alignment. These programs use up 10% of the total budget and often run years behind schedule.

Incremental business model
This government-funded business model does not trigger new and radical thinking to achieve an outcome. Companies involved get paid anyway for the activities they work on.

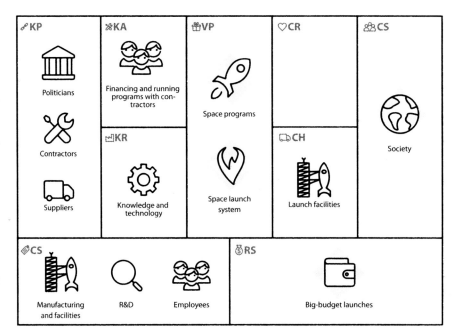

⌀ KP
Politicians
Contractors
Suppliers

🗱 KA
Financing and running programs with contractors

🗍 KR
Knowledge and technology

🎁 VP
Space programs
Space launch system

♡ CR

🖏 CH
Launch facilities

🎗️ CS
Society

⌀ CS
Manufacturing and facilities
R&D
Employees

💰 RS
Big-budget launches

A new way to drive innovation in space exploration is to turn to fixed-price contracts for some activities. If NASA would have outsourced the resupply of the International Space Station to SpaceX, they would have poured about $4 billion in a cost plus contract. This is 10 times more than the $400 million that SpaceX invested in the Falcon 9.

Open innovation

For NASA, working with SpaceX and other commercial companies is the only way to create a sustainable space-born economy. As such, a marketplace can be created for space transport and breakthrough space technologies. We need this new way of thinking and the resulting exponential

technologies to spur innovation across the board. This is required to turn the Moon into an industrial base, which can be used as a springboard to the rest of the solar system. This incremental business model happens to perfectly align with SpaceX's vision of turning humankind into a multi-planetary species.

To Mars, here we come!

SpaceX aims to bring down the costs of space travel significantly by using reusable launch systems. The company already has more than 100 launches contracted and is growing fast. SpaceX is also using its reusable rockets to launch hundreds of satellites for its Starlink business. Starlink will offer broadband internet for the entire planet.

Reusable passenger rockets
SpaceX started to develop its new Starship in 2019, with which Musk hopes he can launch people and cargo into Earth's orbit, to the Moon, and eventually to Mars. The first flight is planned for 2023, when Japanese businessman Yusaku Maezawa and his guests will fly around the Moon.

In this century, Elon Musk aims to bring over a million people to Mars and make living on that planet possible. The city created on Mars could be funded by Starlink's revenues, which are now estimated at $35 billion in 2025. All of this seems to be a good start for making space travel possible for everyone.

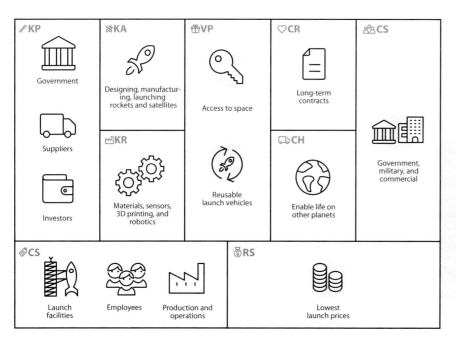

Space
Enabling life on multiple planets by offering the transportation infrastructure (Starships) for goods and peope.

10x effect
Elon Musk and his team questioned everything about the design process of building rockets and redesigned the whole production process. Through in-house development and production, and experimentation, they found new ways to produce rockets more cheaply by orders of magnitude.

Snackable cases

Waze is using the data of its 115 million community members to reduce traffic congestion and pollution. The live location of the drivers and passengers are being used to predict traffic flows in order to avoid traffic jams and provide you with the best and fastest route possible.

You control the news

Reddit is bringing the latest and most interesting news to you by using its **430 million active monthly users** to decide what kind of news this is. The community posts content and comments on content, and can vote on the most interesting content.

By using co-creating and open innovation, Local Motors succeeded in

bringing the first co-created, self-driving, electric, 3D-printed and cognitive shuttle Olli to you.

Enabling 3D products

Shapeways already enabled over 1+ million businesses creating 3D products in a fast and flexible way. Via the website, you can easily update your design, and Shapeways will take care of the rest. A global network of manufacturing and material partners is being used to produce these customized products and deliver them to you.

Do you know that feeling of having that great business idea in your head? Quirky helps with that. Quirky already brought 321,000 products to life and paid

over $11 million to these inventors.

Local Loans

Almost 2 billion people around the world don't have access to financial services. **Kiva** is enabling those people to do amazing things by providing them access to loans. Via Kiva you can start lending as little as $25 to someone and enable that person to make a difference. Already $141 billion is funded in loans through Kiva, boosting local economies all around the world.

Website?

Start building your free website today with **WordPress**. Via WordPress you can create your personalized website, without having to have any technical knowledge. Today, **WordPress** powers 35% of the internet.

4 Short case studies

Short. Crisp. Fast. Clear.

1 Stellar Biotech.

CEO Frank Oakes	**Total revenue** <$1 million	**Founded 1999** Port Hueneme, California	**Scale** To be achieved

2 Khan Academy

CEO Salman Khan	**Total revenue** Nonprofit	**Founded 2008** Mountain View, California	**Scale** 71 million users

3 GitHub

Owner Microsoft	**Total revenue** $160 million	**Founded 2008** San Francisco, California	**Scale** 40 million active users

4 Netafim

CEO Ran Maiden	**Total revenue** $1 billion	**Founded 1965** Hatzerim, Israel	**Scale** 4,300 people

Stellar:
Modern medicine

Stellar has the unique ability to sustain and reproduce KLH without harming the natural source animal."

Frank Oakes, CEO

Whatever the disease or malady, traditional medicine has not kept pace to address diseases—especially new ones—all that effectively. This led to a paradigm shift in medicine in the late 1990s, whereby treatment strategies focused on helping the body's own immune system target disease. This shift increased demand for a specific protein, KLH, which was problematic because there was only one source, the Giant Keyhole Limpet. This marine animal is a scarce snail that is only native in the Pacific waters of Southern California and Baja California, Mexico. Its existence was and is still threatened by uncontrolled fishery and bad manufacturing practices.

Cutting edge tech
Protecting and growing this magnificent, lifesaving sea creature and its habitat became the cornerstone of the business model of Stellar Biotechnologies. Stellar's ambition is to power the growing field of disease-targeting immune therapies. With its partners Stellar is working on more effective treatment of diseases like cancer, Crohn's disease, and Alzheimer's disease.

Stellar has production facilities right next to the natural habitat of the snail. Stellar's marine scientists developed complex methods to successfully grow multiple generations of this marine species in land-based aquaculture. They pioneered the extraction, purification, and separation of the KLH molecule, without killing or even harming this animal.

Protect and grow
Stellar invests in protecting and preserving the natural habitat of the snail. Their innovative approach and technology have successfully averted depletion of the wild source species. In addition, Stellar has even enlarged the natural habitat of the Keyhole Limpet. Scientists are able to pursue their ambition to power the important field of immunotherapy and at the same time protect the ecosystem.

Curing the world with a snail

10x effect

The extracted KLH protein could be more effective than any of the currently available cancer therapies with the advantage that the product avoids the harm linked with chemotherapy. The therapy, therefore, offers far better quality of life for the patient. KLH is much more desirable and effective because it achieves similar goals to synthetic drugs, while being noninvasive and nontoxic. This might well be the 10x impact we are hoping for in medicine.

Health

Combining cutting-edge technology from aquaculture and biotech to nurture a unique snail for generations, of both the species as well as humans, to come.

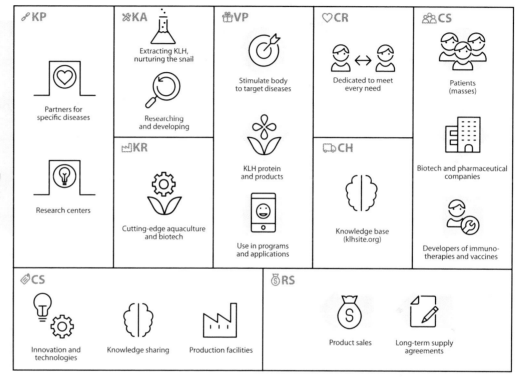

✎ KP	⚒ KA	🎁 VP	♡ CR	👥 CS
	Extracting KLH, nurturing the snail	Stimulate body to target diseases	Dedicated to meet every need	Patients (masses)
Partners for specific diseases	Researching and developing			Biotech and pharmaceutical companies
	🏭 KR	KLH protein and products	🚚 CH	
Research centers	Cutting-edge aquaculture and biotech	Use in programs and applications	Knowledge base (klhsite.org)	Developers of immuno-therapies and vaccines

✎ CS			💰 RS	
Innovation and technologies	Knowledge sharing	Production facilities	Product sales	Long-term supply agreements

Traditional medicine is hitting its boundaries, while the number of people hit with diseases like cancer, Alzheimer's disease, autoimmune disorders, and inflammatory diseases keeps growing. These health problems are clearly developing exponentially. Like cancer, the growth rate of these diseases has already been defined as epidemic. Yet effective treatments for Alzheimer's disease and various types of cancer are still lacking. This is why the paradigm shift towards immunotherapy is so important. Incremental innovation will not be sufficient to address these growing health issues for the masses.

Stellar is well on its way in their good fight against these epidemic diseases. Investors see the importance of immunotherapies as well. When Stellar merged with Edesa Biotech in 2019, their stock price went up 78%. With seven new vaccines in various stages of development, Stellar holds a lot of potential to heal the world with its snails.

"

There is no magic formula to make kids more creative; rather, it's a way to give light and space and time to the creativity that already exists in each of us."

Sal Khan, founder

Khan Academy: Education for everyone

Mathematics was difficult to master for Nadia in high school. Her cousin, Salman Khan, decided to help by tutoring her over the phone and via Yahoo Doodle. Nadia's grades began improving and word quickly spread. Soon Salman was receiving more requests for tutoring sessions than he could handle, causing him to upload the videos to YouTube so that his students could learn on demand. Khan Academy was born.

You can learn anything
At Khan Academy, there is the deep belief that anybody can learn anything. Its site provides instructional videos from basic to advanced, covering subjects such as arithmetic, algebra, engineering, computing, economics, and history. Students take lessons through a digital blackboard, which, over the course of a ten-minute lesson, is gradually filled up with neon-colored scrawls illustrating key concepts. Students study at their own pace, get insights into their knowledge gaps and progress through a learning dashboard, and are incentivized through gamification. Khan academy is also part of the curriculum of classrooms globally. It helps teachers to see where kids are struggling, so that they can be more effective in giving instructions. Students like it because of the immediate feedback on their progress. In 2015, Khan Academy began offering test prep for critical standardized exams. Students, regardless of high school level, gender, race, ethnicity, or parental education level, all achieve much higher scores.

Spreading change
In 2016, Khan Academy started Khan Lab School, a physical school to break out of the factory model of education. Students pursue mastery-based, personalized learning with a lot of focus on skills like entrepreneurship and creativity. They also work in mixed groups to build stuff. Everything they do and learn about what works in education (or not) is open-sourced and shared.

Building a global classroom

A lot of money is spent on education. Global spending is $3.9 trillion, or 5.6% of planetary GDP, according to a report from the President's Council of Economic Advisers. Throughout the years, traditional reform programs required more and more money only to produce declining results.

Khan Academy is fully committed to address the grand challenge in education. Children all over the world crave education. By digitizing educational content, Khan Academy is able to reach millions of people. It helps teachers to introduce new concepts, track student progress, and intervene when needed.

The combination of technologies like the internet, fast handheld devices, and data science is changing how people learn. This is why John and Ann Doerr, The Bill & Melinda Gates Foundation, Reed Hastings, Fundación Carlos Slim, and others happily invest and contribute to this new learning model.

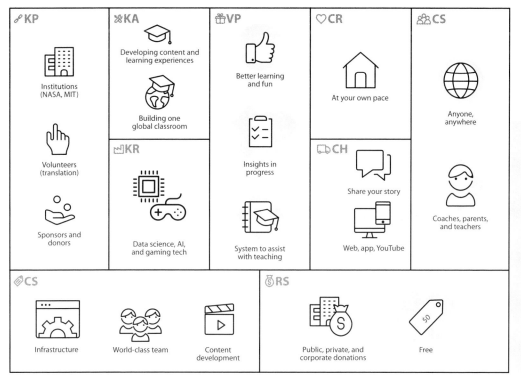

Learning
Access to education that is free, personalized, visualized, and gamified. Self-paced learning that is helping everyone master anything they want.

10x effect

As laid out by Sal Khan in *Forbes* in 2012: Khan Academy reaches about 10 million students annually in a meaningful way, using a $7 million operating budget. For $1, about 1.5 students get a tremendous boost in learning. Khan Academy is supported by a community of fans, who translated videos into 36 languages. Today, it has 71 million registered users from 190 countries and 1.5 million very active learners monthly, a number that has been growing steadily. Every child now has access to a fun, enjoyable, and rewarding learning experience.

> The developer community that collaborates on GitHub transcends languages, time zones, cultures, and more."

GitHub: Community of developers

Before GitHub, when developers contributed to open-source code, they put in a tremendous effort. Before they began coding, they downloaded all the code. Then they made their changes locally, made a list of changes (called a *patch*), and sent an email to the person who maintained the code, who would review developers' changes. The person who maintained the code might not have a relationship or know anything about the developer sending in the patch. A lot of manual labor was involved to work on a piece of code together.

As easy as 1, 2, 3

GitHub makes software version control easy, seamless, and collaborative. GitHub has integrated an array of third-party tools and apps to make coding easier and stress free. The power of GitHub lies in the millions of minds that help improve and innovate on each other's code. Its community of 40 million members work together to create and improve the amazing software that powers the internet, home automation, games, and so much more. GitHub's paid value proposition is its private *Git repositories,* which are code repositories that individuals and companies can use to work on private projects. For these customers, paying Github for hosting is a no-brainer.

Collaborative innovation

From a functional perspective, GitHub is a graphical online tool that acts as a host for code in the form of Git repositories. By having access to source code from millions of projects, developers around the world can contribute to and innovate on each other's ideas. The usefulness of GitHub made them the largest host for source code in the world. From a broader perspective, GitHub is a platform that has innovated the coding and development process. GitHub is also a way for developers to showcase their abilities and portfolio in an extremely practical way. GitHub has brought together millions of developers, empowering collaborative innovation and pushing the envelope of value creation with software. In addition, they add security, ease, and transparency to the world of open-source development.

The future of software development

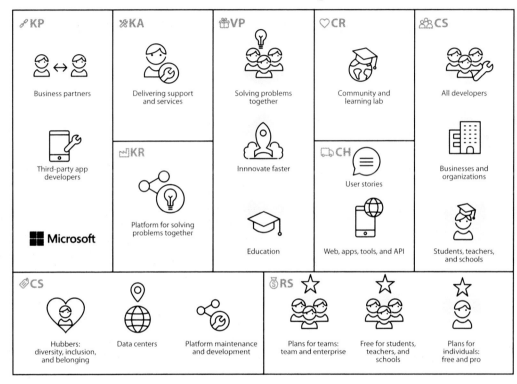

⚭ KP	✂ KA	🎁 VP	♡ CR	🔗 CS
Business partners	Delivering support and services	Solving problems together	Community and learning lab	All developers
Third-party app developers	🖉 KR	Innnovate faster	🚚 CH	Businesses and organizations
	Platform for solving problems together		User stories	
▮▮ Microsoft		Education	Web, apps, tools, and API	Students, teachers, and schools

⚭ CS			💰 RS		
Hubbers: diversity, inclusion, and belonging	Data centers	Platform maintenance and development	Plans for teams: team and enterprise	Free for students, teachers, and schools	Plans for individuals: free and pro

10x effect

Over the years, the number of code repositories hosted by GitHub grew exponentially:

46 thousand	1 million	5 million	10 million	100 million
2009	2010	Jan 2013	Dec 2013	2018

Increasingly, people and companies are adopting the collaborative innovation model. Companies that have adopted the model include Alibaba, Microsoft, Alphabet, IBM, Intel, and many more. In 2012, Andreesen Horowitz led a series A investment of $100 million at a valuation of $750 million. The exit price of $7.5 billion makes that a 10x result.

All patterns
Most technology companies have adopted this collaborative innovation model, from Alibaba to Alphabet to Intel.

GitHub is the place where companies, organizations, and developers are brought together to help tackle each other's problems. This level of collaboration has a direct impact on how fast grand challenges are addressed. GitHub reflects what people are working on and as such is a good reflection what society at large is interested in. On Github, you can find Bitcoin for cryptocurrency; a particle detector for CERN's Large Hadron Collider; gaming projects like Space Station 13, and a gaming engine—Godot; education projects like Open edX and Code.org; web and mobile app building projects like WordPress and Joomla; databases to store your content for the web; a Home Assistant; and a search engine to navigate through content—Elasticsearch. GitHub plans to turns the world of coding into a living, breathing organism that is the product of the world's minds collaborating. A catalyst for innovation, GitHub is the future of software, which is exactly what Microsoft acquired for $7.5 billion in the summer of 2018.

Netafim:
Feed the planet

"

We can outproduce the best ground in this area with some of the poorest soils."

Dan Luepkes, Corn farmer, USA.

Farming is quite a challenge. As a farmer, there are many things you have to get right: quality of seeds, soil, water, and sun. This is not easy as the forces of nature come into play and inevitably change over time. A successful harvest cannot be guaranteed. During the season, a farmer is faced with challenges such as groundwater depletion and lack of access to water reserves. Growing food in the desert seems like a mission impossible. Yet, the Negev desert in Israel is exactly where Netafim started. Being farmers first and innovators second, they know what it's like to farm in extreme conditions. Their own struggle taught them a great deal about precision irrigation, agronomics, and innovation. All of this turned into the business that it is today, helping farmers grow more of any crop, in any climate, with less.

The incremental way of growing more food is to add more fertilizer, labor, or land. The exponential way is to deliver the perfect amount of water and nutrients straight to the roots of each plant—not the soil. Netafim's vision is to provide solutions to fight scarcity of food, water, and land. Netafim provides diverse solutions—from state-of-the-art drippers to advanced automated systems, accompanied by agronomic, technical, and operational support.

Helping farmers help themselves
Currently, Netafim is leading the way in digital farming. NetBeat™ is the first digital farming solution to enable automated irrigation, fertigation, and crop protection. NetBeat is a modular platform that lets farmers easily monitor, analyze, and control their irrigation system from wherever they are. The system integrates over 50 years of agricultural and hydraulic knowledge into intelligent Dynamic Crop Models™. This digital system supports farmers in making better decisions by sending them irrigation strategies personalized to their crops. Insights from the field are turned into profitable decisions that lead to bigger gains season after season.

Grow more with less

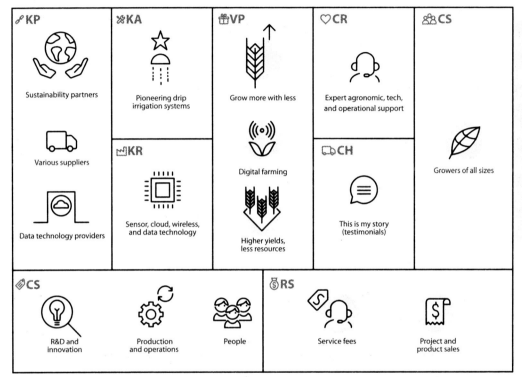

KP

Sustainability partners

Various suppliers

Data technology providers

KA

Pioneering drip irrigation systems

KR

Sensor, cloud, wireless, and data technology

VP

Grow more with less

Digital farming

Higher yields, less resources

CR

Expert agronomic, tech, and operational support

CH

This is my story (testimonials)

CS

Growers of all sizes

CS

R&D and innovation

Production and operations

People

RS

Service fees

Project and product sales

10x effect

With Netafim, no water is wasted. A typical crop like corn requires a huge amount of water per hectare to grow until harvest. Using drip irrigation slashes water use by more than 50%. Yields increase by more than 25% and crops are healthier.

Farmers can grow more food using fewer resources. They can use agriculture to climb out of poverty and generate more profit, and live healthier, more empowered lives.

Food
The drip revolution is a paradigm shift towards low-flow agricultural irrigation, leading to a food production system that does not waste nutrients, land, and water.

Water is life

Everything on the planet needs water, yet so much of it is wasted every day. Since Netafim started to grow food in the desert, the farmers who run it are unstoppable. If growing food succeeds under such extreme conditions, precision irrigation can be used successfully all over the world. It is badly needed to shift towards precision irrigation. With water and arable land already in rapid decline, using precision irrigation seems to be the only way to double food production by 2050.

Sustainability is what Netafim does as expressed in its purpose, vision, and values. To date, Netafim has produced over 150 billion drippers used by more than two million ambitious farmers, irrigating over 10 million hectares of land. Its goal is to make precision irrigation the most accessible and effective solution for growers around the world.

Ask yourself the following questions . . .

How can you think differently about your production system or supply chain, and shrink its footprint?

Beyond Meat lets people eat what they love. It turned out that meat does not have to come from animals. As long as burgers look and taste like meat, the masses dig in just fine. The plant-based production system needed to feed the world with plant-based food is substantially dematerialized. Both inputs and facilities needed are a fraction of the animal-based system, reducing the footprint by 10x or even 100x.

Where can you be extraordinary? What commitment can you make to solve a huge problem for the masses?

Alphabet shows that exponential growth is deceptive. A team might be completely unaware that they are working on a business model that has the potential to grow exponentially in terms of users, impact, and revenues. Even if you have an exponential mindset, it is crucial to get really clear on what impact you want to make with your businesses.

What experiments can you perform to learn how to apply exponential technology to solve customer problems?

SpaceX proves that you can pursue your dreams, even when the whole world thinks it can't be done and tells you you are crazy. Elon Musk pursued his dream, and Space X became a truly disruptive force in the space industry. Most of the things SpaceX accomplished through rigorous experimentation were declared almost impossible a few years beforehand.

What strong partners can you work with to spread the positive impact of your business exponentially?

Stellar Biotechnologies takes a totally different approach to fighting diseases. Diseases have become epidemic. By sustainably growing snails, Stellar provides a sophisticated protein that activates our bodies to fight disease. It focuses on nurturing snails and producing protein. Together with strong partners, it develops applications and vaccines for specific diseases that improve the quality of life for the masses.

What can you digitize and spread in a fun way to everyone on the planet?

Khan Academy believes that anyone can learn anything, providing world-class education is available to everyone. Education is a right, yet so many people do not have access to good education. Digitizing educational content makes it universally accessible. Gamifying the experience and giving students deep insight into their learning journey makes it rewarding and fun.

What can you democratize by bringing it into the open-source domain and improving it together?

GitHub makes working together a wonderful experience. Corporate companies used to be fairly closed, trying to protect their competitive advantage. Today, all the big proprietary players—Google, Apple, Microsoft, Facebook, Baidu, and Alibaba publish open-source projects on the platform. Developing great code just works better when you do it together.

What if water were demonitized (free), and no human on the planet had to worry about water anymore?

Netafim was able to grow food in the desert without wasting water or sacrificing food nutrients despite the hostile growing conditions of the desert. We are running out of water. Netafim is committed to growing more with less, making sure every drop of water is used and no water goes to waste.

High level strategic choices

1

 Adopt an exponential mindset

Think much, much, much bigger about your business: the grand challenges to address, and the masses to serve, in a digital and unique way.

Challenge existing beliefs and assumptions about why things cannot be done. An exponential mindset will figure out how to develop and use technology to do the impossible.

2

 Focus on a big problem

There are still many problems unsolved in the world. Grand challenges that require radically different thinking and technology to effectively address them.

Focus on solving such a big problem. Look at the list of global grand challenges as defined by Singularity University and zoom in on the one that you are excited about.

3

 Digitize value creation

Physical items and assets are difficult to handle and scale. Digital products, services, and assets can be multiplied, distributed, and scaled very easily.

Explore what and how to digitize value propositions and the underlying assets. Create and deliver new value through digitization.

to drive this shift.

4 — 5 — 6 —

 Develop an algorithm

Algorithms help make sense of data from customer interactions to logistic operations.

Analyze and automate routine activities to speed up manufacturing, distribution, and delivery of value. Learn from those interactions to deliver even more value.

 Find unusual partners

Exponential value creation requires multiple perspectives in order to understand and solve the problem.

Seek partners in unusual places. Work with a variety of partners to achieve the breakthrough that is needed.

 Build a community of fans

You are working on a tough challenge in an extraordinary way. This is innovation that the media wants to talk about.

Turn followers and customers into fans: customers because you solve their problems; followers because you do amazing things that are cool to talk about.

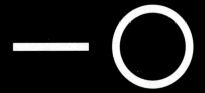

From linear to circular

Our traditional economy has limited growth potential because linear business models exhaust resources to make products that eventually go to waste. Circular business models overcome these limits and build an economy where business growth and a positive socio-environmental impact reinforce each other.

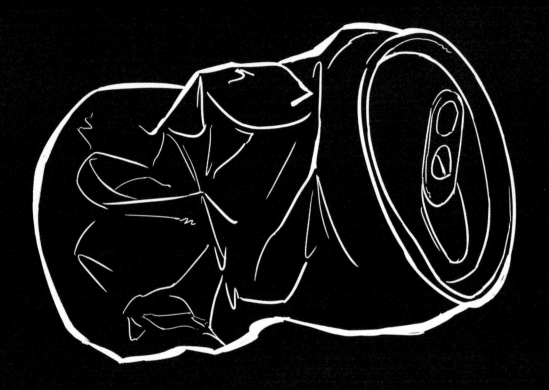

linear →

The *circular shift* is a business model strategy that aims to **close the resource loop.** When undertaking a circular shift, the producing company takes **full responsibility for its use of resources and works to ensure that no resource, material, energy, or water is wasted.** The ultimate goal of this strategy is to have a business model that creates healthy profit margins while also reducing its footprint and generating a positive socio-environmental impact by design. Paradoxically, as circular businesses increase in revenue and size, they see increasing restorative effects on the context they operate in. Unlike other business model strategies, a circular shift decouples growth from any negative effects of achieving that growth.

Shift stories
Large
↗ Nike

Medium
↗ Signify
↗ Interface

Short
↗ Elmhurst
↗ Patagonia
↗ Fairphone

circular

Resources are finite

Circular businesses rethink conventional producer-consumer relationships and the structure of value chains. Environmental and social factors are an integral part of the strategy of circular businesses. When designed properly, circular business models can be extraordinarily profitable for the producer of goods and services, as they reuse materials that would otherwise be wasted.

Resources are finite. There are limits to growth, and given the transparency most businesses practice today—and the speed at which information disseminates—most people have seen firsthand what happens to companies that negatively impact society, the economy, and the environment. But this negative impact isn't about scandals. The model most economies are built on is born of the successes of the Industrial Revolution which more often than not is stuck in a take-make-dispose paradigm. Whether your ambition is to reduce the footprint of your business or make a positive dent in the universe, a great place to start is by designing a business model that aims to reuse resources to create more value. Done properly, a circular business model is both increasingly profitable and simultaneously generates a positive socio-environmental impact.

Strategic questions
Who is the customer that is consciously aware of the negative effects of the current production-consumption system? Who are the customers that are committed to changing their behavior? How can less conscious customers be convinced? How might you design a return channel that brings back used products to your company? How might you design waste out of production in the first place, and what can you learn from nature? What do employees need to make better decisions in using materials, energy, or other resources to make your products or offer your services? What can you learn and apply from companies that have already made this shift?

Looking beyond the current take-make-waste extractive industrial model, a circular economy aims to redefine growth, focusing on positive society-wide benefits. It entails gradually decoupling economic activity from the consumption of finite resources, and designing waste out of the system."

Ellen MacArthur foundation

From linear

The linear business model takes resources and turns them into a product that is sold. Customers use the product until it breaks or becomes outdated, upon which it is disposed of, ending up in a landfill.

Sell more to grow

A typical linear model targets customers that want material goods or perishable stuff. In many cases, these customers don't ask themselves: "Do I really need this?" and "How is this produced?" Customers are offered fairly low-quality goods or products that lose their relevance quickly.

Revenues are generated from products sold. The company can only grow the business by producing and selling more. This model generates little or no positive socio-environmental effects. The company just reports its environmental impact and the initiatives to reduce those impacts in order to comply to rules and regulation and social pressure.

Produce as much as possible

In a linear business model, the focus is to increase production so that the company can focus on selling, while also improving the product so that the next version can be sold to new customers or existing customers with defunct products or outdated versions. Production is outsourced to suppliers in countries with cheap labor. The supply chain

is put under a lot of pressure to reduce cost so that margins stay healthy.

Sooner or later, resources become scarcer, driving up costs for acquiring them. Managing waste is also an important cost. This business model produces many negative socio-environmental effects, such as pollution, high energy and water use, waste, and climate change.

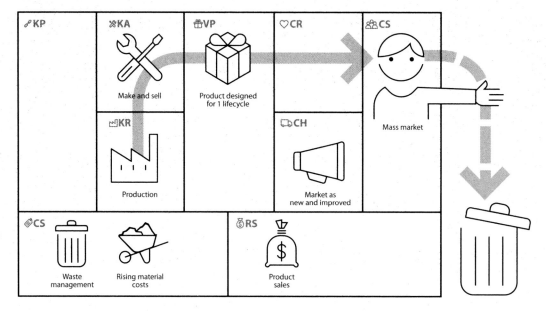

to circular

Effectively reusing resources after the initial value exchange and considering the entire lifecycle of materials, circular business models enable companies to lower environmental footprints while also creating new value propositions.

Closing the loop

A key activity in a circular business model is promoting and tracking usage as well as retrieving products from customers that no longer use them (to bring them back into the loop, shown in the image below). Circular-minded companies continually ask, "can we make this more circular?" spending effort upfront to come up with products that can be used (not owned), used much longer, easily reused and/or dismantled into their components. Circular-minded companies also look for ways to use waste from different sources as raw materials. Partners that share a circular ambition are crucial to get breakthroughs, achieve results, and impact. Costs are made for gaining and sharing knowledge and employing new production techniques. Material costs and costs for dealing with waste are reduced.

Conscious consumption

The value proposition is a product designed to last or a service based on a high-quality and durable product. By using the product or service, customers contribute to a better world. Customers are people who care about the environment and climate change. They want to change themselves and have set their own sustainability goals, personally or as a company. Customers are connected to the company because they feel part of its mission to drive substantial change. The waste bin where customers disposed their products has been replaced by a collection bin of some sort. The company has a dedicated return channel to bring used products back into the system.

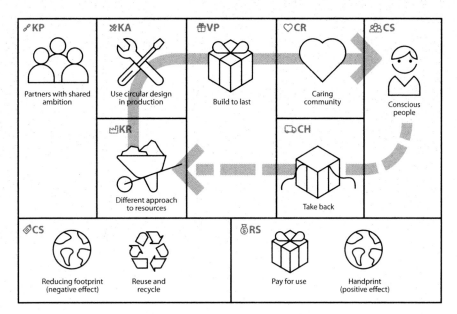

Use it, not own it

 Use it together

 Use it longer

1

The company rents or leases a product to customers to ensure that the product is used to maximum potential. Companies own and manage products in a pool that is used to provide a service to multiple customers over time. Products are designed for repeated use to ensure a positive customer experience. Customers get the products they want, with the features they want, when they want (or need) them—all without the hassles inherent in owning those products.

Examples: Nike Adventure Club, Signify, Streetbank

2

Companies provide a platform for customers who own assets to connect with others who borrow those assets from them. The company facilitates customers finding each other, sharing assets, and returning the assets after an agreed upon amount of time. The company ensures that expectations are met by asset owners and users. Customers review each other on the platform.

Examples: Erento, SnappCar, Streetbank, Warp It

3

This business model is for companies aiming for the highest quality. Repair instructions or services are offered to keep the product in good shape. A product can also be taken back, cleaned and repaired, and sold secondhand. *Upcycling* is taking back, upgrading, and selling it at a higher price. Remaking is taking back, disassembling, putting it together again with new components where needed and selling as good as new.

Examples: Nike Adventure Club, Patagonia, Warp It, Streetbank, Fairphone

Patterns

 Use that by-product

 Use it again

 Use it again, elsewhere

The company produces a product for a customer segment. The waste from the production process of that product is used as input for another production process or the waste in itself is a product. Waste can be energy that is generated in a primary production process, material waste, or CO_2. The by-product meets a whole other need of a second customer segment, generating a second revenue stream.

Examples: Black Bear Company, Elmhurst

The company produces a product for a customer segment. This product is taken back from the customer or returned by the customer. The product is broken down to its components or materials, which are used to produce the same product. A reward might be used to incentivize customers to return the product.

Examples: Nike Grind, Interface, Xerox, Patagonia

The company produces a product for a customer segment, takes it back, and breaks it down to its components or materials. These components or materials are now used in entirely different products or can even be used as input (feedstock) in a production process in a completely different value chain.

Examples: Nike Grind, Nike Adventure Club, Interface, Close the Loop

Nike

How one coach and his athlete turned his quest for performance into the largest and most recognized sports brand. Now the quest is on to shift to a business model that produces zero carbon and zero waste.

Founders Bill Bowerman, Phil Knight **Founded 1964** as Blue Ribbon Sports	**Total revenue** $39.1 billion (2019)	**Industry** Sporting goods and apparel	**Scale** 700 shops 45 countries 73,000 employees

1964
Blue Ribbon Sports

The company is founded by Bill Bowerman and Phil Knight and officially became Nike, Inc., on May 30, 1971.

1971
The Swoosh

Carolyn Davis designs the famous swoosh for $35 and later receives 500 shares. Phil famously said, "Well, I don't love it, but maybe it will grow on me."

1978
Victory

Company name officially changes to Nike, which means "victory." In 1980, the company goes public. At this time, they have a market share of about 50% in the US.

1984
Michael Jordan

Michael Jordan signs his endorsement contract. By the end of 1985, $100 million in revenues is generated as a result.

I've always believed that businesses should be good citizens."

Phil Knight

co-founder and

former chairman of Nike

On a quest for performance

The story about how Nike started is well-known. The athletic shoe company founded by Bill Bowerman and Phil Knight in 1964, called Blue Ribbon Sports, has become the largest and most recognized sports brand in the world.

What most people don't know is that Nike is also a leader in the circular economy. The story of Nike's shift from a relatively simple linear business model to a set of circular business models is not only interesting; it's groundbreaking when you consider how Nike has managed to pull from its core (once linear) elements to develop incredibly innovative, customer-centric, circular business models.

From the company's beginning, Nike products have been designed for performance.

As Phil Knight said, "We wanted Nike to be the world's best sports and fitness company. Once you say that, you have a focus. You don't end up making wing tips or sponsoring the next Rolling Stones world tour." It goes without saying then, the company has continually sought after and invented new materials and processes that help to deliver better performance.

Of course, it's not just better materials that have enabled Nike to grow. By sponsoring athletes like Michael Jordan (a star American basketball player) and national sports leagues, like the National Basketball Association (NBA) and the National Football League (NFL), Nike's "Just Do It!™" attitude has created mass appeal and, in turn, mass expansion of the brand and its products.

1988
Just Do It!

Nike launches the "Just Do It!" campaign. The campaign does very well. More and more people feel connected to the brand. Eventually, "Just Do It!" becomes Nike's slogan.

1990
Sweatshops

Nike is criticized for contracting with sweatshops and the use of child labor leading the company to overhaul its oversight of manufacturing partners and processes.

Commitment to innovation

Leadership at Nike wants Corporate Social Responsibility (CSR) to go beyond greenwashing, seeing CSR as a vehicle to fuel innovation. They use it to seize early leadership in growth opportunities driven by sustainability.

Linear business model
The initial Nike business model was a linear design and production model, turning raw materials into great products that are eventually discarded by customers.

Push the limits

The business model that has enabled Nike to scale to the powerhouse it is today is anchored by Nike's "Just Do It!" attitude and associated value propositions. The underlying products have also expanded from athletic shoes—made for athletes—to entire apparel lines designed for every sport as well as casual settings. The engine behind all of this: elite internal design and development teams that continually push the Nike brand into new realms and tight, ever-expanding partnerships with global manufacturers.

Nike, Just Do It!

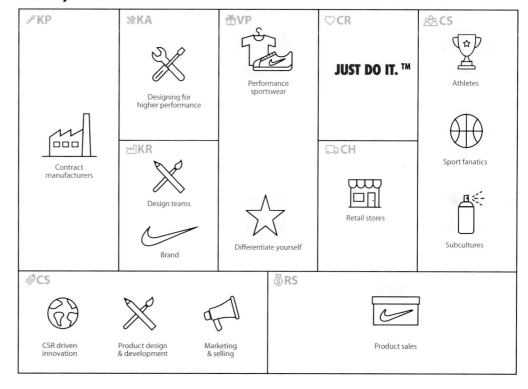

1993
Nike Grind

A shoe should not be wasted. Nike shifts its linear model by launching the Reuse-A-Shoe™ program and the launch of Nike Grind.

2004
Considered line

Nike releases the Considered Boot. Nike's first concept shoe in this new line that was designed and produced by explicitly considering environmental impact.

2007
Climate friendly

Ranked in the top 3 for most climate friendly company by Clean Air, Cool Planet. Receiving praise and recognition from Climate Counts.

Due to lack of oversight in its offshore manufacturing practices, the company found itself in hot water in the 1990s, wherein several of its contract manufacturers were found to have used child labor to assemble its popular shoes.

To gain more control over its supply chain, Nike reduced the number of factories it worked with. At the same time a number of people at Nike realized that amid the reorganization of its supply chain, an entirely new opportunity existed to clean up its manufacturing mess. With this, Nike "envision[ed] a world without waste."

To support this ambition, the company searched for new ways to create value. In 1993, an employee named Steve Potter came up with Reuse-A-Shoe: a sneaker recycling program that collects worn shoes from consumers and breaks down the shoes into the high-performance materials they are made of. This program turned into an entire new business model, Nike Grind.

Leaders at Nike challenged designers to design products that offered great performance and a reduced footprint, to which they created a new way to select materials with lower environmental impact, partly provided by Nike Grind.

From shoes to purpose.

Nike's purpose is to commit to creating a better, more sustainable future for our people, planet, and communities through the power of sport. Without a planet, people cannot do sports. This purpose motivated Nike employees to design with an eye toward sustainability.

At the same time, Nike Grind employs a number of the company's core elements, namely leadership committed to being good citizens, retail stores for drop off in the Reuse-A-Shoe bin, and the problem-solving mindset of their designers.

Appealing to everyone brings mass responsibility. Design out waste!

2008
Air Jordan XX3

Nike releases Air Jordan XX3. The design was done by applying the Considered Design ethos. Nike Trash Talk a shoe made entirely from waste, launches and is promoted by Steve Nash. The Trash Talk shoe is intended to create more environmental awareness.

Limitless potential

To Nike, nothing should be wasted. The company's materials and waste are designed for high-performance and have limitless potential beyond the first use.

Waste is not waste

Nike spends a lot of effort to come up with shoes and apparel that boosts the performance of their customers. This can only be done with the best materials. At their end-of-life, these high-performance materials should be used again. This is what the Nike Grind business model makes possible. Nike takes back shoes from any brand through hundreds of stores in the US, Canada, Spain, and Italy. These shoes are broken into their components and used for various Nike Grind products, such as shoes and apparel.

Use it again
Nike Grind provides Nike designers materials that score high in physical and environmental performance.

Use it again, elsewhere
Grind granules are the base material for athletic surfaces, offered to premium surface manufacturers.

Nike Grind: turning waste into products

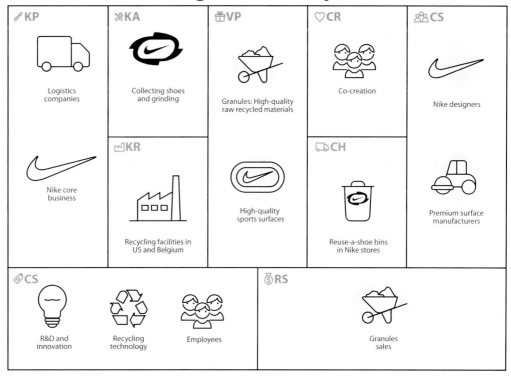

We have an obligation to consider the complete design solution: how we source it, make it, use it, return it, and how we reimagine it."

John Hoke, Nike's Chief Design Officer

Just design differently

Circularity is not just about new materials. It's also about designing new business models that create entirely new customer experiences and interactions. As a multi-tiered subscription service built for parents and kids, this is what Nike Adventure Club does.

In a linear business model, companies protect their intellectual property and keep design and manufacturing knowledge to themselves. What Nike learned about circular design has been shared to inspire and guide other designers and companies. To that end, Nike created a white paper on its website, "Circularity: Guiding the Future of Design," which presents 10 actionable principles to rethink and redesign products to have a positive impact on our planet.

In addition to sharing knowledge, Nike has nudged other players to innovate and join a movement that designs a better future. Nike's innovation challenge, launched in 2018, invited other designers, engineers, scientists, and makers to join the company in creating a circular future: (1) how might we design new products using Nike Grind materials, and (2) how might we develop new technologies to advance footwear recycling?

2016
Ellen MacArthur

Nike becomes a global partner of the Ellen MacArthur Foundation, finally achieving a channel to talk about what they are doing and accelerate towards a truly circular economy.

Shift in the mindset

According to product design lead Deborah Castel: "New business models are just the evolution of product design, especially around circularity and sustainability."

The end is just the beginning

Nike Grind keeps shoes out of landfills and protects the future of play. Twice a year, Nike Adventure Club ships a prepaid bag to send back your worn out shoes, which are then recycled through Nike Grind. If they are still in good condition, they are refurbished and donated to families in need.

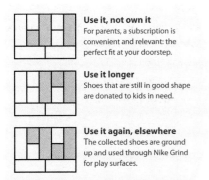

Use it, not own it
For parents, a subscription is convenient and relevant: the perfect fit at your doorstep.

Use it longer
Shoes that are still in good shape are donated to kids in need.

Use it again, elsewhere
The collected shoes are ground up and used through Nike Grind for play surfaces.

Nike Adventure Club: shoe subscription model

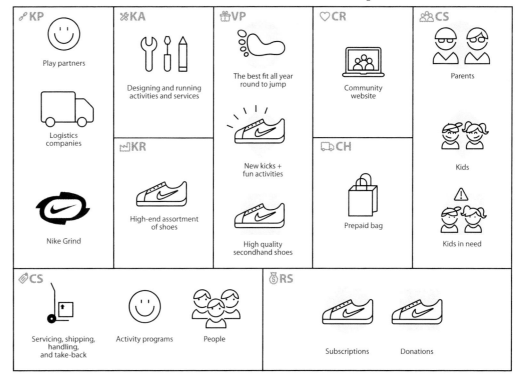

Design out waste

It's not easy to shift to new business models when your company has successfully executed the same business model for half a century. What's become clear though, when looking at the Nike Grind and Adventure Club business models, is that Nike still uses many of the core business model elements that made it the powerhouse that it is.

Nike Grind is driven by a mindset that CSR should fuel innovation and challenges designers to use materials that deliver performance for the user and the environment. The Adventure Club combines its well-known brand, huge assortment of shoes, and Nike Grind to offer an entirely new circular out-of-the-box subscription model for kids, their parents, and the communities they live in. These new business models infuse the organization with new elements, such as partnerships, design practices, and return channels, that can be used to create new value.

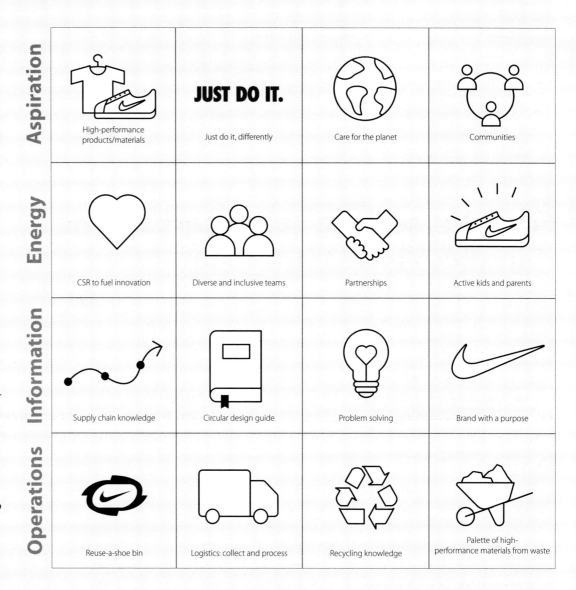

Aspiration

High-performance products/materials	Just do it, differently	Care for the planet	Communities

Energy

| CSR to fuel innovation | Diverse and inclusive teams | Partnerships | Active kids and parents |

Information

| Supply chain knowledge | Circular design guide | Problem solving | Brand with a purpose |

Operations

| Reuse-a-shoe bin | Logistics: collect and process | Recycling knowledge | Palette of high-performance materials from waste |

2018
Open Innovation

Nike introduces the Circular Innovation Challenge, an open innovation challenge to extend value creation with Nike Grind and advance recycling of footwear.

2019
Grind and Adventure Club

Nike celebrates 26 years of closing the loop with Nike Grind and launches the Adventure Club, a shoe subscription model to encourage children to live a more active life.

Future
Move to Zero

Move to Zero is Nike's restated purpose to help protect the future of sport, reframed as a journey toward zero carbon and zero waste. 100% renewable energy is to be achieved by 2025.

For Nike, serving customers means that there is no finish line.

Nike Grind is a fully validated business model, but with only 292 out of 700 stores globally collecting used shoes, the model has plenty of room to scale (and Nike has plenty of shoes to recycle). At the same time, through Nike Adventure Club, the company is beginning to prove out that with the right business model, people will collect and return shoes.

The Nike Adventure Club is a business model in the early stages of growth and needs to gain traction in the market. It's a mission-based model that aims to achieve three things: (1) more adventure, (2) more community, and (3) less waste. It is also fo-cused on the future, ensuring that recycling worn-out shoes is easy for consumers. This business model requires Nike to double down on logistics—both forward and reverse—to ensure that customers get what they need when they need it, and can just as easily return to Nike what they have used.

More than ever, Nike is committed to making a circular shift. It has even developed a circular design guide, called "Circularity: Guiding the Future of Design" (available for download at https://www.nikecirculardesign.com) to show other companies how to think different-ly and just do it . . . on their own. The company makes a clear case for taking climate action by showing how climate change is affecting athletic performance in negative ways, which is supported and endorsed by top athletes.

Over time, the company has employed its core and new elements to create new circular business models. Likewise, Nike has always used design to ensure that athletes perform better and sponsored them along their journey. Now, these athletes are supporting Nike to take performance to the next level. It's not about performance of everyone. It's about preserving the planet so that everyone can enjoy life on Earth.

Interface

Interface was a traditional manufacturing company with a founder that radically changed his mind after realizing the devastating impact that his business had on the environment. He decided to turn his business around, working extremely hard with his team to bring impact to zero.

Facts

Founder
Ray C. Anderson

Founded 1973
LaGrange, Georgia

Total revenue
$1.2 billion (2018)

Industry
Carpet tiles and flooring

Other information
Top 3 Corporate Global
Sustainability leader
since 1997

Scale
4,000 employees
40 global offices and
showrooms

> **Lesson 1: shoot for the moon. If you want to transform, set a goal that you don't know how to achieve yet."**
>
> Lessons for the future: The Interface guide to changing your business to change the world

Interface was founded by Ray Anderson to bring the concept of well-designed modular carpets to the masses. Anyone with a floor was a target for Interface, for which the company sold both the carpets and carpet design. What made Interface's business model work so well was that carpets can be custom designed to replace existing carpets. For decades, the company happily grew the business using traditional manufacturing methods, which used a lot of toxic materials, all of which fell within regulatory guidelines.

What about sustainability?

While Interface's business was progressing nicely, in the early 1990s, a customer asked how sustainability played into Interface's strategy. Neither Anderson nor his colleagues had an answer other than, "we follow the rules." However, Anderson also knew the numbers behind his industry. Namely,

that 4 billion pounds of carpet end up in landfills every year in the US alone. With this question, Anderson realized that simply "following the rules" would end up costing society and his company a lot of resources.

In 1994, Interface began an inspiring journey. The company developed Mission Zero®, a bold vision that sought to transform its business to have zero negative impact on the planet by the year 2020. Now, 25 years later, Interface has achieved its mission by transforming the company into a purpose driven flooring company anchored by sustainable designers, makers, and storytellers. Interface has greatly reduced the impacts of the business and operations while also transforming its supply chain, its products, and business models. These EcoMetrics became communications tools—something everyone could understand, recall, and act upon.

Bold and aggressive

Interface truly became a sustainability leader by making bold choices and doing the hard work every day. In 2019, the company fulfilled Mission Zero. Mission Zero required various frameworks, shared goals, and internally driven programs, all of which took a holistic, systematic approach to the business. But most of all, it was rewriting the company's story. A new and completely different future was clearly envisioned and communicated. This was accompanied by setting aggressive targets in many areas: zero waste to landfill, zero fossil fuel energy use, zero greenhouse gas emissions, and greatly reduced water usage. EcoMetrics were subsequently used to report progress to employees and the world.

Draining the planet

Taking materials from the earth and using the company's key resources, such as factories and supply chain know-how, paired with unique custom-designed expertise, Interface was able to deliver value (and capture value therein) from just about anyone with a floor, from consumers to businesses. Via this traditional take-make-waste business model, Interface grew to the largest modular carpet manufacturer in the world.

Linear business model
A production model relying on toxic, petroleum-based materials, requiring a lot of energy to turn them into onetime use carpet tiles

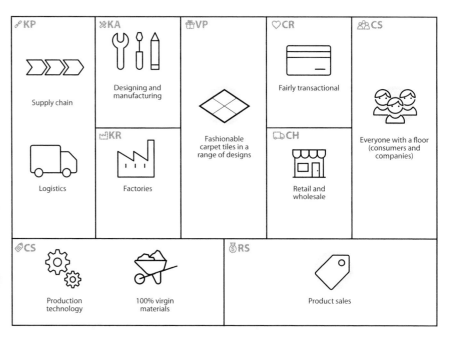

KP — Supply chain — Logistics

KA — Designing and manufacturing

KR — Factories

VP — Fashionable carpet tiles in a range of designs

CR — Fairly transactional

CH — Retail and wholesale

CS — Everyone with a floor (consumers and companies)

CS — Production technology — 100% virgin materials

RS — Product sales

Mission Zero

Interface knew designing a circular business model was essential. This approach included changing the inputs and putting in place technology and systems to use recycled materials. A part of this shift is to use raw materials that can be reused and recycled effectively. In addition, recycled materials are used in many carpet components. Today, 60% of the raw materials in Interface carpets come from recycled or biobased sources.

Of course, it wasn't always smooth sailing. Under the FairWorks™ initiative, the company introduced a new line of products, a range of eco-friendly grass and bamboo-woven floor tiles, sourced from artisan weavers in India. Despite market testing and early enthusiasm from customers, sales were disappointing. Because the products were made from unusual materials, customers felt they would be harder to maintain or might not perform as well as carpet tiles made from nylon.

Redesign everything

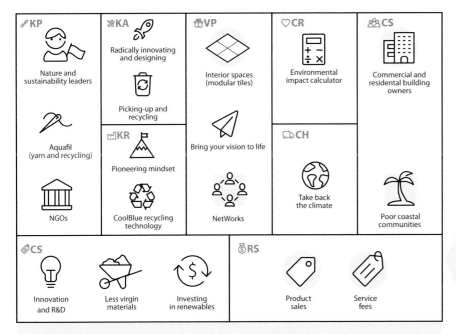

Interface sells designs that turn interior spaces into a pleasant and energizing space to work or live in. The savings from using waste funded the R&D and innovation needed to redesign and transform the company.

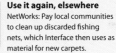

Use it again
ReEntry: Reclaim/recycle Interface products from customers and turn them into brand-new products.

Use it again, elsewhere
NetWorks: Pay local communities to clean up discarded fishing nets, which Interface then uses as material for new carpets.

Negative effects (footprint)
To date, Interface has diverted 13 million pounds of post-consumer carpet from landfills, while shifting to use 98% recycled or organic material for its flooring. As of 2019, its carbon footprint is zero.

Positive effects (handprint)
Interface's circular business model makes for happier people and a healthier planet. It's helped to collect and recycle 317,000 pounds of fishing nets (46% of plastic) and moved to 100% renewable energy.

Regenerate
Interface's new mission is the "Take Back the Climate" initiative. Through this initiative, Interface develops products that capture carbon. The company provides tools and frameworks to other businesses to help them shift their respective business models in this direction as well.

Signify

Signify's purpose is to unlock the extraordinary potential of light for brighter lives and a better world. Signify wants to make light an intelligent language that connects and conveys meaning. The company offers a broad range of lighting products and services.

"I'm not interested in the product, just the performance: light, and not the bulbs."

Thomas Rau, Architect

Starting with carbon-filament lamps, Philips (which later became Signify) has been a pioneer and industry leader in technological innovation since 1891. The company has invented hundreds if not thousands of products, from electric shavers to video recorders, from the Compact Audio Cassette, Laser Disc, and Compact Disc, to chip production machines (now ASML), and from semiconductors (now NXP) to medical equipment.

As with most companies that manufacture lightbulbs, Philips employed a linear business model, organized around technology, and had been quite successful, continually replacing old products with new ones. It goes without saying, this is a resource intensive business model. Of course, Philips, known for quality, has never seen its linear business model as a way to develop inferior products. Quite the contrary. The company has invested billions into developing new and improved lighting solutions. During the energy crisis of the 1970s, Philips Research invented energy-saving lamps. Low energy LED lights were introduced in 2005. And, around 2010, with the introduction of the Philips Hue, lighting was made intelligent for consumers and businesses.

In 2011, Architect Thomas Rau did not want to buy for his new Amsterdam office expensive lighting infrastructure that he would only need to replace and dispose of later. He approached Philips and explained: "Listen, I need so many hours of light in my premises every year. If you think you need a lamp, or electricity, or whatever—that's fine. But I want nothing to do with it. I'm not interested in the product, just the performance. I want to buy light, and nothing else." Given its customer-centric focus, Philips worked with Rau to create a minimal lighting plan that maximized the use of daylight. In addition, the Philips engineers installed a combined sensor and controller system to optimize lighting and energy use throughout the building.

The pilot with Thomas Rau inspired Philips to develop this into a new value proposition and related business model. As a result, Circular Lighting was developed to provide a new value proposition where customers pay only for what they use, generate instant savings, and are able to achieve their own sustainability goals (faster). And, at the end of the day, most commercial customers really only want and need light.

Under this business model, Signify is fully responsible for delivering light performance and thus owns all of the equipment necessary to light a building. Not only does this require Signify to develop superior quality lighting—so it's not overextended in human resources required to replace lights on customer site—but the company also collects data, enabling it to deliver insights, benefits, and new services to its customers.

Pushing technology

The Philips linear model was organized around technology and was successful for a long time, spitting out innovative products all the time. For more than 100 years, Philips invested significant resources into researching and developing new and improved lighting solutions. For example, in the energy crises in the 1970s, Philips Research invented energy-saving lamps.

Linear model
After use, high-end products end up in the landfill, while materials like gold and other precious metals become scarcer and more expensive.

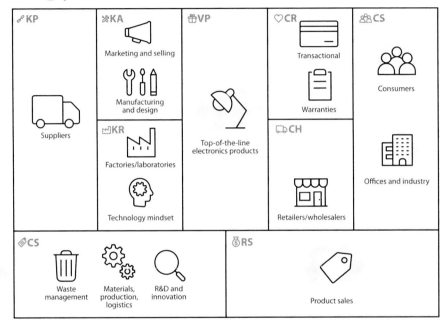

So much energy wasted

Fifteen percent of electricity globally is used for lighting homes, stores, industrial buildings and plants, offices, and cities, mostly with traditional lighting systems. The equipment is thrown away at its end-of-life. Traditional lighting equipment wastes a tremendous amount of energy and materials.

Throughout its history, Philips has been leading the evolution of lighting. Every new product has been designed to outperform and disrupt the previous one in terms of energy use. Low energy LED lights were introduced in 2005. LED lights are a breakthrough in energy efficiency and intelligence, as the light is actually built

into a microchip. Light based on chips can create and deliver new value in many ways. In 2012, intelligent lighting for consumers (Philips Hue) was introduced as an Apple Store exclusive.

Driving value through services

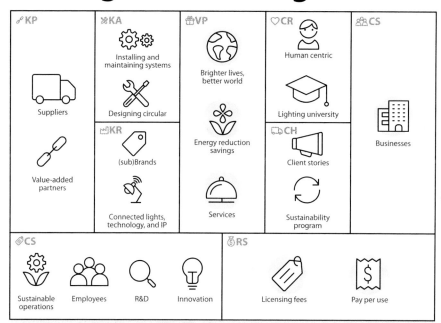

Lighting as a service helps customers achieve their goals in that they don't pay for products, infrastructure, or maintenance; they pay instead only for what they need. Signify is a partner to many within the entire supply chain. The company also provides light to communities that lack access and resources.

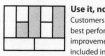

Use it, not own it
Customers always get the best performance. Upgrades, improvements, and innovations are included in the service.

The light revolution
Today, Signify's circular business model is not focused on pushing technology in the form of products. It values reusing and renewing technology in an endless loop of innovation that benefits customers. Signify's purpose is to unlock the extraordinary potential of light for brighter lives and a better world, and the company seeks to make light more intelligent, ensuring that humans have the light they need when they need it. The development of a circular business model was a necessity to bring the lighting industry into a new century.

Negative effects (footprint)
To date Signify has reached 95% sustainable supplier performance and recycles 82% of manufacturing waste. By the end of 2020, it plans to be carbon neutral and get 89% of its energy from reusable sources.

Positive effects (handprint)
With the lighting services Signify provides, people see, feel, and function better. This has helped to catalyze recreation, productivity and growth. By the end of 2020 80% of Signify's revenue will be recurring.

Snackable cases

From tires to energy!

Black Bear recovers the carbon black from end-of-life tires that are destined for the landfill. Black Bear also uses the high-calorific gas created during the process to generate green energy.

Since 2003, **Erento has made it as easy as possible for people to rent everything imaginable online, including mobile homes, sports cars, event technology, and tools.**

Unused cars

Snappcar facilitates peer-to-peer carsharing. These car owners are able to charge a fee to rent out their vehicles when they are not using them. The goal of Snappcar is to reduce the number of cars in Europe by 5 million by 2022. **Having fewer cars creates more space to live and reduces CO_2.**

Too many perfectly good items are being thrown away. Warp It provides a network where organizations keep their equipment, assets, and "stuff" circulating to reduce spend, waste, and environmental impact.

Close the Loop turns old printer cartridges and soft plastics into roads that last up to 65% longer than roads made with traditional asphalt.

Every kilometer of road, uses the equivalent of 530,000 plastic bags, 168,000 glass bottles, and12,500 printer cartridges.

Instead of ending up in landfill, all that waste is given a new life.

Streetbank helps with:

1. **Giving things away**—find a grateful neighbor for stuff you no longer need.
2. **Sharing things**—get the most use from things like ladders and drills that go unused much of the time
3. **Share skills**—help neighbors with things like DIY, languages, and gardening.

Xerox sells contract print services rather than printers.

Printers are designed to be remanufactured and reduce waste in operation.

Dutch company DyeCoo has developed a process of dyeing cloth that uses no water at all, and no chemicals other than the dyes themselves.

3 Short case studies

Short. Crisp. Fast. Clear.

	CEO	Total revenue	Founded 1973	Scale
1 Patagonia	Doug Freeman	€1 billion	Ventura, California	1,000 employees
2 Elmhurst	CEO Henry Schwartz	Total revenue $26 million	Founded 1925 New York, New York	Scale 105 employees
3 Fairphone	CEO Eva Gouwens	Total revenue $14 million (2017)	Founded 2010 Amsterdam, Netherlands	Scale 100K+ phones sold

Patagonia: Making the best product

> **"We embrace risk and act to protect and restore the stability, integrity, and beauty of the web of life."**
>
> Patagonia website—mission statement

Patagonia, Inc., "an American clothing company that markets and sells outdoor clothing," has made it its mission to promote sustainability and circularity throughout its business practices, investments, and stories. Though Patagonia is small when compared to the largest outdoor apparel company, VF Corp., which owns well-known brands like The North Face, SmartWool, and Eagle Creek, the company aims to shift to 100% renewable and recycled raw materials and recycles nearly twenty thousand pounds of gear annually and repairs some forty thousand garments. To do this, Patagonia runs the largest apparel repair plant in North America.

The company promises to make products that endure, and to repair, resell, or recycle them as necessary, while it hopes its customers buy only what they need, and to similarly steward their purchases from new garments to storied heirlooms to the recycling bin. Via its Portland, Oregon, store, Patagonia is testing secondhand clothing sales as well and has made product repair and recycling an essential part of its business model.

Patagonia isn't only focused on shifting its outdoor gear business model either. Via its Patagonia Provisions division, which produces and sells quality products that address the ecological consequences of farming, fishing, and livestock husbandry, Patagonia is "imagining a point out in the future where that business is probably going to eclipse the apparel business." As Rick Ridgeway, Patagonia's vice president of environmental affairs, described to the *New Yorker* in 2015, Patagonia Provisions exist "where the biggest problems reside, and that's also where the biggest solutions reside." The bigger Patagonia gets, the more impact it can create".

Save our home planet

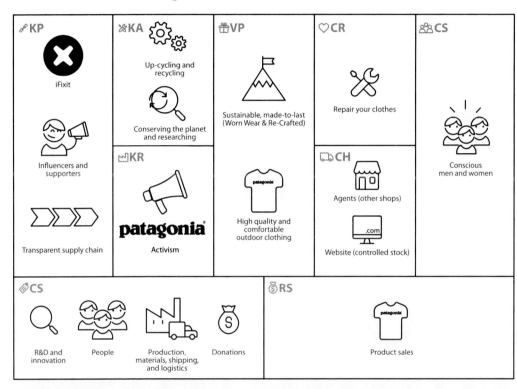

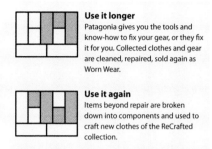

Use it longer
Patagonia gives you the tools and know-how to fix your gear, or they fix it for you. Collected clothes and gear are cleaned, repaired, sold again as Worn Wear.

Use it again
Items beyond repair are broken down into components and used to craft new clothes of the ReCrafted collection.

Negative effects (footprint)

In the US Patagonia uses 100% renewable electricity and 76% globally. Sixty-nine percent of Patagonia's product line includes recycled material with plans to shift to 100% recycled or renewable materials by 2025.

Positive effects (handprint)

Patagonia has donated more than $105 million to grassroots projects to preserve and conserve nature and support youth climate activists. The company also invests in carbon-capture projects, like reforestation, across the globe.

A carbon positive future

Patagonia is very aware of the negative impact their business creates. In order to save the planet, the vision is to become "carbon positive"—taking more carbon out of the atmosphere than the company puts in, even as the company grows. Patagonia is also investing in start-ups with regenerative business models through Tin Shed Ventures. This all fits in the bigger scheme of regenerative organic agriculture as a source of raw materials for its apparel and food for Patagonia Provisions. Through various certifications, Patagonia promotes the creation of healthy topsoil. Via its ever more circular business model, Patagonia is helping to ensure we have a place to live in the future.

"

As awareness and demand for vegan products continues to grow, we're seeing plant-based options become mainstream."

Henry Schwartz, CEO Elmhurst

Elmhurst:
From cows to nuts

The industrial food production system is broken and requires lots of input, i.e., water, land, animals, and antibiotics, to produce food. At the same time, this system generates plenty of negative effects, such as sick animals, pollution, deforestation, and degradation of ecosystems. What's more, some of the global pandemics we're experiencing are often the result of this broken system. Although most consumers are unaware of all these factors, one thing is clear: people have been shifting en masse to using plant-based alternatives, like nut milks.

Expiration date has passed

Experiencing firsthand what customers really want and need is a great reason to shift your business model . . . even if your company supplies milk to more than 8,300 grocers and 1,400 public schools in NYC, producing over 5.6 million quarts a week.

After producing and selling milk since 1925, Henry Schwartz, the founder of Elmhurst,

decided to shift Elmhurst's business model from cow milk to nut-based milks in 2017. Elmhurst went all-in to the plant-based market, producing milk in a more sustainable way (for the business model and planet), and addressing its consumers' needs in a way others cannot. Today, Elmhurst is the fastest growing plant-based "dairy" company in the US.

Zero waste

Producing milk from plants is quite different from producing milk from cows. Ironically, producing plant-based milks from nuts has a lower footprint than its animal-based counterparts. Due to the fact that all parts of the nuts, grain, or seeds are used in the process, it produces no waste. This is made possible by the HydroRelease™ method, invented by food technologist Dr. Cheryl Mitchell, which does not require additives to hold the product together, which results in a clean and natural-looking product.

Plant-based dairy

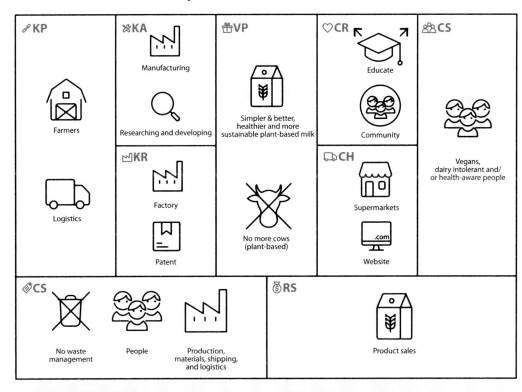

Negative effects (footprint)

Elmhurst produces no waste as every part of the nut or grain is used. Peanuts are especially sustainable as they require very little water to grow.

Positive effects (handprint)

Using different nuts and grains as the source of milk leads to better farming because multiple crops are grown, instead of just a single crop.

Healthier food

For the past decade, consumers have been switching from dairy milks to plant-based alternatives at an accelerated rate. And, although dairy-based products still make up the bulk of most milk sales, the dairy industry has actually been in decline while the plant-based industry continues to grow at more than 10% annually. It's not that there are fewer cows. It's that consumers want plant-based alternatives.

Use that byproduct
The HydroRelease method uses the entire nut to produce sustainable and healthy milk.

The future of food

Schwartz believes that the future is plant-based. It's Elmhurst's goal to improve nondairy alternatives by making them better than their counterparts. In doing so, Elmhurst provides households everywhere sustainable, healthy options. In the future, Elmhurst plans to expand into other plant-based products made from seeds and legumes.

Fairphone:
Awareness about fairness

"

The ultimate business model is if we would not sell any phone anymore.''

Bas van Abel, Founder Fairphone

Fairphone is not just a smartphone company. The primary goal of the company is to create awareness about the wars in Democratic Republic of the Congo caused by the mining of resources for the electronics industry. Bas van Abel wanted to make awareness physical, rather than just a mental exercise. So he invented the first sustainable, modular smartphone: the Fairphone.

The story is the product

The Fairphone is designed as a storytelling device that (re)connects consumers with the products they use, connecting them with the supply chain that is behind the product. In 2015, the company received the Tech5 award for being the fastest growing start-up in Europe. Its story was in the hands of 17,418 customers within 2.5 months. Fairphone began its work by designing a modular, easy-to-repair smartphone in an effort to create more ethical, reliable, and sustainable electronics. Fairphone strives for a usage period of 5 years, in contrast to

regular smartphones that are designed to be used for only 2 years. Users can order parts online and replace parts that frequently break (screen) or require upgrading (camera). Currently, Fairphone partners with iFixit, which provides open source repair guides for consumers, contributing to Fairphone's vision to use phones much longer.

Fairphone is on a journey to change the electronics industry; the key to this is its community. The company has built a community across the entire supply chain, starting with the manufacturers that produce the phone in a sustainable way and put people first and ending with consumers and businesses that buy and use the phone to make a statement. Social responsibility initiatives and NGOs are also part of their community, driving awareness and spreading the story.

Phones with a story

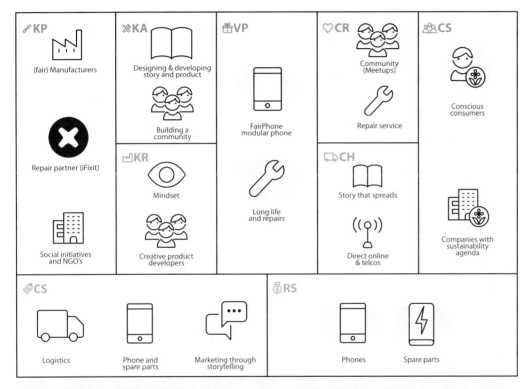

✒ KP	✂ KA	🎁 VP	♡ CR	ஃ CS
(fair) Manufacturers	Designing & developing story and product	FairPhone modular phone	Community (Meetups)	Conscious consumers
Repair partner (iFixit)	Building a community		Repair service	
Social initiatives and NGO's	**KR** Mindset / Creative product developers	Long life and repairs	**CH** Story that spreads / Direct online & telcos	Companies with sustainability agenda

✎ CS			⑤ RS	
Logistics	Phone and spare parts	Marketing through storytelling	Phones	Spare parts

Consumers and companies who want to champion sustainability and fairness in the world are the primary customers of Fairphone. They use their phones for a long time. They also use their phones to change an industry, spread the story about fairness, and create awareness and change in consumer behavior.

Use it longer
Focus on longer use: design a phone that is modular and easy to repair and upgrade.

Negative effects (footprint)
Fairphone is producing phones to last at least 5 years. Doing this will help to reduce e-waste. The company recycles old phones and turns collected plastic into furniture.

Positive effects (handprint)
Fairphone incentivizes recycling electronic waste, urban mining, Fairtrade certified gold, and conflict-free mining. All of this is done to improve worker welfare and foster economic development.

A new standard
Fairphone is not about phones, but about setting a new standard for consumers and producers. The hope is that one day, Fairphone can stop telling stories. That is the day that all producers will manufacture electronics that are 100% ethical and consumers will use their phones for 5 years consecutively.

Ask yourself the following questions ...

What is your responsibility in contributing toward a sustainable future?

Nike shows that you have to go beyond implementing what everybody else is doing. CSR has long been and still is without a lot of meaning or business sense. Leadership at Nike used CSR to fuel innovation and rethink how their products are designed and produced, with the goal to design out waste completely and as a competitive advantage.

How would you close the loop and drive your footprint to zero in your industry?

Interface's production system had a huge and devastating footprint, although it still complied with all the rules and regulations. By the way: this means regulators could do more to accelerate the circular economy! Now, it is a business that has zero negative impact and offsets greenhouse gas emissions with a new mission to reverse climate change. Any industry can be transformed from extractive to restorative.

What if you stopped selling products and started delivering performance as a service?

Signify created a new offer. We used to live in a world where every organization acquired technical infrastructure, systems, and products, and employed highly paid facilities engineers to screw in light bulbs. Signify has a much better offer: they light up the day and night of their customers by managing all the hardware and software for them.

What part of your business model doesn't make sense anymore and could be eliminated?

Elmhurst eliminated animals from their business completely, replacing them with nuts. Eating habits are changing. More and more people demand higher quality, natural food and are shifting to a diet that is more plant-based. Elmhurst realized that milk from cows had lost its relevance and faced the hard fact that their business model was dead.

What needs to change in order for your products to stay in use forever?

Patagonia urges consumers to stop draining the planet. Fast fashion is draining the planet. Production of clothes is very resource intensive, yet clothes are sold and used as throw-away items. Patagonia challenges consumers to think hard about whether they really need new clothing. They offer the highest quality and free repairs, so that their clothes last a lifetime. Patagonia wants consumers' mindset to center on usage, not consuming.

What needs to change in your supply chain to make it fair for people and planet?

Fairphone is making people aware that the electronics industry has a bad reputation and is offering a phone that drives change from within—a phone made from materials that are sourced with respect for people and the planet and designed in a modular way. Buy the change and use your phone for 5 years instead of just 1.5 years.

High level strategic choices

1

 **Adopt a
new mindset**

Forget about traditional production
systems. Circular is about making unusual
combinations to produce in completely
new ways.

Look at nature to discover new materials
and inspiration to redesign processes and
deal with waste. Interact with experts
from different fields who have already
implemented circularity in their business.

2

 **Be specific
about your goal**

Be clear about the fundamental change
you seek. Articulate a circular vision and
quantify what you want to achieve.

Define the bold steps you need to take to
achieve your vision and break them down
into specific actions you can take. Be sure
that you have circularity metrics in place to
measure progress.

3

 **Keep the focus
on customers**

A circular business is also just a business,
meaning you need to live up to high
expectations from your customers.

Connect your efforts to become circular to
value for your customers. Define what the
benefits are for customers in becoming
more circular. Test the customer willingness
to pay for those benefits.

to drive this shift.

4
5
6

 Develop circular skills

Design helps to explore new ways to create sustainable, resilient, long-lasting value in the circular economy, giving you the confidence to redesign the world around you.

Challenge your people to unlearn and acquire circular design skills. Design waste and pollution out of your business model. Design a business model that is regenerative and restorative.

 Work together

Working with the right partners is crucial. Look for those partners that share your vision and can contribute meaningfully to your business model development.

Make a list of companies that you could partner with and discuss why these specific companies. Identify what value they add to your business and vice versa.

 Celebrate progress

The media is looking for real stories that show what the circular economy is all about. Tell stories about what you want to achieve and what you are working on.

Work with the media to spread your story and grow your business. Make explicit what positive social, economic, and environmental effects your business generates.

Where value is shifting!

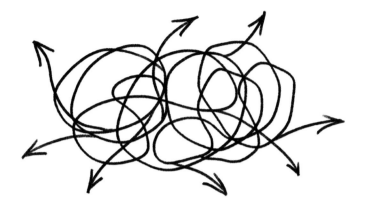

Understanding shifts

If you've reached this page, having read the other chapters, no doubt you can see that business model shifts have been undertaken by all types of organizations in many industries. And, in every case, those business model shifts were undeniably designed by the organization to deliberately create, deliver, and capture new value.

Likewise, given that change is nonlinear, business model shifts in every case must take into account technology acceleration and the changing needs and expectations of people. Wielded properly, technology then can help organizations create new connections between customers, employees, and other stakeholders, thereby helping organizations to shift to new business models.

Six ways to shift

As you can see, threaded through many of these case studies are technologies that helped the organizations undergoing some business model shift to create tighter connections between business model elements and streamline processes, thereby making value creation, delivery, and exchange more efficient and easier for customers.

For instance, in the services shift, BMW used mobile technology to help create on-demand mobility services. Clearly, digital shifts, like the one the *New York Times* is undergoing, would not be possible without investing in technology to connect people. In fact, none of the companies whose case studies are presented in this book would have been able to create such monumental business model shifts were it not for the availability of new technologies.

Make your own shift

Of course, technology alone does not make the business model shift. The shifts described in this book require bold steps that include stepping up and exploring new ways to create, deliver, and capture value, and even bolder steps to make the business model shifts happen. After all, the journey towards a successful business model shift is often littered with uncertainty and failures. In writing this book, we hope to have helped illuminate the path by creating a North Star for others to follow.

Shifting is about asking: where is value . . . next?

As previously mentioned—and demonstrated via the case studies—business model shifts require those who are making the shifts to search for new value. This is different and a separate set of activities to executing the current business model. Whereas executing the current business model relies on known knowns, when searching for new value, the search must focus on a problem worth solving, for both customers and your organization, that isn't being solved today in the current business model. This value may exist in adjacent or even radically new markets.

Searching for new value can be an uncertain endeavor requiring patience and humility. Most of all, it requires a lot of watching, questioning, and listening. Do customers have problems that are worth solving or a real need that must be fulfilled? What solution or value proposition is attractive and desirable for customers? Can you deliver that proposition in a viable way? Is it feasible to organize all the moving parts to deliver the value repeatedly?

In all cases, this search is not meant to be accomplished with a big bang approach, where vast sums of money and other resources are thrown at it. Rather, business model innovation should be performed in a structured and systematic way, using what we call a *double loop process*, as outlined in our book, *Design a Better Business: New Tools, Skills, and Mindset for Strategy and Innovation* (Wiley) and shown in the diagram on the right side of this page.

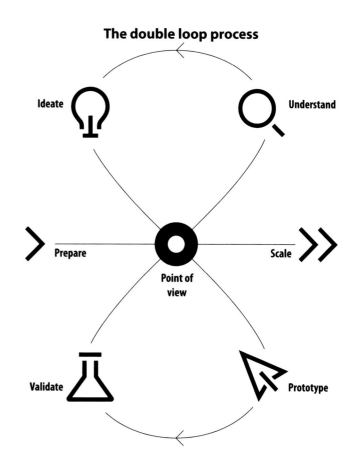

The double loop process

Ideate · Understand · Prepare · Point of view · Scale · Validate · Prototype

Manage your business model portfolio

If nothing else, the gist of this book is that along with business model shifts, organizations can no longer afford to stick with a single, static business model and expect to live very long. In fact, with compounding change, organizations must develop a portfolio of varying business models that provide a way to continually find ways to create, deliver, and capture future value while divesting of older business models that no longer provide value.

With business model portfolios, organizations can assess the health of current business models, begin to play in spaces that may be disruptive, and make more sound business model investment decisions. That said, for many companies, it's natural to execute multiple business models simultaneously. However, what's often missing is a business model assessment and investment approach that would enable the company to make strategic choices about what business model shifts to invest in and when.

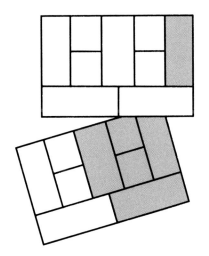

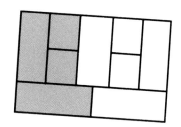

How to drive your own business model shift

Continuous innovation

A great way to visualize and manage multiple business models and business model shifts at once is to use a business model growth curve. This curve is a dynamic view, broken up into seven stages, each denoting a level of business model maturity and thereby pointing out what's next.

The business model growth curve is also multi-dimensional, bringing to the fore a few things all at once. First, the business model growth curve shows how, over time, business models begin to lose their ability to capture value as they once did. This has as much to do with market dynamics as it does the company's focus. Second, the curve depicts a number of stages meant to represent what the organization should focus on based on the maturity of its business model. For each stage, like "learn," a business model canvas denotes where the organization's focus should be placed. Third, for each stage, there is a milestone that denotes what the larger set of activities should be focused on, like "problem-solution fit."

Using a maturity curve like this can help an organization make decisions about where and when to invest resources as part of continuous innovation.

Discover

Stage 1 – Find the customer and the problem.

The goal of this stage is to discover a problem worth solving, and more importantly, the people who have that problem and are your potential customers. However this is performed, the most important metric to be measured is the number of potential customers that truly have the problem worth solving.

Design

Stage 2 – Explore the solution.

The goal of this stage is to iteratively design a value proposition that addresses the customer problem in a unique and compelling way. This is often performed by running objective, time-boxed experiments using simple prototypes that make visual and tangible what you have to offer. The most important metric is customers wanting to use and pay for your innovative solution.

Grow

Stage 3 – Validate value creation.

The goal of this stage is to validate the building blocks (and interconnectivity therein) on the right-hand side of your new business model. The more customers that are interested and actually buying your product/service, the closer you are to achieving product-market fit. Depending on your offering, it often takes several years to achieve this milestone.

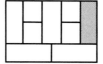 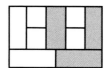 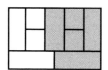

Business model growth curve

Problem validation   **Problem-solution fit**   **Produ**

258

Operationalize

Stage 4 – Validate value delivery.

The goal of this stage is to validate the building blocks on the left-hand side of your new business model. Though you already have resources, partners, activities, and a cost structure, this stage is about structuring these elements such that you can validate your ability to operation-alize cost effectively. At the end of this stage, the business model is fully validated.

Amplify

Sustain

Divest

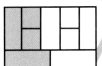

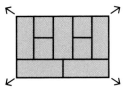

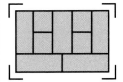

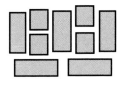

Stage 5 – Let the machine scale the model.

This is the stage wherein validated business models become business models that are executed by the larger organizational machine. Whereas during the search stages, your business model was being fine-tuned, at this stage, it's ready to be amplified and scaled to meet full market demand. This likely means more marketing, sales, and production.

Stage 6 – Keep the engine turning.

As new business models move into the execution bucket, currently executed business models must also be managed such that they can continue to grow to their full potential.

Stage 7 – Reuse and remix.

At some point every business model must be sunsetted or divested of. This is not about throwing it away completely. At this stage, customers must be made aware of the plans to sunset the product/service and the organization should find ways to utilize constituent elements from the old business model in new business models where applicable.

rket fit　　**Prepare to scale**　　**Market saturation**　　　　**Market disruption**

Example:
Alibaba's business model portfolio

As you may have observed in many of the case studies in this book, most organizations develop new business models while executing other business models in parallel. In some cases, organizations are reactive, developing new business models as a reaction to their own needs or market changes. For example, BMW introduced mobility business models when it noticed customer behavior changing due to urbanization and the trend from ownership to access.

Several of the organizations with case studies in this book began developing a portfolio of business models from their inception. Alibaba introduced the Taobao business model connecting different groups of buyers and sellers only four years after its founding date.

In its short existence (so far) Alibaba has developed one platform business model after another. Given that they're multi-sided with value propositions connected to both the supply and demand sides, platform business models are famously tough to develop. Alibaba has been able to pull this off time after time, even connecting all its business models in an ecosystem of value creation, which has turned into an economy of its own. This is all a result of Alibaba's dedication to continuous innovation combined with a deliberate portfolio management strategy.

Alibaba has lots of ideas incubating and being validated, such as AMap, TMall Genie (voice assistant), Xianyu (secondhand).

Problem validation   Problem-solution fit   Prod

Operationalize   **Amplify**   **Sustain**   **Divest**

Taobao started in 2003, also based on the known customer needs of prosumers all around China to trade with each other. Remember, eBay was also trying to fulfill this need. Taobao matured within 4 years or so, forcing eBay to give up on China, by focusing on developing value propositions that deeply resonated with how the Chinese want to do business.

Alibaba.com moved through the stages fairly quickly. Within 3 years, it became cashflow positive. From the start, it was clear that there was a huge need from small- and medium-sized Chinese manufacturers to trade with the rest of the world. The customer problem for both sides was already validated and though an iterative approach, the value propositions for both could be improved along the way.

天猫 TMALL.COM   淘宝网 Taobao.com

1866.com and TMall are in this stage.

arket fit   **Prepare to scale**   **Market saturation**   **Market disruption**

Trends

Though shifting business models is not easy, when we seek to understand needs and wants of our (future) customers, designing the future becomes attainable. To that end, here are some of the trends that our friends at Trendwatching.com believe you should watch and design for next . . . and now.

Green pressure

We are at a tipping point at the moment of awareness where people care about the environment. This shift is moving from eco-consumption as a status play (see Patagonia, Nike, and Beyond Meat) to the mainstream, for both B2C and B2B companies. What's more, companies that include environmental, social, and governance policies as part of their culture and operations will be seen as viable alternatives to legacy companies that don't move in this direction.

Brand avatars

Humans are social animals and seek to connect with one another as well as with the brands that personify their interests. Whether these are B2C and B2B, people expect to engage with brands in new ways through digital channels, like websites, games, apps, bots, and virtual assistants (i.e., AI-fueled conversations). In addition, in order to remain relevant, brands must exist in multiple channels, and even in the media, such that customers are reminded of their relationship and relevance therein.

Civil media

If COVID-19 has proven anything, it's that our need for community transcends physical connection. And, while social media promised to be a utopia of sorts, it's turned out to be toxic and uninviting. Civil media then is about fostering the creation of trusted, niche communities that enable people to connect with other people (mostly virtually) to share insights, stories, and points of view. Whether accomplished via online conferences or virtual meeting spaces, the communities you foster will create long-lasting customer relationships.

Metamorphic design

Though every customer must feel they are relevant to the brands they do business with, this trend is about utilizing digital technology to create unique, personalized experiences for every customer . . . which are constantly updated to meet the new reality. This goes for both digital and physical experiences (e.g., iPhones are personalized by Apple and third-party, or individual, app developers). Eventually this trend may lead to new relevance-as-a-service business models that offer personalization for other services.

The burnout

Like connection, well-being is a basic human need. Though digital technology has always promised to make people more efficient, thereby gaining time for themselves, in reality we work in an always-on environment. With the paradigm shift brought about by COVID-19, people in every industry have refocused on their own well-being while also getting work done. The companies that foster employee experience in the same way they do customer experience will be perceived as long-term partners rather than people factories.

We cannot predict the future, but we can invent it."

Dennis Gabor

Creating the right ecosystem to shift

Undergoing business model shifts while growing and managing a business model portfolio requires that organizations also develop an internal innovation ecosystem that supports all functions necessary for change, as well as strategies to invest time and resources into change. This ecosystem is made up of six interconnected foundations.

Ambition

Making a business model shift requires a bold ambition and clear vision of the future you want create. Clear visions also become rallying cries within organizations. Therefore, before embarking on a journey of exploration and innovation, a clear vision must be developed in order to inspire, motivate, and activate people to move the business forward together, while also enabling teams to make strategic choices and daily decisions.

Teams

In just about any organization there are various teams focused on different functions of the business. Well-defined innovation ecosystems require four specific kinds of teams. The first are teams responsible for running the current businesses. These teams execute and optimize, innovating incrementally within current business models. Most often these teams are held accountable with traditional key performance indicators (prof-

It, revenue, and margins) generating returns on the short term.

The second are teams responsible for growing new businesses. These teams innovate and validate, continually working on the next business models, often focused on adjacent innovation. New business teams are held accountable using innovation metrics (traction), generating returns on the mid-term.

The third are teams responsible for exploring new businesses. These teams experiment and pivot, working on radical, completely new business models, and are held accountable using innovation metrics (validated learnings about value creation) potentially generating returns in the long term.

The last is the Management Team/Board, which is responsible for managing the entire portfolio of businesses, including making decisions about when to divest of outdated business models that no longer contribute or are losing relevance in the eye of the customer.

Process

In *Design a Better Business: New Tools, Skills,* *and Mindset for Strategy and Innovation* (Wiley), we outlined an entire process, called the double loop, that is designed to help anyone in any company find, create, deliver, and capture new value. This is a systematic and iterative process meant to support continually learning. Whether organizations use the double loop or another process, what's important is that there's a system in place that outlines what the organization expects when searching for new value.

Metrics

Metrics should be set for each business model innovation and validation journey. You can't improve what you don't understand. The right set of metrics helps teams involved in innovation to understand how successful they are and what they need to improve upon. Additionally, metrics can be used to systematically de-risk innovation.

Skills & mindset

People create business model shifts, plain and simple. Innovation requires the right talent and mindset from both leadership and innovators themselves. In addition, each stage of the maturity of a company's business model demands a different skillset in order to become successful. While many organizations employ people that are skilled doers, just as many lack people with an entrepreneurial mindset and skills needed for exploration, prototyping, and validation. On the left side of the maturity curve, where new, potentially disruptive businesses are being invested in, organizations need true entrepreneurs, risk-takers, visionaries, anthropologists, growth hackers, developers, and designers. Of course, these are also skills that can be taught to anyone willing to take the leap.

Resources and funding

Innovation projects can be organized in myriad ways, from accelerators to co-innovation to venture funds. Business leaders must be committed and accountable for bringing new business models to life. Innovation requires leadership to unlock the right investment in people, money, and time . . . at the right time. With a metered investment approach, organizations can manage their innovation portfolio as an investment fund. For this to work, the organization will need a small but experienced investment board tasked with managing the business model portfolio. Moreover, this investment board must have C-level commitment and be responsible and accountable for the innovation budget.

References

Besides sourcing from our own experience and cases, we also used general public sources like company websites, Wikipedia, and more general articles from business websites and popular media as research for this book.

Green, Innovative, and Profitable: A Case Study Of Managerial Capabilities At Interface Inc.
Tommi Lampikoski – timreview.ca   234

Guiding the Future Of Design.
purpose.nike.com   224

H

Heart-warming Story Of the Hamieds, Who Set Up Cipla and Have Been Saving Lives.
nationalheraldindia.com   78

Here Are 5 Ways Apple's App Store Changed How We Use Smartphones. Shara Tibken – cnet.com   156

Here's How the World's Largest Money Manager Is Overhauling Its Strategy Because Of Climate Change. Pippa Stevens – cnbc.com   68

How A Founder's Story Fueled Medtronic's Growth From A Tiny Garage To A $120b Brand.
Carmine Gallo – forbes.com   28

How Alphabet Became the Biggest Company in the World. Alex Hern – theguardian.com   182

How Alibaba Is Using Ai To Power the Future Of Business. Jennifer O'Brien – cmo.com.au   142

How an Indian Tycoon Fought Big Pharma To Sell Aids Drugs For $1 a Day.
Katherine Eban – qz.com   78

How Beyond Meat Made It Into the Meat Aisle.
Danielle Wiener – edition.cnn.com   192

How Connecterra Is Getting Thousands Of Cows Online. connecterra.io   124

How Dollar Shave Club's Founder Built a $1 Billion Company That Changed the Industry.
Jaclyn Trop – entrepreneur.com   38

How Duolingo Built a $700 Million Company Without Charging Users. producthabits.com   122

How EBay Failed In China.
Helen H. Wang – forbes.com   142

How GitHub Conquered Google, Microsoft, and Everyone Else. Cade Metz – wired.com   206

How GitHub Democratized Coding and Found a New Home At Microsoft. Hiten Shah – usefyi.com   206

How Grab Is Becoming an Everyday, Everything App in Southeast Asia.
Dipen Pradhan – entrepreneur.com   152

How Kickstarter Became One Of the Biggest Powers in Publishing.
Richard Lea – theguardian.com   162

How Khan Academy Is Changing the Rules Of Education. Clive Thompson – wired.com   204

How Nike's Circular Design Aims To Save the World. Jim McCauley – creativebloq.com   224

How Rent The Runway Built an $800 Million Business in a Mom-and-pop Industry.
Sam Hollis – jilt.com   42

How Salesforce Built a $13 Billion Empire from a CRM. Hiten Shah – usefyi.com   100

How Storytelling Turned Dollar Shave Club Into a Billion Dollar-brand. Zontee Hou
convinceandconvert.com   38

How Tech's Richest Plan To Save Themselves After the Apocalypse.
Douglas Rushkoff – theguardian.com   248

How The New York Times Is Clawing Its Way Into the Future. Gabriel Snyder – wired.com   114

How to Bring Sustainability To The Masses: Tony's Chocolonely's Impact Strategy.
Jeroen Kraaijenbrink – forbes.com   82

How Wechat Became China's App For Everything.
Alex Pasternack – fastcompany.com   166

I

Ida Reduces Antibiotic Usage in New Trial!
ida.io   124

Impact of 1% for the planet: How We Fund.
patagonia.com   244

Interface Announces Mission Zero Success, Commits To Climate Take Back.
floortrendsmag.com   234

Interface Unveils Prototype Carpet Tile To Inspire New Approaches To Address Climate Change.
interface.com   234

Is Spacex Changing the Rocket Equation?
Andrew Chaikin – airspacemag.com   196

It All Started With a 12-year-old Cousin.
Claudia Dreifus – nytimes.com   204

K

Kickstarter Focuses Its Mission on Altruism Over Profit. Mike Isaac – nytimes.com   162

L

Lessons From the Rise and Fall Of Toms Shoes.
Chavie Lieber – businessoffashion.com   72

The makers behind the book

Patrick van der Pijl

Patrick is CEO of Business Models Inc. producer of the worldwide bestseller *Business Model Generation* and co-author of *Design a Better Business*. He is passionate to help entrepreneurs, leaders, rebels, and corporate companies to innovate their business model and design a future strategy.

🐦 @patrickpijl
in ppijl

Roland Wijnen

Roland is fanatic about understanding how businesses are evolving. As a long-time Business Designer at Business Models Inc. in the Netherlands, he uses those insights to challenge and support companies to go make their shift.

🐦 @rolandwijnen
in rolandwijnen

Justin Lokitz

Justin Lokitz is an experienced Strategy Designer and Managing Director of
the Business Models Inc. San Francisco
office. He leverages his experiences
across a wide range of industry sectors
to help companies design innovative,
sustainable business models and
strategies for the future.

 @jmlokitz
 jmlokitz

Maarten van Lieshout

Maarten van Lieshout is a passionate
design thinker and strategic storytell-
er. He is the designer of the bestseller
Design a Better Business. His visual and
design skills helps companies to dive
into uncertainty and explore new
strategic futures and create value for
their customers.

 @maartenvl
 mvlieshout

The contributors

Core team

Jeroen Bosman, research

Leroy Spiekerman van Weezelenburg, design, research and iconography

Lotte de Wolde, illustrations (pages 148, 156, 188 and 196) and iconography

Oliver Holding Fay, research

Niek Otten, portfolio management content

Niki Seelen, research

Scott van den Berg, research

Special thanks

Michael Anseeuw, BNPPF (BE);

Dirk Ramhorst, Wacker (GER);

Henry Mason, Trendwatching.com (UK);

Richard Narramore, Wiley (USA);

Diego Gil, Singularity University (Spain/Italy)

Raymond Slaughter, Route2Pi project (GER)

Ron Kersic, ING (NL)

Patrick Willer, Salesforce (NL)

Ynzo van Zanten, Tony's Chocolonely

Team Hotelschool The Hague, led by Jeroen Bosman

Iulia Tuica

Miriam Seng

Louis van Hyfte

Daan van Zanten

Our proofreaders

Adriana Lakatosova

André Bolland

Angelique Kuut

Arjan Molenkamp

Bart Sutorius

Daisy Rood

Ditmar Kroezen

Erik Bottema

Erik Schipper

Erik van Busschbach

Fabienne van Leiden

Francis Windt

Frank E. Soe-Agnie

Giovanni Caruso

Jacobo Senior

Jan-Maarten in 't Veld

Jeroen Bosman

Joeri van Cauteren

Joris Smidt

Lotje van der Kooij

Marco Tistarelli

Patrick Marcelissen

Paulus Tangkere

Petra Wullings

Reiner Walter

Remo Knops

Robert Viegen

Ron Kersic

Scott van den Berg

Serdar kara

Stefan Buijsingh

Susan Schaper

Ton Willems

Will Gordon

Ying-Tsung Lee

Yolanda Verveer

What are you going to shift?

The future of your organization—and all organizations—is waiting to be created. And that future comes by way of new business models and business model shifts. It's up to you, your team, your leadership, and your organization's culture to take the reins and begin to deliberately create, remix, and remake the next versions of the value creation, delivery, and capture mechanisms that will **enable your organization to delight customers in the long term.**

Although in no way is this book meant to be a compendium of every business model shift that has ever happened, the case studies covered here definitely hint at where the future is headed when it comes to business models and where you might find value next. What's more, although likely not all of the organizations that made it into this book will be around in the next decade, the ones that are will come up with even more new ways to create value.

In our estimation, with the right tools, skills, and mindset, **everyone who reads this book is also capable of doing the same. After all, understanding that the change we're experiencing is accelerating is half the battle.** Armed with that knowledge, and using these case studies as fodder, we invite you to execute your own shift and create a future with more value for your customers and stakeholders.

Index A-Z

Index A-Z